Saviour Siblings

Genetic screening technologies involving pre-implantation genetic diagnosis (PGD) raise important questions about selective reproduction and the welfare of the child to be born. How does selection impact on the identity of the child who is born? Are children who are selected for a particular purpose harmed or treated as commodities? How far should the state interfere with parents' reproductive choices?

Currently, concerns about the welfare of the child in selective reproduction have focused on the individual interests of the child to be born. This book re-evaluates the welfare of the child through the controversial topic of saviour sibling selection. Drawing on relational feminist and communitarian ethics, Michelle Taylor-Sands argues that the welfare of the child to be born is inextricably linked with the welfare of his or her family. The author proposes a relational model for selective reproduction based on a broad conception of the welfare of the child that includes both individual and collective family interests. By comparing regulation in the UK and Australia, the book maps out how law and policy might support a relational model for saviour sibling selection.

With an interdisciplinary focus, *Saviour Siblings: A Relational Approach to the Welfare of the Child in Selective Reproduction* will be of particular interest to academics and students of bioethics and law, as well as practitioners and policymakers concerned with the ethics of selective reproduction.

Michelle Taylor-Sands is a Senior Lecturer at the Melbourne Law School, University of Melbourne and has advised the Victoria government on assisted reproductive treatment. Michelle has published in the field of saviour sibling selection and the welfare of the child to be born.

Biomedical Law and Ethics Library
Series Editor: Sheila A. M. McLean

Scientific and clinical advances, social and political developments and the impact of healthcare on our lives raise profound ethical and legal questions. Medical law and ethics have become central to our understanding of these problems, and are important tools for the analysis and resolution of problems – real or imagined.

In this series, scholars at the forefront of biomedical law and ethics contribute to the debates in this area, with accessible, thought-provoking, and some-times controversial, ideas. Each book in the series develops an independent hypothesis and argues cogently for a particular position. One of the major contributions of this series is the extent to which both law and ethics are utilised in the content of the books, and the shape of the series itself.

The books in this series are analytical, with a key target audience of lawyers, doctors, nurses, and the intelligent lay public.

Available titles:

Human Fertilisation and Embryology
Reproducing regulation
Kirsty Horsey & Hazel Biggs

Intention and Causation in Medical Non-killing
The impact of criminal law concepts on euthanasia and assisted suicide
Glenys Williams

Impairment and Disability
Law and Ethics at the Beginning and End of Life
Sheila McLean & Laura Williamson

Bioethics and the Humanities
Attitudes and Perceptions
Robin Downie & Jane Macnaughton

Defending the Genetic Supermarket
The law and ethics of selection the next generation
Colin Gavagham

The Harm Paradox
Tort law and the unwanted child in an era of choice
Nicolette Priaulx

Assisted Dying
Reflections on the Need for Law Reform
Sheila McLean

Medicine, Malpractice and Misapprehensions
V.H. Harpwood

Euthanasia, Ethics and the Law
From the conflict to compromise
Richard Huxtable

The Best Interests of the Child in Healthcare
Sarah Elliston

Values in Medicine
What are we really doing to patients?
Donald Evans

Autonomy, Consent and the Law
Sheila A.M McLean

Healthcare Research Ethics and Law
Regulation, review and responsibility
Hazel Biggs

The Body in Bioethics
Alastair V. Campbell

Genomic Negligence
An interest in autonomy as the basis
for novel negligence claims
generated by genetic technology
Victoria Chico

Health Professionals and Trust
The cure for healthcare law and policy
Mark Henaghan

Medical Ethics in China
A transcultural interpretation
Jing-Bao Nie

Law, Ethics and Compromise at
the Limits of Life
To treat or not to treat?
Richard Huxtable

Regulating Pre-Implantation
Genetic Diagnosis
A comparative and theoretical analysis
Sheila A.M McLean & Sarah Elliston

Bioethics
Methods, theories, domains
Marcus Düwell

Human Population Genetic
Research in Developing
Countries
The Issue of Group Protection
Yue Wang

Coercive Care
Rights, law and policy
Bernadette McSherry & Ian Freckelton

Saviour Siblings
A relational approach to the
welfare of the child in selective
reproduction
Michelle Taylor-Sands

Forthcoming titles include:

Human Population Genetic
Research in Developing
Countries
The issue of group protection
Yue Wang

Stem Cell Research and the
Collaborative Regulation of
Innovation
Sarah Devaney

The Jurisprudence of Pregnancy
Concepts of conflict, persons and
property
Mary Neal

Regulating Risk
Values in health research governance
Shawn Harmon

About the Series Editor
Professor Sheila McLean is International Bar Association Professor of Law and
Ethics in Medicine and Director of the Institute of Law and Ethics in Medicine at
the University of Glasgow.

Saviour Siblings

A Relational Approach to the Welfare of the Child in Selective Reproduction

Michelle Taylor-Sands

Routledge
Taylor & Francis Group

LONDON AND NEW YORK

First published 2013
by Routledge
2 Park Square, Milton Park, Abingdon, Oxfordshire OX14 4RN

And by Routledge
711 Third Avenue, New York, NY 10017

First issued in paperback 2015

Routledge is an imprint of the Taylor & Francis Group, an informa business

British Library Cataloguing in Publication Data
A catalogue record for this book is available from the British Library

Library of Congress Cataloging in Publication Data
Taylor-Sands, Michelle.
Saviour siblings : a relational approach to the welfare of the child in selective reproduction / Michelle Taylor-Sands.
pages cm. -- (Biomedical law and ethics library)
Includes bibliographical references and index.
ISBN 978-0-415-53571-7 (hbk : alk. paper) -- ISBN 978-0-203-70870-5
(ebk : alk. paper) 1. Procurement of organs, tissues, etc.--Law and legislation.
2. Preimplantation genetic diagnosis--Law and legislation. 3. Human reproductive
technology--Moral and ethical aspects. 4. Human reproductive technology--Law
and legislation. 5. Fertilization in vitro, Human--Law and legislation. 6. Brothers
and sisters. 7. Biomedical ethics. I. Title.
K3611.T7T39 2013
176--dc23
2013009263

ISBN13: 978-1-138-93531-0 (pbk)
ISBN13: 978-0-415-53626-4 (hbk)

Typeset in Garamond
by Taylor & Francis Books

For my family, past and present

Contents

Foreword

From the very start of the enterprise, bringing children into the world has always involved at least two people and, typically, the co-ordinated and enduring work of several. Reproduction is the paradigm instance of our deep need for others, including their very bodies, to provide the most fundamental features of our own lives. Physically, every one of us takes shape within women's wombs; socially, virtually all of us take shape within families.

Much more recently, assisted reproduction technologies – for example, *in vitro* fertilisation, and pre-implantation genetic diagnosis – have introduced a new dimension to the relational process of conceiving, begetting and bearing children. The ways in which lives can hinge on the bodies of others have newly increased as well. We now live in a time when otherwise unavoidable death – often enough, a child's death – may be forestalled with infusions of human stem cells, and when the best way to obtain useful cells may be from the body of a brother or sister – 'saviour siblings' – whose conception and birth are carefully orchestrated to achieve just that purpose.

Michelle Taylor-Sands' exceptional book explores the dramatic overlap of these new dimensions in how we can reproduce ourselves, and how we can draw on each other's bodies to sustain lives. I find her work particularly compelling for the distinctive ways it weaves together thoughtful, highly informed attention to philosophical and ethical complexities, with legal expertise and policy savvy. The result is a superb guide to both thought and practice concerning the moral and political complexities of a striking new human power: bringing children into the world to provide tissues uniquely tailored to be vital therapeutic resources to their siblings, or other family members. Despite the complexities of its topic, her book is marvellously clear, and notwithstanding its scholarly heft, it is a riveting read.

What I find most striking about *Saviour Siblings*, though, is its thoroughly realistic grasp of its basic topic – the moral relationships that constitute families, and in particular, that sustain the connections between parents and children. Realistic theory and policy about families are scarce. As this book makes almost painfully plain, much of UK, Australian and US law, policy and ethics that touch on families and on children reads as though it was written by people who have tried as hard as they can to forget their own experience as children, as sisters or brothers, or as mothers or fathers.

Taylor-Sands reminds us that humans do not spring up fully formed from the ground, as in Hobbes' infamous mushroom metaphor from *De Cive*, 'come to full maturity without all kind of engagement to each other'. The notions that animate much of social thought and political theory – that our chief interests all revolve around making a narrow conception of ourselves better off, that all our responsibilities are fundamentally a matter of our free choices – are revealed for the fantasies they are if we keep some of the most basic features of our own lives in view. Not everyone is born as an orphan, waiting to be chosen to be someone's child; we do not choose our parents or our siblings; and even if we influence the timing or other circumstances of births, we cannot choose our children as we can our friends, our hobbies, our political affiliation, our careers. Nor are the obligations with which family life encumbers us always experienced as alienating burdens. On the contrary, very many people avidly seek out just the chance to be 'encumbered' in that way, and find 'freedom' from such bonds to be extraordinarily painful.

While it is very tempting to speculate about why so much of the West's moral and political wisdom seems so out of touch with these unmistakable and centrally important facts, Taylor-Sands grasps them fully and firmly. Good thinking, good policy-making and good practice involving families and children must proceed along the lines that she sketches. In the small-scale social institutions called families, as she powerfully argues, many interests are shared, entwined and interwoven; some of them can reasonably be thought of as interests of the family itself, rather than of any of its members solely. A regulatory regime that constrains how parents and children interact along the lines of a conception of the child's 'best interests' that tacitly supposes an image of mutually indifferent agents manoeuvring to advance their own agendas, is either ideologically motivated or just flatly divorced from reality; in either case, it is morally flawed.

In families, our needs, desires, hopes and fears overlap, reinforce, weaken or directly collide with each other. This very familiar element of life means that determining what actually constitutes a child's welfare – and, accordingly, what compromises within families are necessary, reasonable, dubious and intolerable – is a much more complex matter than standard law and policy, and even a good deal of mainstream bioethics, is able to accommodate.

Taylor-Sands' book provides precisely what is needed: an elegant and plausible theoretical foundation for a pragmatic regulatory framework that *is* able to handle these complexities. With emotional as well as intellectual precision, though without a shred of sentimentality, she keeps squarely in sight what much of the law in different nations, and much Western bioethics struggle to glimpse: that even in a digitalised, globalised world, where foetuses can be conceived, sorted and gestated into children whose stem cells may keep a sibling from untimely death, love and intimacy remain deeply important aspects of many people's lives.

At the same time, Taylor-Sands vividly appreciates that new technologies can present threats, not only to individual children, but also to the attitudes and practices that support the structures in which familial intimacy can thrive. Selective reproduction generally, and 'saviour siblings' in particular, are 'ethically complex' matters, as she insists, for just these reasons. Conceiving a child to be a tissue donor presents risks to the 'saviour sibling' in particular, and to families grappling with the serious illness of a relative in general.

For instance, readers of *Saviour Siblings* will learn of new research indicating at least theoretical reason to fear that removing a cell from the early embryo to test for genetic compatibility may raise the chance of damages that manifest in later life. Further, some saviour siblings might not merely supply the stem-cell rich blood from the umbilicus – a procedure involving very little discomfort or risk – they might also be subjected to repeated peripheral blood and bone marrow draws. Much more problematically, some saviour siblings might be seen as sources of non-renewable tissues needed by their ill relations. It is also possible that even the well-matched tissues that their sibling provides may not save a sick sister or brother, and that some families might not be able to prevent their new child from being the focus of their grief and disappointment.

Taylor-Sands also very effectively addresses what may be an even more pressing concern than harm: disrespect. Children, she recognises, are vulnerable to other ills than merely pain, sickness or stress. Like adults, they can be the victims of respect offences. If children are treated in ways motivated solely by other people's interests, or it is conveyed that children's real value resides in what they can provide for others, rather than being cherished for themselves as well, they become, as Taylor-Sands puts it, kinds of 'commodities'. When a child has been thus commodified, he/she has been wronged, even if not otherwise harmed. Imagine, for example, a child brought into the world by a family who needed her stem cells, that her cells are harvested to good effect, and then is immediately relinquished for adoption. Absent some unusual circumstances, it would be hard to argue that the family valued that baby as anything other than a therapeutic resource, and thus that they treated her disrespectfully, even if she ends up as a much loved child of a doting family.

In addition to her realism about the character of familial interests and relationships, and her clarity about the challenges that the practice of therapeutically oriented selective reproduction faces, Taylor-Sands makes another powerful contribution to good thinking about saviour siblings. She sets aside various points that are often mistakenly seen as highly important to responsible thinking about selective reproduction in general. While, in my view, the moral complexities introduced by families and children into healthcare practice and policy are typically unappreciated, sometimes they receive too much emphasis of the wrong sort, thus triggering their own distortions.

Consider, for example, the persistent intuition, shared by some ethical theorists and widely represented among the population as a whole, that we do wrong if we attempt to tailor our children too precisely to a list of specifications. The effort to have 'designer babies' is taken to erode the idea that children are gifts, not artefacts, and to interfere with the attitude of loving acceptance that children deserve. It might seem that the effort to match a new sibling to an existing child's genetics is a clear example of just this kind of disturbing design orientation toward human beings.

But insofar as this designer objection is taken to be a knock-down, drag-out argument against selective reproduction as such, Taylor-Sands makes a simple yet powerful reply: people have children for a great variety of perfectly acceptable reasons, very few of which are thoroughly altruistic. Children who are conceived because of another child's medical need, and who emerge from a process of embryo screening to ensure compatibility, can be loved as thoroughly as that (rare) child whose birth was desired for the most selfless of reasons. More specifically, she points out that the worry that bringing children into the world to save the life of another person will coarsen our love for children generally is highly speculative at best; refusing a chance to save a child's life on such a basis seems a confused expression of love. Whatever one might think about the ethics of using reproductive technologies to affect appearance, height or intelligence, or to determine the sex of one's children, the motivation in saviour sibling cases could hardly be dismissed as trivial.

A more technical concern that has become a staple of professional discussions of the ethics of bringing children into the world is the 'non-identity' problem. The trouble here starts from the observation that a particular child necessarily emerges only from the specific pair of gametes that were actually involved in its conception – any other pair, and possibly any single other gamete, and the resultant child is not merely different in this or that respect, but is a wholly different being. This thought prompts the further idea that unless someone's life is so thoroughly and unrelentingly miserable that it would be better for that person never to have existed at all, no one can coherently object to the conditions that were necessary for him/her to exist. It then seems to follow that even if a child from a specifically selected embryo experienced some disagreeable or bad effects owing to the circumstances of her conception, she could press no reasonable complaint. Anything that anyone might have done to change those circumstances would not have improved *her* life, but rather have simply precluded *that very child's* existence. It might seem that being chosen as a saviour sibling is a necessary condition of that particular child's existence, and hence is unlikely to be the source of any valid complaint.

Taylor-Sands' treatment of this argument seems definitive to me, at least insofar as it concerns selective reproduction. Among her several rejoinders, I focus on one that is particularly telling. She makes it clear that many of the threats of harm or disrespect to potential saviour siblings are not in fact necessary conditions of their existing at all. For example, removing a cell from an early embryo for the purposes of determining whether it would become optimally suited to provide stem cells is not a necessary condition of its existence as such. If such procedures were known to carry significant risk, a resulting child who suffered such harm could reflect that *her own life* – not merely the life of some other child – could well have been better had she not been biopsied.

The reply that without the biopsy, the embryo would not have been implanted or even created in the first place is not successful. Imagine a child born into slavery objecting to her lot, and her 'owner' replying that, had the child not been conceived to be a slave, she would not have been conceived at all. That a person's sole motive in starting a pregnancy was to do something morally dubious to any resultant child does not give that person a *carte blanche* to do so. A child may not be able to object coherently to having had the biological parents she in fact had, but she can certainly object to how they treat her once she is a part of the world.

With arguments of this sort, and several others, Taylor-Sands makes plain that the use of our new powers to try to save desperately ill children is neither a violation of an ethically and legally defensible standard of the best interests of the child, as it would surely seem to be were such standards to be taken at face value. Nor is it a completely innocent use of technology, unable to threaten any interest of the new child we have reason to respect. Rather than at such extremes, the truth lies in the broad middle ground, delineated by the need to realise that people have serious interests other than those that focus on promoting their individual well-being, and that even our individual well-being requires a profound level of involvement with other people. As Taylor-Sands sees so well, our interests in our own welfare and in our own autonomy need to be understood in ways that fully acknowledge the deep and abiding importance of relationship in our lives. When we come into the world, unless we are very unlucky, we are always already part of a family. We are not thrown on the mercy of strangers, relying on their charity until we develop the clout to negotiate mutually beneficial deals with them. Rather, the quality and character of our lives are inextricably linked to the character and quality of the lives of a particular set of other people.

Drawing imaginatively on the work of those bioethicists and feminist theorists who appreciate this point, Taylor-Sands develops this relational view of human reality and human welfare, engages it with the specifics of the controversies about saviour siblings, and provides a basis for extending it further to selective reproduction in general. Her distinctive contribution extends to providing a model for guiding deliberation about saviour sibling efforts that focuses on the interests of the family as a whole, makes a default assumption of co-operation and mutual support rather than conflict, and aims to bolster rather than further stress families grappling with fraught decisions.

Her relational, inclusive, supportive model in turn gives rise to a detailed outline of how selective reproduction for therapeutic ends can be reasonably regulated to achieve its profound benefits safely and respectfully. Strategically inserting consulting bioethicists into her system, not in the guise of moral experts, but as what Margaret Walker has called 'architects of open moral spaces' in which productive deliberation can be fostered, she aims to use regulation not to judge who is 'worthy' of a chance to save his/her child, but to improve the position of parents to think carefully about difficult issues, and to help families to cope with the challenges they confront. Developed in creative contact with much of the most careful thinking on the bioethics of families available, and contrasted with devastating effect against existing policies, the regulatory framework Michelle Taylor-Sands details in this book would do a great deal to help families and their members, both born and yet to come. Her work also does much to vindicate the promise of bioethics itself, demonstrating how theoretical reflection can be transformed into new, practical ways in which what families and medicine understand by 'care' can co-operate and converge.

James Lindemann Nelson

Acknowledgements

This book grew out of my doctoral thesis, undertaken for the PhD degree at the University of Melbourne. I am indebted to my principle supervisor, Christine Parker, for her wonderful feedback, support and encouragement along the way. I would also like to thank Loane Skene and Margaret Coady who generously imparted their own expertise in relation to different aspects of my interdisciplinary research.

I owe a very special thanks to my PhD examiners, James Lindemann Nelson and Belinda Bennett, for their thoughtful comments and suggestions that helped me further refine my line of argument in my doctoral thesis and reshape it into a book. I also received invaluable feedback from several anonymous referees about revising my thesis for publication as a book, for which I am extremely grateful. I am very appreciative of the encouragement and editorial advice I received from Routledge, with particular thanks to my commissioning editor, Katie Carpenter, and the series editor, Sheila McLean.

Writing a book requires financial support and dedicated time. I would like to thank the University of Melbourne for awarding me a Melbourne Research Scholarship, without which I would not have completed my PhD thesis. I am extremely grateful to Carolyn Evans and Andrew Kenyon in the Melbourne Law School for their support during my PhD candidature and for allowing me to take my study leave in 2012 to work on this book. I would also like to thank Monash University Publishing for granting me permission to republish parts of Chapter 3, which were first published in September 2010 as 'Saviour Siblings and Collective Family Interests' 29(2) *Monash Bioethics Review* 12.1–12.15.

I received assistance from various other people within the Melbourne Law School. A very heartfelt thanks to the Law Research Service at the Melbourne Law School, especially Robin Gardner and Louise Ellis, for their tireless research support throughout the writing process and particularly towards the end. I am also very grateful to my Melbourne Law School friends and colleagues for their encouragement and advice – especially Jacqueline Horan, Michelle Foster, Tania Voon and Deborah Whitehall. Thanks also to Simon French for generously reviewing an earlier draft of this work with a keen eye for detail, and Suzanne Vale for brainstorming titles.

Last but not least, I would like to thank my family. A major theme throughout this book is the intrinsic value of family. I am grateful to my parents and family, not only for their love and support over the years but also for providing me with an insight into family relationships and for fostering an inquiring mind. I have been able to draw on my own experience, as the member of an intimate family, in writing this book.

In more recent years, I have been fortunate enough to have formed my own family, who are the heart of who I am. I would like to thank my husband, Michael, for his unerring support and respect for my work and for dedicating many hours over his summer holiday to reading my manuscript. Lastly, thank you to my three beautiful children and muses – Gabriel, Amelie and Juliet – who inspire me every day!

List of abbreviations

AAP	American Academy of Pediatrics (US)
ACART	Advisory Committee on Assisted Reproductive Technology (NZ)
ACT	Australian Capital Territory
AHEC	Australian Health Ethics Committee
ART	Assisted reproductive treatment
ART Act (NSW)	Assisted Reproductive Technology Act 2007 (NSW)
ART Act (SA)	Assisted Reproductive Treatment Act 1988 (SA)
ART Act (Vic)	Assisted Reproductive Treatment Act 2008 (Vic)
CEC	Clinical ethics committee
COAG	Council of Australian Governments
CORE	Comment on Reproductive Ethics
Cth	Commonwealth of Australia
DI	Donor insemination
ECART	Ethics Committee on Assisted Reproductive Technology (NZ)
HFEA	Human Fertilisation and Embryology Authority (UK)
HFE Act (UK)	Human Fertilisation and Embryology Act 1990 (UK)
HGC	Human Genetics Commission (UK)
HLA	Human leukocyte antigen
HREC	Human research ethics committee
HRT Act (WA)	Human Reproductive Technology Act 1991 (WA)
HSC	Haematopoietic stem cells
ICSI	Intracytoplasmic sperm injection
ITA	Infertility Treatment Authority (Vic)
IT Act (Vic)	Infertility Treatment Act 1995 (Vic)
IVF	*In vitro* fertilisation
NHMRC	National Health and Medical Research Council (Australia)
NSW	New South Wales
NT	Northern Territory
PGD	Preimplantation genetic diagnosis
SA	South Australia

STC	House of Commons Science and Technology Committee (UK)
UK	United Kingdom
UNCRC	United Nations Convention on the Rights of the Child
US	United States
VARTA	Victorian Assisted Reproductive Treatment Authority
Vic	Victoria
VLRC	Victorian Law Reform Commission
WA	Western Australia

1 Introduction

In October 2000 in the United States (US), Adam Nash was the first saviour sibling reported to have been born using a form of genetic screening technology known as preimplantation genetic diagnosis (PGD).[1] Adam's sister, Molly, was suffering from Fanconi's anaemia, a rare hereditary blood disease. Doctors treating Molly's parents used PGD to select an embryo that was both free of Fanconi's anaemia and a direct tissue match for Molly. After four attempts, the couple conceived a healthy son. Adam's cord blood was successfully transplanted to his sister Molly, which cured her disease. For the Nash family, Adam's birth was a triumph of modern reproductive medicine that saved their daughter's life. Despite its success for the Nash family, Adam's birth opened up a new area of controversy in assisted reproductive treatment (ART) and raised ethical concerns about the welfare of the child to be born.

The welfare of the child is a fundamental principle in assisted reproduction and a key feature in ART regulation in the United Kingdom (UK) and Australia. The use of ART for selective reproduction[2] raises particularly complex questions about the welfare of the child to be born. For example, how does selection impact on the identity of the child to be born? Can being brought into existence ever harm a child? Are children who are selected for a particular purpose treated as commodities? These questions require us to re-think the roles played by parents and the state in promoting the welfare of the child. For instance, should prospective parents be allowed to select a child with particular traits or characteristics? If so, what type of trait-selection is legitimate and where do we draw the line? Finally, who is in the best position to make decisions about the welfare of the child to be born? Is it the parents, clinicians or the state? The use of PGD to select saviour siblings has re-focused the debate on the welfare of the child to be born in recent years and compelled ethicists, policymakers, legislators, regulators and courts in the UK and Australia to reconsider the nature and role of the welfare of the child principle in assisted reproduction.

To date, concerns about the welfare of the child in selective reproduction have focused on the individual interests of the child to be born in being treated with respect and protected from harm. This book re-evaluates the welfare of the child principle in the context of selective reproduction using applied ethics. It focuses on the controversial topic of saviour siblings as a case study for an in-depth evaluation of the welfare of the child born as a result of selective reproduction. There are several reasons for this.

First, saviour sibling selection has been more widely accepted than other types of selection, such as social sex selection and selecting in disability. This is because, for many people, saving the life of an existing child represents a legitimate reason for selective reproduction. To put it another way, saviour sibling selection more 'plausibly falls within societal understandings of parental needs and choice in reproducing and raising children'.[3] As a consequence, saviour sibling selection has been carried out in several countries, including the US, the UK and Australia, advancing the legal and ethical debate surrounding this form of selective reproduction considerably during the last 10 years.

A second reason for focusing on saviour sibling selection is that much of the debate about saviour siblings centres on the welfare of the child to be born. Saviour sibling selection is currently permitted in the UK and Australia, subject to ART regulation that promotes the welfare of the child to be born. There is therefore a wealth of academic, legal and policy debate on saviour siblings from these two jurisdictions on the welfare of the future child.

A third and final reason for using saviour sibling selection as a case study is that it enables discussion to remain focused on welfare of the child concerns without becoming side-tracked by broader societal concerns about 'designer babies' that arise more commonly in relation to other types of selection. The 'designer babies' objection to selective reproduction, based on concerns about eugenics and slippery slopes, is not a major issue for saviour sibling selection. Saviour siblings are not selected to 'improve stock' but rather to save the life of an existing child and the incidence of saviour sibling selection is likely to be very low.[4] The debate about saviour siblings has therefore remained more focused on the welfare of the child and not been obscured by the ethical concerns about 'designer babies' that arise in relation to other more controversial applications of PGD.

There are two primary ethical concerns about the welfare of the child selected as a saviour sibling. The first is that the child is treated as a commodity. The second is that the child may be harmed physically, psychologically or socially. These two concerns, which have shaped the development of law and policy on selective reproduction in the UK and Australia, focus on the individual interests of the child to be born and pay little regard to the collective interests the child shares with his/her family. This book critiques the prevailing individualistic approach to the welfare of the child in assisted reproduction and proposes an alternative relational approach. It argues that a child living in an intimate family is both an individual and the member of an intimate collective and the welfare of the child to be born is inextricably linked with the welfare of his/her family. Instead of focusing on the individual interests of the child to be born, the child's interests should therefore be considered *in connection with* the interests of other family members. As previously mentioned, a third concern raised more broadly in relation to selective reproduction is that of 'designer babies', which reflects broader societal concerns about parents selecting the traits of their children.

In Chapter 2, I describe how these three main ethical concerns – commodification, harm and 'designer babies' – have shaped the debate about selective reproduction. I also explore the non-identity problem and reject the argument, commonly used to justify selective reproduction, that it is better to be born than not. I then introduce saviour sibling selection as the primary case study for an in-depth analysis of the welfare of the child principle in selective reproduction. I briefly explain some current regulatory approaches to saviour sibling selection that attempt to promote the welfare of the child to be born. In particular, I focus on the UK and Australian regulatory frameworks in which the welfare of the child to be born is a foundational principle. Although there is no clearly articulated ethical approach to the welfare of the child in either UK or Australian regulation, UK policy on the welfare of the child reflects a 'harm-based' approach, whereas at least some Australian jurisdictions promote a 'best interests' approach. I introduce an alternative 'relational approach' to the welfare of the child that highlights both individual and collective family interests. My relational approach, which is based on relational feminist and communitarian ethics, is explored in more detail in the second half of the book.

Given the strong focus in assisted reproduction on the welfare of the child to be born, it is important to understand what 'welfare of the child' means in this context. In Chapter 3, I examine the role and relevance of the welfare of the child principle in ART regulation. I begin by exploring the origins of the welfare principle in ART legislation in the UK and Australia. I then explore in detail the two key ethical concerns about the welfare of the child that have dominated the debate about saviour siblings – commodification and harm. I conclude that concerns about commodification and harm reflect an individualistic approach to the welfare of the child to be born, whose interests are treated as largely separate to and distinct from the interests of other family members. While the individual interests of the child to be born should be protected, a purely individualistic approach to the welfare of the child fails to adequately take account of the interests of the child as part of a family. Furthermore, given the interests of other family members in selective reproduction, a broader consideration of interests and relationships beyond those of the individual child to be born is necessary. I argue that, in the context of saviour sibling selection, the interests of the parents, their existing ill child, and any other siblings likely to be affected should be considered in connection with the interests of the child to be born in being treated with respect and protected from harm.

In Chapter 4, I propose an alternative relational approach to the welfare of the child to be born, which situates the interests of the child within the context of his/her family. Drawing on relational feminist and communitarian ethics, I argue that the welfare of a child is inextricably connected to the welfare of the intimate collective that is his/her family. A comprehensive account of the welfare of the child therefore requires consideration of both the individual interests of the child to be born as well as the collective interests the child shares with his/her family. By recognising the importance of connection and interdependence within a family, this broader approach to the welfare of the child not only protects the child to be born but also the family that enables the child to flourish. Recognising that the welfare of the child to be born is not necessarily synonymous with the welfare of the family as a whole, I examine the role of familial duty as a justification for compromising some individual interests of family members in favour of the welfare of the family as a whole. However, given the vulnerability of the child to be born, I argue that there should be limits on how much parents can ask of a child in order to protect that child from exploitation, abuse or neglect.

Applying my relational approach to the welfare of the child developed in Chapters 3 and 4, I propose a relational model for selective reproduction in Chapter 5. I argue that a relational model, which recognises and accommodates individual and collective interests within a family, is more appropriate for regulating selective reproduction than a 'harm-based' or 'best interests' model. My relational model requires consideration to be given to the interests of all family members, not just those of the child to be born, in making decisions about selective reproduction. In particular, I emphasise the importance of developing an effective *process* to assist prospective parents in exploring the various interests within their family and deciding whether or not to select a child with specific genetic traits. There comes a point, however, at which compromise becomes sacrifice and the child to be born should be protected from exploitation, abuse or neglect. I therefore propose that the state should provide a threshold level of protection for the child to be born. I draw on the two main ethical concerns about saviour siblings discussed in Chapter 2 to formulate a threshold level of respect and protection from harm for the child to be born.

Chapter 6 addresses issues associated with the implementation of a relational model for selective reproduction by outlining a framework for regulating saviour sibling selection. I begin by raising a preliminary question about whether selective reproduction should be regulated at all. I argue that regulation is justified insofar as it protects the welfare of the child to be born and ensures high standards in treatment services. I then draw on elements of UK and Australian regulation to 'map out' my regulatory framework. I propose a permissive regulatory framework that protects the child to be born from exploitation, abuse and neglect and promotes a robust decision-making process without unnecessarily restricting reproductive choice. I conclude that decisions about saviour siblings should be made on a case-by-case basis by parents in collaboration with their healthcare team, in accordance with legislation and policy guidelines. The healthcare team should support parents in the decision-making process by providing information, counselling and clinical ethics consultation. Decisions should also be subject to ethical oversight by clinical ethical committees to ensure the welfare of the child is adequately protected. Lastly, I explain how a relational framework for saviour sibling selection is less restrictive and more responsive to the individual circumstances of each case than current regulatory frameworks in the UK and Australia.

I conclude in Chapter 7 by highlighting the benefits and burdens of a relational model for selective reproduction and identifying areas where further research is needed. I explain that the relational framework for saviour sibling selection proposed in this book is intended as a starting point only, to trigger debate about how ethically complex decisions about selective reproduction might be made in the future. Other types of selection will no doubt raise additional concerns to those associated with saviour sibling selection and will require careful consideration and debate. In particular, selecting a child for non-therapeutic reasons, such as social sex selection or selecting for disability, challenges the way in which many people view the nature of reproduction and the parent/child relationship. By situating the child within the context of his/her family, a relational model offers a more realistic and transparent lens through which to view the thorny issues posed by selective reproduction in the future.

Notes

1 Y Verlinsky *et al*, 'Preimplantation Diagnosis for Fancomi Anemia combined with HLA Matching' (2001) 285 *Journal of the American Medical Association* 3130.

2 I use the term 'selective reproduction' to refer to the practice of selecting a child with particular traits or characteristics. In this book, I focus on selective reproduction involving PGD. There are, however, other biotechnological means for enabling parents to select in (or out) specific traits or characteristics, which raise similar concerns. These include an array of prenatal testing technologies, sperm sorting (for sex selection) and sperm donor selection.

3 J A Robertson, 'Extending Preimplantation Genetic Diagnosis: Medical and Non-medical Uses' (2003) 29 *Journal of Medical Ethics* 213. The fact that society supports a particular use of PGD does not necessarily make it ethical. However, societal acceptance has certainly influenced the debate and law and policy reform in the area of selective reproduction.

4 As at the beginning of 2010, 24 licences had been issued to use PGD for saviour sibling selection in the UK and only two births were recorded: Human Fertilisation and Embryology Authority (HFEA), *Minutes of Authority Meeting* (20 January 2010), [10.6]. In Australia, the statistics as at 2010 are similarly low. In Victoria, for example, there had only been two applications for saviour sibling selection, of which one was withdrawn and the other did not go ahead: email from Tracey Petrillo (Policy Officer, Victorian Assisted Reproductive Treatment Authority) to Michelle Taylor-Sands, 13 May 2010.

2 Selective reproduction: ethics and the law

2.1 Introduction

Adam Nash's birth is not the only case in which ethical concerns have been raised about selective reproduction. Embryo screening using PGD has been available for over 20 years and has sparked debate about how much choice prospective parents should exercise about the genetic characteristics of the children they conceive. The process of PGD involves an embryo biopsy to determine the genetic composition of embryos created through *in vitro* fertilisation (IVF) in order to select a suitable embryo for implantation. In the past, PGD has most commonly been used to screen out heritable genetic disorders that would lead to serious disease, disability or increased risk of miscarriage. In these cases, ethical concerns about the procedure are considered by many to be outweighed by the therapeutic benefits. Regulation in the UK and Australia allows prospective parents to use PGD to detect serious genetic conditions and improve ART outcomes.[1] What constitutes a serious genetic condition or disability is, however, a contentious issue.[2] The extent to which PGD might be used in relation to susceptibility or late-onset conditions,[3] for example, has led to concerns about where the line should be drawn in selective reproduction.[4]

Selecting a child for non-therapeutic reasons is even more controversial. Whereas saviour sibling selection has a clear therapeutic benefit for the existing child (if not for the child to be born), there is no obvious therapeutic benefit in using PGD for sex or disability selection. Social sex selection and selecting for disability is currently prohibited in the UK and Australia.[5] Attempts by couples to seek social sex selection in these two jurisdictions have been unsuccessful to date. In 1999, Alan and Louise Masterton approached the UK Human Fertilisation and Embryology Authority (HFEA) about using PGD to select a female embryo. The Mastertons, who had four sons, lost their only daughter in a bonfire accident and wanted another daughter to restore the gender balance in their family. The HFEA would not consider their application as no UK clinic was prepared to apply for a licence.[6] More recently, an Australian couple applied to the Victorian Patient Review Panel to obtain access to PGD for social sex selection. Similar to the Masterton family, the

Australian parents wished to conceive a girl following the death of their only daughter. They already had three boys and had aborted twin male foetuses conceived through IVF prior to their application.[7] The Patient Review Panel dismissed the application and the parents appealed, unsuccessfully, to the Victorian Administrative Appeals Tribunal.[8] Although there are no reported cases of prospective parents seeking PGD to conceive a child with a disability in the UK or Australia, a 2008 survey revealed that deliberate selection of children with a disability occurs in the US.[9]

As scientific advances present new opportunities for prospective parents to select the genetic traits of their future offspring, there is an increasing need for public debate about the ethical implications of selection and the role of the state in regulating selective reproduction. In sections 2.2 to 2.4 of this chapter, I explore three key ethical concerns that have dominated the debate about selective reproduction – 'designer babies', commodification and harm. The first is a broad societal concern about our future humanity, whereas the latter two concerns specifically relate to the welfare of the child to be born. In section 2.5, I introduce saviour sibling selection as a case study for analysing the welfare of the child principle in selective reproduction. As mentioned in Chapter 1, saviour sibling selection is currently regulated in the UK and Australia. I briefly explain the science behind saviour sibling selection before outlining the regulatory frameworks in the UK and Australia in which the welfare of the child is a foundational principle. In section 2.6, I propose a relational ethical approach to the welfare of the child that includes both individual and collective family interests. I explore in detail the individual and collective interests of the child to be born in the context of saviour sibling selection in Chapter 3.

2.2 'Designer babies'

Selective reproduction raises fears about a future in which children are selected for potentially eugenic or trivial reasons, which may ultimately threaten our understanding of what it is to be human.[10] The notion of 'designer babies' reflects a myriad of concerns based on a range of religious, political and ethical views about the impact of selection on society at large or particular groups within it. Specific objections include: religious opposition to 'playing God'; secular concerns about interfering with nature; that children are treated as products rather than 'gifts'; that selecting individual traits devalues the notion of 'unconditional parental love'; and that selecting out particular impairments discriminates against particular groups within society. A detailed examination of these harms to broader society is beyond the scope of this book, which focuses primarily on the welfare of the child to be born. In this section, however, I briefly examine the main arguments against 'designer babies' as they are relevant to some types of selection and, for some people, the 'designer babies' concern provides a reason to prohibit all forms of selective reproduction.[11]

Many of the broader societal concerns associated with 'designer babies' are less of an issue for saviour sibling selection as only a very small number of parents will attempt to conceive a saviour sibling, and saving the life of an existing child is generally widely endorsed.[12] As Jonathon Glover states, where the life of a child is at stake, 'you have got to have a very powerful reason to resist the means by which that life can be saved'.[13] Concerns associated with 'designer babies' are more relevant to selection for other purposes, in particular selecting out disability and sex selection. These concerns are likely to increase as PGD becomes more broadly available and will need to be addressed in more detail in debates about particular types of selection. I have roughly divided the 'designer baby' objection to selective reproduction into concerns about eugenics and slippery slopes, although these two categories are clearly interrelated.

2.2.1 Eugenics

The eugenics concern is complex and problematic because, although commonly relied on by opponents of selective reproduction, there is no clear single definition of 'eugenics'. The term is most commonly associated with atrocities committed in Nazi Germany and other eugenic practices carried out in the US and Europe in the early twentieth century.[14] It is therefore not surprising that eugenics is 'widely regarded as a dirty word'.[15] Although the idea of eugenic states can be traced back to Plato, the term was first used in 1883 by Francis Galton to describe the 'science of improving stock'.[16] More recently, eugenics has been defined as 'any policy that alters the composition of the human gene pool',[17] a definition broad enough to cover any type of selective reproduction. While state-imposed coercive eugenic programmes of the past have been justifiably condemned and serve as a caution in relation to genetic selection, it does not necessarily follow that all forms of eugenics are morally wrong.[18] As the House of Commons Science and Technology Committee in the UK (STC) stressed in its report to the UK Government on ART, eugenics should 'not be used as an emotive term of abuse to obscure rational debate'.[19]

The charge of eugenics is most commonly levelled at using PGD to select out genetic disability and disease.[20] This is not surprising, given the parallels with previous government-led eugenic practices in the US and Europe. One critical difference is that PGD is not imposed by the state but is a matter of individual patient choice. Isabel Karpin and Kristin Savell question, however, the 'realness' of reproductive choice amidst medical and social pressure on women to 'manage their pregnancies and potential pregnancies' to ensure the 'best' possible outcomes in terms of a healthy child.[21] This pressure is potentially compounded by ethicists who argue that potential parents have a moral reason to select a child with the best chance in life based on the 'principle of procreative beneficence'.[22] Whether or not selecting out disability ultimately constitutes eugenics is arguably a question of degree. As Gregory

Pence points out, '[j]ust because the Nazi regime went to extremes trying to create one racial phenotype, doesn't mean it's a form of eugenics to give mothers folic acid to prevent their babies from having neural-tube defects'.[23]

The primary concern associated with using PGD to select out disability or disease is that, compulsory or not, it discriminates against people with the conditions that are screened out. A secondary concern raised by David King is that screening out disability and disease will harm society more broadly by eliminating diversity.[24] Some disability activists argue that an increased use of PGD to screen out genetic disorders within society will inevitably lead to decreased support for and/or acceptance of people with disabilities.[25] Concerns about discrimination are generally divided into the 'loss of support' objection (disabled people will be worse off if fewer people are born with disabilities) and the 'expressivist' objection (using PGD to screen out disability de-values disabled lives).[26]

There are various counter-arguments to disability-based objections, including a lack of empirical evidence for the loss of support objection[27] and the fact that choosing not to have a disabled child does not necessarily equate with a discriminatory attitude towards disabled people. Furthermore, prenatal screening tests are already routinely used by prospective parents in order to detect genetic abnormalities.[28] The reasons people may have for choosing to have a child, or a child with particular traits, are complex and varied. While many potential parents may choose to screen out a disability, others may choose to have a child with a disability.[29] In this book, I argue that complex reproductive decisions are best left to prospective parents in conjunction with their healthcare providers, subject to ethical guidance and independent review. In a pluralistic society, people will no doubt make different choices about selecting out disability that will vary according to their religious beliefs, cultural background and individual circumstances. However, just because people may not *make* the same choices does not mean that they cannot *respect* one another's choices. According to Robert Boyle and Julian Savulescu, allowing people to make their own choices about PGD is, in fact, the best way to prevent state-enforced eugenics.[30]

2.2.2 *Slippery slopes*

The slippery slope objection to selective reproduction is, in some ways, an extension of the eugenics objection. A subtle distinction can be made, however, between these two objections. While eugenics is often associated with discriminatory policies, the slippery slope objection is directed more broadly at an increased use of genetic screening technologies, particularly for trivial reasons. Aside from whether selective reproduction can be classified as 'eugenic', careful consideration must also be given to the extent to which screening technologies like PGD are made available and whether a line should be drawn to preserve humanity. Instead of focusing on whether a selection decision is 'eugenic', Scott suggests it would be more helpful to 'reflect on the

reason or justification for it'.[31] Implicit in this approach is the notion that some reasons are sufficiently important to justify PGD, whereas other reasons do not warrant the use of selective screening technology.

At one end of the slippery slope, there is considerable support for using PGD to select out life threatening diseases where the child born will have little or no quality of life, such as Tay Sachs disease and Lesch-Nyhan disease.[32] Selecting out less debilitating conditions such as Down's syndrome or spina bifida, whilst more controversial, is also often justified on the basis that the parents' lives or the lives of existing children may be seriously compromised.[33] Further down the proverbial slope are late-onset and susceptibility conditions, such as early onset Alzheimer's disease and *BRCA1* and *2* susceptibility for breast cancer. The therapeutic benefit in selecting out late-onset and susceptibility conditions is more uncertain as the child may have a healthy 30–40 years before the disease manifests itself and, in the case of susceptibility conditions, the child may never develop the disease.

In the UK *Quintavalle* case, Mance LJ raised what he considered to be a crucial distinction between 'screening out abnormalities' and 'screening in preferences'.[34] The shift from PGD for therapeutic to non-therapeutic reasons raises concerns about the increased use of genetic selection and enhancement technology for social or trivial reasons.[35] A substantial increase in the number of 'designer babies' invokes dystopias such as those depicted in Aldous Huxley's *Brave New World*[36] or Andrew Niccol's 1997 film *Gattaca*, where people are no longer appreciated for who they are but are valued in terms of their genetic inheritance.

When PGD was first used to create saviour siblings, concerns were raised about stepping onto the slippery slope of 'designer babies'.[37] While saviour sibling selection represents a controversial shift in focus from the health of the child to be born to the health of the existing child, the shift does not take us very far down the slippery slope of 'designer babies'.[38] Parents seeking a saviour sibling for an ill child are simply acting on basic parental instincts to care for their children and preserve life. This point is illustrated in the following plea by Anna's father in Jodi Picoult's popular fiction novel, *My Sister's Keeper*:

> We didn't ask for a baby with blue eyes, or one that would grow to be six feet tall, or one that would have an IQ of two hundred. Sure, we asked for specific characteristics – but they're not anything one would ever consider to be model human traits. They're just *Kate's* traits. We don't want a superbaby; we just want to save our daughter's life.[39]

Wanting to save the life of an existing child could not be described as a trivial or social reason for using PGD. The more controversial aspect of saviour sibling selection is the shift in focus from the welfare of the child to be born to the welfare of the existing child, although the two should not be viewed as mutually exclusive. I explain, in Chapter 4, how a relational approach to selective reproduction involves considering the interests of the child to be born in connection with the interests of other family members.

The slippery slope objection has been raised more persuasively in relation to PGD for social sex selection. Choosing the sex of a child for social reasons represents a clear shift from the welfare of any existing or future child to parental preferences for a particular 'type' of child. Allowing PGD for social sex selection is potentially a critical step on the slippery slope towards 'designer children'. If social sex selection becomes accepted practice, it is less of a stretch to allow prospective parents to select other traits for their children, such as hair colour, sexual orientation and intelligence (assuming this becomes possible). In the UK, there is strong public opinion against allowing parents to choose the sex of their child for social reasons. The HFEA conducted a public consultation in 2002 as part of its review of sex selection policy, which revealed strong opposition to non-medical sex selection.[40] Some opponents argue that allowing social sex selection is likely to lead to a disproportionate number of males in some cultures, which may compound already existing injustices between men and women.[41] Others argue that selecting the sex of a child is inherently sexist and therefore harmful to women generally.[42]

As with fears about screening out disability, many of the concerns about social sex selection are empirically unsubstantiated.[43] Furthermore, well-considered regulation can insure against morally unacceptable types of selection. Restricting the use of PGD for family balancing would largely address concerns about sex selection related to gender disparity.[44] In 2005, the STC recommended to the UK Government that sex selection be allowed for family balancing, although this was ultimately rejected in the UK Government's reforms to ART law.[45] Sex selection is similarly prohibited in Australia, although the National Health and Medical Research Council (NHMRC), a Commonwealth statutory authority,[46] has committed to reviewing the 2005 moratorium on sex selection in Australia.[47] Using PGD to select sex raises complex ethical issues that require robust and well-informed public debate. The Victorian Civil Administrative Tribunal in Australia highlighted the lag between science and ethical debate in this area,

> The scientific or medical advances which have led to the ability to determine the sex of an embryo have occurred well in advance of public debate and discussion about the broader ethical, moral, social and cultural issues involved.[48]

Apart from any potential negative impacts on society or particular groups within it, increased selective reproduction also raises ideological concerns about how we value life and view parental love. Michael Sandel cautions that 'what began as an attempt to prevent a genetic disorder now beckons as an instrument of improvement and consumer choice'.[49] Ideological opposition to 'designer babies' is often associated with religious, conservative or dignitarian[50] concerns that it is inherently wrong to select the traits of your children. Commentators draw on notions such as the 'giftedness of life' and 'unconditional parental love' to support their position against many types of selection. For example, in its inquiry into human cloning, the President's Council on Bioethics in the US cautioned that selecting a child's genetic make-up in advance treats the child as a 'product' that is manufactured rather than a 'gift'.[51] Sandel argues that selective reproduction undermines the 'norm of unconditional love', a central tenet of parenting, and thereby 'disfigures the relation between parent and child'.[52]

The assumptions on which ideological objections to selective reproduction are based have been challenged in detail elsewhere[53] and I do not intend to repeat the broad philosophical debate in detail in this book. It is worth noting, however, that some form of trait-selection occurs in all human conceptions. At a very basic level, we influence our children's traits when we choose the other parent from whose gene pool our children will draw. If we accept that parents have legitimate interests in the 'project of parenthood',[54] then parental interests should at least be given some weight alongside those of the child to be born. Whether or not selection is justified in any given case is inevitably a question of degree and will depend on the reasons for selection and the individual circumstances of the case. Human cloning justifiably raises concerns about manufacturing children as it involves selecting the *entire* genetic make-up of a child. In contrast, using PGD to choose only one characteristic such as sex or human leukocyte antigen (HLA) compatibility with a sibling does not necessarily treat the child as a 'product' and may be justified in individual cases. Furthermore, selection at the stage of conception does not necessarily prevent parents from loving their child in the same way as any other parent once the child is born.

2.3 Commodification

The second major concern associated with selective reproduction is that it commodifies the child to be born. This objection is commonly raised against saviour sibling selection on the basis that the child to be born is treated as simply a means to save the life of his/her sibling. Claims about commodification have also been made against social sex selection. Prospective parents who want to select the sex of their child are sometimes criticised for treating the child as a means to satisfying their own gender preferences rather than an individual in his/her own right.[55] The commodification objection is closely related to the concerns about the 'giftedness of life' and 'unconditional parental love' discussed above, which focus on the nature of the parent/child relationship and parental virtues and duties.[56] In this section of the chapter, I discuss the deontological objection against commodification that stems from Immanuel Kant's second formulation of the categorical imperative to treat people 'never simply as a means, but always at the same time as an end'.[57]

The Kantian injunction against treating people simply as a means to an end has heavily influenced debate about the welfare of the child to be born in the context of selective reproduction. The commodification objection is essentially about treating the child to be born with respect. In contrast to a harm-based analysis of the welfare of the child to be born, the child is *wronged* if Kant's principle is offended, even if no *harm* flows to the child as a result.[58] As Colin Gavaghan points out, even 'if all parties involved are net beneficiaries in terms of harms and benefits, we may have done something ethically wrong if, in the process, we treated some of them as mere instruments'.[59] The parental motivation in wanting the child in his/her own right therefore becomes morally significant.

Policymakers in both the UK and Australia have raised concerns about commodification and the welfare of the child in the context of regulating saviour sibling selection. In 2001, the UK HFEA Ethics Committee stated that 'positive consideration of the welfare of the child requires respect for beings as ends and that the putative child be treated not simply as a means to further an end but also as an "end in itself".[60] In Australia, the former Victorian Infertility Treatment Authority Ethics Panel had similar concerns about saviour sibling selection and emphasised the importance of ascertaining parental motivation for saviour sibling selection to ensure that parents want a child in his/her own right and not simply as a donor for an existing child.[61] Ethical Guidelines on ART published by the NHMRC (NHMRC ART Guidelines) specifically require ethics committees advising clinics on saviour sibling selection to ascertain whether parents desire another child in his/her own right and not merely as a tissue source.[62]

Arguments against selective reproduction based on commodification have been widely discredited for being based on an incorrect interpretation of Kant's categorical imperative. According to Tom Beauchamp and James Childress,[63] Kant's dictum has often been misinterpreted to mean that we should never use another person as a means to our ends, whereas it in fact prohibits treating another person *exclusively* as a means to an end. Kant's formulation envisages that people may be treated as a means, provided they are also treated as an end. It is therefore acceptable to use someone as a means, provided you 'do not lose sight of the fact that s/he is also an end in him/herself'.[64] Selective reproduction would not, therefore, offend Kant's categorical imperative if the parents desire a child in his/her own right even though they may also desire a child for a particular purpose, such as saving the life of an existing child or satisfying a long-held desire to have a daughter.

Ultimately, the commodification objection to selective reproduction based on a strict interpretation of Kant's categorical imperative is weak. The objection raises, however, important questions about parental motivation for having a child that may impact on the welfare of the child to be born. In Chapter 3, I examine in more detail parental motivation for selecting a saviour sibling when I explore the child's interest in being treated with respect.

2.4 Harm

The third major objection to selective reproduction is the risk of harm to the child to be born. In contrast to the deontological concern about commodification, the harm objection focuses on the potential consequences for the child selected using PGD. The principle of non-maleficence, which asserts an obligation not to inflict harm intentionally, is one of the principal precepts of medical ethics.[65] For instance, the principle of non-maleficence is reflected in the Latin edict *primum non nocere* (meaning 'first, do no harm').[66]

According to the Victorian Law Reform Commission (VLRC) in Australia, the need to protect children from harm is '[t]he most common justification for regulation of ART'.[67] This is consistent with a liberal approach to regulation whereby state intrusion into people's private lives is only justified if it prevents harm to others.[68] In the UK, HFEA policy reflects a 'harm-based' approach to the welfare of the child to be born by conferring a threshold level of protection on the future child.[69] Following its review of the welfare of the child principle in 2005, the HFEA stated that there is now a 'presumption to provide treatment unless there is evidence that any child born to an individual or couple, or any existing child of their family, would face a risk of serious harm'.[70] This approach is reinforced in the HFEA's Code of Practice, which requires assessments about the welfare of the child to be born to focus on factors that are likely to cause a risk of significant harm or neglect to the child.[71] Clinics should refuse treatment where a risk of significant harm or neglect exists.[72] By way of contrast, the 'best interests' approach to the welfare of the child in at least some Australian jurisdictions[73] seems to imply something more than protection from significant harm or neglect, although exactly what 'best interests' encompasses is unclear.[74]

There are risks of physical and/or psychosocial harm to the child born as a result of selective reproduction. First, there is a risk of physical harm associated with ART and the embryo biopsy process used for PGD. Second, there is a risk of physical and/or psychosocial harm associated with being selected for a particular purpose. In the remainder of this section, I outline the risks of harm associated with the process of PGD and selection. I provide a more detailed discussion of specific risks of harm associated with being selected as a saviour sibling in Chapter 3.

2.4.1 *Risks of ART and embryo biopsy*

Several studies have identified that there are risks of physical harm to the child to be born as a result of ART, although findings vary. In Australia, children conceived by ART are more likely to be stillborn or to die shortly after birth, although outcomes differ depending on the ART procedure used.[75] This higher death rate is largely attributable to a higher incidence of pre-term delivery and multiple births associated with ART. However, a recent Australian study revealed that twins conceived as a result of IVF are far more likely to need hospital treatment than naturally conceived twins.[76] A Danish study also suggests that women who undergo IVF are four times more likely to have a stillborn baby than those who conceive naturally.[77]

There is also evidence that ART increases the risk of birth defects, although it is unclear as to whether those defects are caused by the IVF process or are associated with the underlying infertility.[78] In 2010, a French study revealed that the birth defect risk is twice as high for children born as a result of ART.[79] This is consistent with an earlier Western Australian study that found that children born as a result of IVF had twice the state average of birth defects.[80] However, a more recent Western Australian study suggests that the prevalence of major birth defects associated with IVF may be decreasing.[81] According to a recent Swedish study, there is a small risk that children born using IVF are more likely to develop childhood cancers than children conceived naturally.[82] Belgian research on the epigenetic differences between children conceived using IVF and children conceived naturally suggests that IVF babies could also be more prone to diseases like diabetes and obesity later in life.[83]

Although current evidence suggests that the physical risks associated with embryo biopsy appear to be minimal, more evidence is needed about long-term outcomes for the child who is born.[84] To date, no rigorous long-term studies have been conducted on the health of children conceived from biopsied embryos. Given that one or more cells are removed from the embryo during the biopsy procedure, trauma is possible. A recent study of mice conceived using PGD suggests that the developing nervous system may be sensitive to embryo biopsy.[85] The study revealed that successful births from biopsied embryos were significantly lower than normal embryos, with some mice from biopsied embryos experiencing increased weight gain and memory decline in adulthood.

Aside from any harm to the child to be born as a result of ART and embryo biopsy, there is also potential harm to embryos that are rejected in the selection process. In the UK and Australia, excess embryos may be stored for future treatment, donated or used in research in compliance with the relevant regulatory regimes.[86] Gavaghan argues that '[t]hose de-selected embryos which will never attain sentience will simply never develop interests of any kind, never attain the capacity to be harmed'.[87] Whether or not one accepts that an embryo is 'harmed' by destruction ultimately depends on the view taken of the status of the embryo.[88] Applying a gradualist view of the status of the embryo,[89] embryo selection (and destruction) is acceptable provided there are legitimate reasons for the procedure. Embryo destruction is arguably less problematic than terminating a more developed foetus following prenatal diagnosis. Objections about harm to excess embryos have been discussed in detail in debates about abortion and embryo research and I do not intend to replay them in this book, which focuses on harm to the child to be born.

2.4.2 *Risks associated with particular types of selection*

Particular types of selection also carry potential ongoing physical and/or psychological risks for the child to be born. A child selected as a saviour sibling, for example, may be exposed to risks of future physical harm associated with peripheral blood and bone marrow donations if the initial cord blood donation is unsuccessful. In addition to the physical risks associated with donation, being selected to save the life of another may also have a negative impact on a saviour sibling's sense of self-worth or identity. A child selected on the basis of sex may similarly feel that he/she was chosen for a particular purpose and feel bound by parental expectations based on gender stereotypes.[90]

Perhaps the most controversial form of selection, in terms of harm to the child to be born, is selecting a child with an impairment or disability. The ethical debate in this area is further complicated by the fact that there is considerable disagreement as to what constitutes a disability.[91] To date, PGD has been used predominantly to *screen out* disease or disability. It is, however, possible to use PGD to *select in* certain traits, such as deafness or dwarfism, which many people consider to be disabling. The primary objection to selecting a child with a disability or impairment is that the child is harmed in cases where the disability causes pain, discomfort or reduced life opportunities. Although using PGD to select a child with a genetic defect or disability is currently prohibited in the UK and Australia,[92] the STC in the UK and the NHMRC in Australia have both acknowledged the need for further debate in this area.[93]

Whether or not a child is harmed by having a disability is ultimately a complex question and depends on a variety of factors, including the child's level of functional impairment, the availability of public facilities accommodating that impairment, private resources available to the parents, and community attitudes. There is also considerable debate as to whether a particular impairment constitutes a disability. Candace Duchesneau and Sharon McCullough, the US couple who selected a deaf sperm donor to maximise their chances of conceiving a deaf child, have defined deafness not as a disability but 'as a cultural identity'.[94] According to Glover, a functional limitation only becomes a disability if 'it impairs capacities for human flourishing'.[95] Careful consideration of these issues will be necessary in determining whether this controversial type of selection should be allowed.

The potential risks of physical and psychosocial harm to children born as a result of PGD will vary according to the type of selection made. Where there are legitimate reasons for selection, some risk of harm is arguably justifiable, particularly if the risk is low. Selection for therapeutic reasons is often regarded as more legitimate than selection for non-therapeutic reasons. For example, many would argue that selecting out embryos that have a serious disease is more legitimate than selecting out female embryos to satisfy parental desires for a male offspring. Some commentators claim that a child selected using PGD is only harmed if his/her life is 'so bad that it is not worth living'[96] – an approach that would render most types of selection acceptable. This approach, which relies on the argument that it is better to be born than not (subject to a life not worth living) is ultimately unconvincing.

2.4.3 Better to be born than not

A commonly cited argument in support of selective reproduction is that the child selected benefits overall as existence is generally better than non-existence, subject to the exception of a life 'not worth living'.[97] This argument is based on the conception of harm proposed by Joel Feinberg in the context of wrongful life cases, whereby a child is only harmed if he/she is caused to be worse off than he/she otherwise would have been (the counterfactual test).[98] So if existence is generally better than non-existence, being brought into existence cannot harm the child if non-existence is the child's only alternative. This relies on Derek Parfit's problem of non-identity, which states that when parents or their doctor select a particular embryo over another, the decision is *identity-affecting* because the alternative for the child who is born is not a different life but non-existence.[99]

In the context of selective reproduction, Sally Sheldon and Stephen Wilkinson state that the philosophical problem of non-identity, ' ... does not necessarily mean that child welfare considerations should be completely disregarded. But it does make it almost impossible to construct a child welfare argument against creating the child whose welfare is under consideration'.[100] Gavaghan similarly argues that the child's interests are already served by being brought into existence and the child 'cannot be harmed by those decisions upon which its very existence is dependent'.[101] John Harris adopts the same reasoning when he states that 'to give the highest priority to the welfare of the child to be born is always to let that child come into existence, unless existence overall will be a burden rather than a benefit'.[102] Similarly, Boyle and Savulescu argue that given the alternative for the child to be born is 'not another life in which he or she was conceived in another way, but non-existence', it is difficult to argue that selection harms the child who is born.[103]

The argument in favour of existence does not apply to 'a life not worth living'. It is therefore worth exploring what this phrase means. Glover explains that 'some kinds of life are perhaps worse than not being alive at all'.[104] Cases involving non-treatment decisions for infants and wrongful life claims have been used as a benchmark for defining 'a life not worth living'. John Robertson argues that few conditions would render a child's life so 'horrible' that his/her interests would be 'best served by never being born'.[105] Feinberg elaborates on the standard adopted in wrongful life cases in the US by referring to the most extreme cases where 'it is rational to prefer not to have come into existence at all', and refers to 'some of the more severely victimised sufferers' of brain malformation, spina bifida, Tay-Sachs disease, polycystic kidney disease and Lesch-Nyhan syndrome.[106]

In a similar vein, Gavaghan refers to 'a life of such wretched quality that, from the subjective perspective of the child itself, it would have been better never to have been born'.[107] He notes that such cases are rare, but suggests that it is plausible to conceive of lives 'affected by genetic disorders that guarantee brief, severely cognitively impaired and pain-filled lives' as being not worth living.[108] Gavaghan refers to UK case law involving non-treatment decisions for infants, in which the courts have recognised that there will be cases where the life of the child is 'so bound to be full of pain and suffering' that life is a burden rather than a benefit and life-prolonging treatment would not be justified.[109]

Margaret Coady describes another way in which a life may be considered not worth living, apart from those lives that are severely affected by genetic disorders. She suggests that it is possible to think of an extreme example where a child is born into a family where there is a very high probability of the child being seriously abused.[110] In such a case, it is conceivable that the child would prefer non-existence.[111] However 'a life not worth living' is defined, Sheldon and Wilkinson argue that the chances of a child born using PGD having a life worse than death are 'surely remote'.[112] Therefore, according to the argument in favour of existence, the child to be born as a result of selective reproduction will generally be better off than had he/she not been born at all.

Although the non-identity problem has been frequently relied on to justify selective reproduction, not all commentators are convinced of its application in genesis cases. James Rachels believes there are significant problems in using the non-identity principle to argue that a child is made better off by being born. He argues that the presumption that you confer a benefit on a child merely by bringing it into existence is easily disputed.[113] I shall provide three reasons why the non-identity problem fails adequately to address concerns about the welfare of the child to be born in the context of selective reproduction.

My first objection is more a preliminary qualification to the application of the non-identity problem. The non-identity problem clearly arises in relation to the risks of harm associated with the child's identity, or the reasons for which the child is selected. An embryo selected because it will be deaf could only ever become a deaf child. There are no other options for that embryo apart from becoming a deaf child, apart from non-existence. However, there are additional risks of harm associated with the PGD process (which involves ART and embryo biopsy) that could be avoided if the child is born naturally. The non-identity problem is not relevant to these risks of harm because there is another option for the child – to be born as a result of natural conception. It is therefore important to distinguish between the harm associated with the child's identity and the harm caused by the PGD process itself. The problem of non-identity is only relevant to those risks of harm associated with a particular child's identity.

My second objection is that Feinberg's assessment of harm based on the counterfactual test is specifically directed at wrongful life claims under tort law and is not readily applicable to selective reproduction. As previously discussed, Feinberg argues in the context of wrongful life cases that a child is harmed only if his/her life is so bad that non-existence is rationally preferable to existence.[114] This very high threshold is only met in the most extreme cases of disability, pain or suffering, where the child's life can be described as 'not worth living'. There are two reasons why I believe this threshold is inappropriate for selective reproduction.

First, Feinberg himself recognises the limitations of his conception of harm by acknowledging that children born with impairments that are not so severe that they render the child's life not worth living 'suffer the continuing residual harms caused by the acts that produced their existence' (even though the child may not be harmed in the way necessary to mount a tort claim for damages).[115] Feinberg states that a child born with an impairment who has a life worth living has no *grievance* (in terms of an infringement of rights) but is justified in feeling *resentment* about being born into a *state of harm* or harmful condition. So the child may not be *harmed* for the purposes of tort law, but the child may still *suffer harm* of the sort that is relevant to decisions about selective reproduction.

Second, wrongful life claims involve a child who is already in existence whereas selective reproduction involves a child who is not yet in existence. There is a difference between saying that a life once commenced is worth living (the test applied in wrongful life cases) and a potential life not yet commenced should be created (the decision you make when you select a child using PGD). Benatar distinguishes between *a life not worth continuing* and *a life not worth beginning* and argues that a higher threshold applies to the first scenario. According to Benatar '[w]e require stronger justification for ending a life than for not starting one'.[116] To put the same argument in a slightly different way, those who already exist have an interest in existing whereas those who do not yet exist have no interest in existing. As Cynthia Cohen states, '[t]he Interest in Existing argument ... is an after-the-fact argument meant to apply at a time when children are already born'.[117] In contrast, when a decision is made to select a child using PGD, the child is not yet born.

My third objection to relying on the non-identity problem in the context of selective reproduction focuses on the morally objectionable consequences of this line of reasoning. By logical extension, almost any form of selective reproduction could be justified, irrespective of the risks of harm for the child to be born provided they fall short of a life 'not worth living'. Recalling Sheldon and Wilkinson's words quoted above, the non-identity problem makes it 'almost impossible to construct a child welfare argument against creating the child whose welfare is under consideration'. A child may have a life of considerable pain and suffering that is still worth living but is it a good thing to bring about such a life? There seems to be something morally repugnant about justifying the use of PGD to select a child who will experience considerable pain and suffering on the basis that his/her life may, overall, be a life worth living.

As already discussed, selective reproduction involves various risks of harm to the child to be born. Given the problems associated with applying the non-identity problem in the context of selective reproduction, it is difficult to argue that a child is better off being born where there is a clear risk of harm to that child. It is therefore important to consider all potential harms to the child to be born when making decisions about selective reproduction in order to determine what level of harm renders a *life not worth beginning*. As the risks of harm associated with selective reproduction will vary according to the particular reasons for selection, the risks must be carefully considered for each type of selection. In this book, I explore an appropriate harm threshold to protect the welfare of the child in the context of saviour siblings.

2.5 Case study: saviour siblings

The debate about saviour siblings has largely focused on the welfare of the child to be born, making PGD for saviour sibling selection an excellent case study for this book. To date, ethical concerns about commodification and harm have dominated the debate about the welfare of the child to be born as a saviour sibling. These two concerns provide valuable guidance on how selective reproduction may impact on the welfare of the child to be born. In particular, they highlight two legitimate interests of the child: (a) an interest in respect; and (b) an interest in protection from harm. In Chapter 3, I examine in detail these two individual interests of the child to be born.

In this section of the chapter, I explore how ethical concerns about commodification and harm have influenced legislators and policymakers in the UK and Australia. I begin by explaining the process for saviour sibling selection and stem cell donation. I then discuss how ethical concerns about the welfare of saviour siblings have been addressed through regulation in the UK and Australia. Despite the strong focus on the welfare of the child to be born, there is no clear ethical approach to the welfare of the child principle articulated in UK and Australian ART regulation. This has, in the past, created confusion for policymakers, clinicians and prospective parents. Lastly, I highlight some key lessons that can be learnt from saviour sibling regulation in the UK and Australia.

2.5.1 The process

Parents can use PGD to conceive a direct donor or saviour sibling for an existing child who requires a stem cell transplant through tissue typing, also known as HLA matching. Where the existing child is suffering from a heritable disease, an embryo biopsy is carried out to screen for genetic disease and select an embryo that is a direct tissue match for the existing sibling. Where the existing child is suffering from a non-heritable disease, tissue typing may be carried out alone.

Children born as a result of this process are described as 'saviour siblings' because they have the capacity to save the life of the existing sibling through umbilical cord blood stem cell donation. Cord blood stem cells are one of three sources of allogeneic haematopoietic stem cells (HSC).[118] The other two sources of HSC are peripheral blood and bone marrow.[119] HSC transplantation has become standard procedure for treating a number of malignant and non-malignant conditions.[120] In cases where a cord blood transplant from a saviour sibling proves unsuccessful, a peripheral blood or bone marrow transplant may need to be carried out at a later date.[121] Although it is possible for parents to conceive a child naturally who is a direct tissue match, there is only a one in four chance of this occurring.[122] PGD enables parents actively to select a child who will be an exact tissue match with an existing sibling, thereby removing the element of chance involved with natural conception.

Tissue-matched siblings are not the only potential source of HSC. HSC may also be obtained from other family members or unrelated donors with a compatible tissue type. In 2010, there were more than seven million living adults on the National Marrow Donor registry in the US and six million additional donors and cord blood units in registries around the world.[123] However, not everyone who needs an HSC transplant will find a compatible tissue donor, particularly if they are from an ethnic minority group.[124] For example, in Australia only 50 per cent of patients for whom a search was initiated through the Australian Bone Marrow Donor Registry between 2003 and 2005 found a suitable unrelated cord blood, peripheral blood or bone marrow donor.[125] Lower success rates were found for patients in the Asian (38 per cent), aboriginal Australian (33 per cent) and Indian (0 per cent) populations.[126] Even where a compatible unrelated donor exists, tissue-matched siblings are generally preferred as donors by physicians because the risks of graft-versus-host disease and other transplant-related complications are more common with unrelated donors.[127]

2.5.2 Regulation

There are various ways in which the welfare of the child born as a result of PGD may be protected. Governments throughout the world have taken different approaches to regulating PGD for saviour sibling selection. At one end of the spectrum, using PGD for selective reproduction is prohibited outright in some countries, including Ireland and Italy.[128] At the other end, there is virtually a free market for PGD in the US, subject to professional regulation and general criminal and civil law.[129] The UK and Australia fall somewhere in between by taking a permissive regulatory approach to PGD, although some states in Australia are more prescriptive than others.[130] In both the UK and Australia, the welfare of the child to be born is a key consideration, which is enshrined in legislation.[131]

The UK HFEA has struggled in the past to apply the welfare of the child principle in saviour sibling cases. Following a comprehensive review of saviour sibling selection and the welfare of the child principle in 2004, the HFEA produced detailed guidelines in its Code of Practice on saviour sibling selection.[132] In Australia, the NHMRC has produced some broad guidelines on saviour sibling selection.[133] However, there is no clearly articulated ethical approach underlying the welfare of the child provision in either UK or Australian regulation. In the remainder of this section, I briefly discuss the UK and Australian regulatory frameworks for saviour sibling selection and highlight some of the problems created by Parliament's failure to articulate a clear ethical approach to the welfare of the child in ART regulation. In section 2.6, I argue that a relational ethical approach is more appropriate than the prevailing individualistic approach to the welfare of the child implicit in UK and Australian regulation.

2.5.2.1 The UK

In the UK, the HFEA licenses clinics to carry out PGD in accordance with the Human Fertilisation and Embryology Act 1990 (HFE Act (UK)) and the HFEA Code of Practice.[134] The HFE Act (UK) sets out broad licensing criteria and confers discretionary decision-making powers on the HFEA, subject to a general duty to consider the welfare of the child to be born. Specifically, the HFE Act (UK) states that 'a woman shall not be provided with treatment unless account has been taken of the welfare of the child who may be born as a result of the treatment (including the need for supportive parenting), and of any other child who may be affected by the birth'.[135] The future child's welfare has been described 'in the broad sense of rights, interests and well-being'.[136] However, because the welfare of the child provision is 'intrinsically discretionary and not supported by a coherent ethical framework', its application has in the past been 'arbitrary and problematic'.[137]

Prior to 2008, the HFE Act (UK) did not expressly authorise the HFEA to grant licences to use PGD for saviour sibling selection and the HFEA's authority to do so was legally challenged in 2002 by Josephine Quintavalle on behalf of the pro-life interest group, Comment on Reproductive Ethics (CORE).[138] CORE contended that the HFEA did not have the authority to issue a licence for the Hashmi family to use PGD in conjunction with tissue typing to conceive a direct tissue match for their son, Zain, who was suffering from Beta-thalassaemia. The challenge, which ultimately failed on appeal,[139] highlighted a need for the UK Parliament to clearly sanction controversial applications of PGD to prevent legal challenges. Following an extensive review of ART law by the UK Government, the HFE Act (UK) was amended in 2008 to authorise the HFEA specifically to license saviour sibling selection where the existing sibling 'suffers from a serious medical condition which could be treated by umbilical cord blood stem cells, bone marrow or other tissue of any resulting child'.[140] PGD is not available, however, to conceive a child as a donor for a non-sibling family member, such as a parent, or to conceive a child as an organ donor.

The HFEA has also been criticised for making inconsistent decisions in cases involving saviour sibling selection. A few months after its decision to issue a licence for PGD to the Hashmi family, the HFEA subsequently refused a licence for the Whitaker family to use PGD solely to conceive a direct tissue match for their existing child, Charlie, who had a non-inherited strain of Diamond-Blackfan anaemia.[141] The contradictory decisions made by the HFEA about saviour sibling selection in these two cases highlight the difficulties faced by the HFEA in applying the welfare of the child principle to PGD. As the Whitakers were not at risk of passing on a heritable condition, there was no need to screen for disease in conjunction with tissue typing. Screening embryos for tissue type alone was not in line with the HFEA interim policy on tissue typing at the time, which was based on the welfare of the child. The HFEA reasoned that, given the concerns about the physical and psychological safety of children conceived using PGD, the invasive and potentially harmful procedure could only be justified where the embryo could be said to benefit from the procedure in the sense that the embryo was free from a genetic disorder. The HFEA therefore restricted PGD for tissue typing to cases where it was used in conjunction with screening to avoid a genetic disorder.[142]

The HFEA's interim policy was widely criticised for being based on a flawed application of the welfare of the child principle. As several commentators have pointed out, the risk/benefit analysis for the child to be born as a result of PGD is the same, whether tissue typing is carried out alone or in conjunction with screening for genetic disease.[143] This is because genetically screening an embryo using PGD does not confer any direct benefit on the embryo in the sense that it 'cures' the embryo in any way. Rather, it simply detects those embryos that are already free from genetic disorders.[144] In either case the embryo is being selected on the basis that it is a direct tissue match with an ill sibling. According to the STC, the HFEA 'tied itself in ethical knots' when it attempted to apply the welfare of the child provision in these two cases.[145] The HFEA reviewed its interim policy in 2004 and removed the arbitrary distinction between PGD for tissue typing in conjunction with screening for disease and tissue typing alone.[146]

Current HFEA policy on saviour sibling selection is significantly improved.[147] The HFEA Code of Practice requires clinics to consider the circumstances of each application for saviour sibling selection individually.[148] Clinics are required specifically to consider the condition of the existing sibling, the possible consequences for any child who may be born as a result of PGD, and the family circumstances of the people seeking treatment.[149] The policy also requires detailed information to be given to patients considering saviour sibling selection about the procedure, associated risks, likelihood of success, likely impact on family members and other sources of treatment.[150] Lastly, HFEA policy requires clinics offering saviour sibling selection to have arrangements in place to facilitate long-term medical and psychosocial follow-up studies of children born as a result.[151] The HFEA reviewed its case-by-case approach to licensing saviour sibling selection in late 2009 and, in January 2010, determined to continue this approach for the time-being.[152] The HFEA was influenced by the fact that 'there are still-unresolved ethical and social concerns' regarding saviour sibling selection and very little information on the benefits and risks of the treatment.[153]

2.5.2.2 Australia

Australia has a similar facilitative regime for PGD to the UK. However, due to federalism, PGD is currently regulated in Australia by a combination of state legislation and national professional standards and ethical guidelines. According to Helen Szoke, 'Australia may be described variously as a rich tapestry of diversity in terms of the regulatory structure, or a patchwork of regulatory stitching lacking cohesion and order'.[154] As in the UK, there is a strong focus on the welfare of the child to be born in Australian ART regulation but no clearly articulated ethical approach to the welfare principle. Fragmented regulatory frameworks with deficient ethical underpinnings operate at a significant cost. Isabel Karpin and Belinda Bennett argue that the complex nature of Australia's regulatory framework for ART 'results in regulatory gaps and general confusion for individuals, clinicians, policy-makers, parents and potential parents'.[155] It also promotes 'reproductive tourism' between states and territories.[156] Greater consistency and certainty could be achieved through uniform national regulation of ART in Australia that is based on clear ethical foundations.

The NHMRC ART Guidelines deal briefly with PGD for saviour sibling selection and thereby provide some level of national consistency.[157] Although the Guidelines themselves do not have the force of law, compliance with them is a key element in the national accreditation system for state- and territory-based ART clinics in Australia and is linked to federal funding.[158] The NHMRC ART Guidelines apply to all Australian states and territories, except to the extent that they are inconsistent with legislation in those jurisdictions.[159] Four states in Australia have expressly legislated in respect of ART – Victoria, South Australia (SA), Western Australia (WA) and New South Wales (NSW).[160] Unlike the UK, saviour sibling selection is not expressly mentioned in the ART legislation in any of these jurisdictions.

The NHMRC ART Guidelines impose a similar regime for saviour sibling selection to that in the UK. Both jurisdictions limit treatment to cases where the existing child is suffering from a serious or life-threatening condition and where the child to be born will be a sibling of the person needing a stem cell transplant.[161] Both require clinics to provide parents with counselling, information on treatment options, the risks associated with treatment for the woman and the child to be born, the likelihood of achieving a successful pregnancy and alternatives to treatment.[162] An additional requirement of the NHMRC ART Guidelines is that clinics must seek advice from a clinical ethics committee (CEC) before providing PGD for saviour sibling selection.[163] The CEC must specifically consider whether the parents wish to have another child as an addition to their family and not merely as a source of tissue.[164] The Guidelines do not impose any eligibility requirements on patients seeking ART services, thereby leaving it up to clinics to develop their own protocols for 'access to, and eligibility for, treatment'.[165]

The availability of PGD varies throughout Australia depending on whether individuals are eligible for ART and the weight attributed to the welfare of the child to be born in each particular state or territory. For example, in Victoria, SA and WA, access to ART is limited by legislation to women who are either: (a) unlikely to become pregnant without ART;[166] or (b) at risk of passing on a genetic disease or abnormality.[167] Accordingly, parents can only use PGD for tissue typing when it is carried out in conjunction with screening for a genetic abnormality or disease. This mirrors the earlier HFEA interim policy on tissue typing in the UK and leads to the anomalous situation whereby parents with a child suffering from a heritable disease (Hashmi family) can use PGD to select a saviour sibling, whereas parents with a child suffering from a non-heritable disease (Whitaker family) cannot. In Victoria, there is also a presumption against treatment where a woman or her partner has been found guilty of a sexual offence, convicted of a violent offence or had a child protection order made against them.[168] The Victorian Patient Review Panel may, however, grant individuals who do not satisfy the eligibility criteria or for whom there is a presumption against treatment access to ART (including PGD) in certain cases.[169]

As in the UK, the welfare of the child is a key principle in ART legislation in Victoria, SA and WA. In Victoria and SA, legislation requires the welfare and interests of the child to be born to be treated as paramount.[170] The strong focus in these two states on the welfare of the child to be born appears to be at odds with saviour sibling selection, a procedure primarily motivated by the interests of the existing child and his/her parents. By way of contrast, legislation in WA requires consideration to be given to the welfare and interests of *both* the participants *and* any child likely to be born as a result of the procedure.[171] This approach appears to be more appropriate for saviour sibling selection. The NHMRC ART Guidelines, which regulate the remaining states and territories, simply require that the use of PGD for saviour sibling selection 'not adversely affect the welfare and interests of the child to be born'.[172]

2.5.3 Lessons from the UK and Australia

There are several lessons that can be taken from the regulation of saviour sibling selection in the UK and Australia, many of which are relevant to selective reproduction generally. First, regulation should clearly address the availability of controversial applications of PGD to prevent legal challenge in individual cases. Second, there is no ethical justification for distinguishing between saviour sibling cases where the existing child is suffering from a hereditary as opposed to non-hereditary condition. The risk/benefit analysis for the child to be born as a result of PGD is the same, irrespective of whether the embryo is screened for genetic disease in conjunction with tissue typing.

Third, in federations such as Australia, a uniform national approach to ART regulation should be adopted to ensure consistency and certainty and prevent potential reproductive tourism. Uniform national regulation is generally viewed as a 'positive objective' in the area of reproductive technology.[173] It not only reduces regulatory duplication but also ensures common clinical and ethical standards in relation to treatment services at a national level. Fourth, further empirical research is needed in relation to the short- and long-term impact of newly emerging applications of PGD on the child who is born. A significant problem faced by the HFEA in formulating its interim policy on saviour sibling selection was the lack of empirical evidence about the risks of physical and psychosocial harm to the child to be born. Robust empirical data requires ongoing monitoring of children born as a result of PGD. Fifth, given the lack of information currently available on the risks associated with new applications of PGD, decisions about access in individual cases should be made on a case-by-case basis.

Lastly, if the welfare of the child is to remain a key principle in ART legislation, the role and nature of this principle should be clearly articulated by Parliament. The welfare of the child principle has been notoriously difficult to apply in the context of PGD, as past experience in the UK illustrates. Some commentators have questioned the relevance of the welfare of the child provision in ART legislation and called for its repeal.[174] The strong focus on the welfare of the child to be born in UK and Australian ART legislation reflects an intention by Parliament to protect the interests of the most vulnerable party – the child to be born. There are, however, other relevant interests at stake in assisted reproduction, including those of the prospective parents and any existing children. In one sense, the welfare of the child provision may be primarily a rhetorical device to ensure that the interests of the most vulnerable party are adequately protected. In the absence of a clear ethical approach to the welfare of the child to be born, however, it is difficult to reconcile the interests of the child to be born with those of his/her family. In section 2.6, I propose a relational ethical approach to the welfare of the child to be born that addresses the child as both an individual and a member of a family.

2.6 A relational approach to the welfare of the child

The Kantian and harm-based concerns about the welfare of the child that have, to date, dominated the debate about saviour siblings provide some useful insights into the interests of the child to be born in the context of selective reproduction. However, children need more than respect and protection from harm in order to flourish. Children are highly dependent on the intimate relationships they have with their parents and other family members. The welfare of the child therefore needs to be viewed more broadly within the social context of the family into which the child is born.

The contemporary interpretation of Kant adopted in the saviour sibling debate, which focuses on parental motivation for having a child, is of limited value in evaluating the overall welfare of the child to be born. The child to be born clearly has an interest in being respected as valuable in his/her own right. A more important question, however, is how the child is treated once born. This question involves a broader exploration of the child's needs and the relationships within the family that supplies those needs. Given that the welfare of a child is inextricably connected with the welfare of his/her family, welfare assessments must take account of the child's relationships with other family members. Moral theories that focus on individual interests are generally ill equipped to explain the moral significance of intimate relationships such as those found in families. This is not meant as a criticism of Kant's ethics, but rather of how contemporary interpretations of Kant's categorical imperative have been applied in the debate about selective reproduction.[175]

Concerns about harm to the child to be born as a result of selective reproduction are legitimate. However, assessing the welfare of the child by simply balancing harms against perceived benefits is problematic. As discussed in section 2.4, there are risks of harm to the child to be born associated with the PGD process and various types of selection. These risks cannot simply be dismissed by the claim that it is better to be born than not. In Chapter 3, I argue that there is potentially no individual net benefit for the child who is selected to be a saviour sibling. Why, then, do many people intuitively feel that saviour sibling selection is morally acceptable? Clearly, the benefits to the family as a whole, in saving the life of the existing child, form part of the reckoning about saviour sibling selection. A more holistic approach is therefore needed to reflect the interrelated interests of family members in selective reproduction. One possible approach is utilitarianism. By removing the focus on the individual interests of the child to be born, a utilitarian approach can take into account other family interests and balance them against those of the child to be born. In the context of saviour sibling selection, other family interests include the interests of the parents, the ill child and any other siblings who are likely to be affected by the death of the sibling. Utilitarianism focuses on bringing about the 'greatest good' in terms of happiness, utility or satisfaction for all concerned.

According to Virginia Held, '[u]tilitarianism is better than Kantian and other deontological approaches in recognising the importance of satisfying needs, because it can weigh them heavily in the calculus of preference satisfaction'.[176] At first glance, utilitarianism seems well suited to deal with the issues arising out of selective reproduction. Selective reproduction generally affects the interests of all members within a family. It is therefore important to consider the interests of not only the child to be born, but also his/her parents and any existing siblings. However, a utilitarian approach would not adequately protect the welfare of the child to be born as his/her interests could potentially be sacrificed in order to achieve the greatest good. For example, the greatest good may be served by allowing saviour sibling selection, even if the child to be born may be seriously harmed as a result. An extreme example might involve using the saviour sibling as a 'tissue farm' for the existing child. The risk of significant harm to the child to be born may still be outweighed by the cumulative benefits to the ill child (whose life may be saved) and his/her parents (who are spared the death of a child). Given the vulnerable position of the child to be born who has no 'voice' in the debate about selective reproduction, it is important to ensure that the welfare of the child is neither overlooked nor subordinated to the interests of others.

Another problem with applying utilitarian principles to selective reproduction is that families are more than 'aggregates of individuals'.[177] As Held states, 'utilitarianism still relies on an abstract universal principle appealing to rational individuals'.[178] Utilitarianism undervalues the moral significance of families and the relationships within them. Families have an inner focus or communal purpose that cannot be measured by the sum of their parts. As Patricia Smith suggests '[a]ggregate good is probably too individualistic an ideal to capture the moral relations of the family'.[179] Alison Jost similarly argues that, 'Good ethical deliberation requires weighing the many competing values in any difficult ethical dilemma. Weighing values doesn't mean pitting them against one another, but considering the contextual and relational heft in a given case'.[180] By failing to situate the child within the context of his/her family, utilitarianism suffers from similar shortcomings to other approaches that focus on the individual interest of the child to be born. A more nuanced approach than utilitarianism is needed to reflect the relational nature of interests within families.

During the last 20 years, there have been various attempts to put the 'relational' into the moral realm, particularly by feminist theorists. Early feminists rejected 'mainstream moral philosophy' in order 'to account for women's moral experience'.[181] More recently, some feminists have revised traditional moral concepts to take account of the relational nature of the self.[182] Held has developed an alternative moral paradigm, based on Carol Gilligan's work on moral psychology and the ethics of care.[183] In contrast to predominant ethical theories that treat moral agents as rational, independent and autonomous individuals, the ethics of care views persons 'as relational and as interdependent'.[184] According to Held:

> A caring relationship requires mutuality and the cultivation of ways of achieving this in the various contexts of interdependence in human life. Noticing interdependencies, rather than thinking only or largely in terms of independent individuals and their individual circumstances is one of the central aspects of the ethics of care.[185]

The ethics of care recognises the moral significance of a person's relationships with his/her family and focuses 'on persons responding with sensitivity to the needs of particular others with whom they share interests'.[186]

Communitarian theory has also influenced the debate about how the welfare of the child should be conceptualised. Some theorists have emphasised the importance of collective endeavour or 'affiliation' to human flourishing.[187]

Family members have certain shared interests that cannot easily be separated. The welfare of a child is therefore inextricably connected with the welfare of the intimate collective that is his/her family. Some commentators have explored the collective welfare of families in the specific context of sibling donations. For instance, Robert Crouch and Carl Elliott argue that:

> [t]he picture of human agent as independent and self-interested that has fuelled so many errors in this context is an inadequate picture of the human agent *within the family*. To think of family members in this way is to miss what is of importance in family life and to human agency.[188]

Other commentators have emphasised that the child to be born should 'not be viewed in isolation'[189] but rather as part of a 'social circle of shared relationships'.[190]

I explore relational feminist and communitarian ethical theories in more detail in Chapter 4 where I propose a relational approach to the welfare of the child to be born.

2.7 Conclusion

New and controversial opportunities for selective reproduction raise legitimate fears about the future of humanity and the welfare of the child to be born. This book focuses primarily on the latter. Saviour sibling selection offers an interesting and current case study for exploring the welfare of the child to be born as a result of selective reproduction. Ethical concerns about commodification and harm have influenced legislators and policymakers in the UK and Australia in regulating PGD to select a saviour sibling. The absence of a clearly articulated ethical approach to the welfare of the child to born in ART legislation has, however, led to some inconsistent decision-making about saviour sibling selection in the UK in the past that could potentially be repeated in Australia. Saviour sibling regulation in the UK and Australia presents a learning tool for developing regulation on selective reproduction in other jurisdictions more generally.

The welfare of the child to be born remains a key principle in ART regulation in the UK and Australia but one that requires further analysis and clarification. In Chapter 3, I examine the nature and role of the welfare of the child principle in UK and Australian ART regulation by exploring its origins and recent review. I also explore the individual interests of the child to be born in the specific context of saviour sibling selection. As foreshadowed in this chapter, however, conceptualising the welfare of the child to be born solely in terms of the child's individual interests is problematic because the welfare of a child depends, at least in part, on the welfare of the family into which the child is born.

It is unrealistic to view the welfare of a child in isolation from the child's family. It is equally problematic to view families as a collection of distinct and separable interests that can be weighed against one another in order to promote the 'greatest good'. Such an approach undervalues the moral significance of families and the relationships between family members. As revealed in this chapter, an individualistic approach to the welfare of the child to be born has led proponents of selective reproduction to rationalise selection on the basis that the child is better off being born than not. This justification is unconvincing and potentially leads to morally unacceptable outcomes. It is not necessary, however, to establish that selective reproduction is in the individual interests of the child to be born if a relational approach to the welfare of the child is adopted.

Notes

1 In the UK, see Human Fertilisation and Embryology Act 1990 (UK), Schedule 2, s 1ZA (1). In Australia, see National Health and Medical Research Council (NHMRC), *Ethical Guidelines on the Use of Assisted Reproductive Technology in Clinical Practice and Research 2004 (as revised in 2007 to take into account the changes in legislation)* (June 2007) (NHMRC ART Guidelines), [12.1].

2 For an in-depth analysis of the concept of 'serious disability', see Isabel Karpin and Kristin Savell, *Perfecting Pregnancy: Law, Disability and the Future of Reproduction* (Cambridge University Press, 2012). Although a detailed discussion of the definition of 'disability' is beyond the scope of this book, I use this term to broadly describe a functional impairment that impacts negatively on a person's well-being by causing pain, discomfort or reduced life opportunities. Scholarship during the last 20 years highlights both the medical and social aspects of disability: see below, n 92. See also Jonathan Glover, *Choosing Children: Genes, Disability and Design* (Clarendon Press, 2006), esp 6–8.

3 Susceptibility conditions are those where the child is born healthy but faces a higher than average risk of serious disease, such as cancer. In relation to late-onset conditions, such as early onset Alzheimer's disease, the child will be healthy for several decades before experiencing any symptoms.

4 Recent PGD testing in Victoria for the *BRCA1* and *BRCA2* gene mutations associated with breast cancer has led to debate about whether PGD should be used when the expression of gene is not 100 per cent: Julia Medew, 'Couples Use IVF to Pick Genes: "Designer Baby" Concerns', *The Age* (Melbourne), 3 July 2012, 1.

5 PGD is only available in the UK and Australia to avoid the transmission of sex-linked disorders, such as haemophilia: Human Fertilisation and Embryology Act 1990 (UK), Schedule 2, s 1ZA(1)(c) and s 1ZB; NHMRC ART Guidelines, above n 1, [12.2]; and Assisted Reproductive Treatment Act 2008 (Vic) (ART Act Vic), s 28.

6 House of Commons Science and Technology Committee (STC), Fifth Report of Session 2004–5, *Human Reproductive Technologies and the Law*, HC7–1 (24 March 2005) (STC Report), 63.

7 Julie Kent, 'Aussie Couple Fights to Have a Baby Girl Through Selective IVF: Have Already Aborted Twin Boys', *Cleveland Leader* (online), 10 January 2011, <http://www. clevelandleader.com/node/15670> (accessed 26 April 2013).

8 *JS and LS v Patient Review Panel (Health and Privacy)* [2011] VCAT 856 (8 April 2011).

9 Three per cent of the US PGD clinics surveyed enabled parents to use PGD to select an embryo with a disability: Susannah Baruch, David Kaufman and Kathy Hudson, 'Genetic Testing of Embryos: Practices and Perspectives of US In Vitro Fertilization Clinics' (2008) 89 *Fertility and Sterility* 1053, 1055.

10 Some commentators express concerns about the impact of increased genetic selection on human dignity. See, for example: Leon R Kass, *Life, Liberty and the Defense of Dignity: the*

Challenge for Bioethics (Encounter Books, 2002); Francis Fukuyama, *Our Posthuman Future: Consequences of the Biotechnology Revolution* (Strauss & Giroux, 2002); Bill McKibben, *Enough: Genetic Engineering and the End of Human Nature* (Bloomsbury, 2003).

11 By way of contrast, Colin Gavaghan argues that the term 'designer babies', although catchy, 'contributes little to the debate about PGD': Colin Gavaghan, *Defending the Genetic Supermarket: Law and Ethics of Selecting the Next Generation* (Routledge-Cavendish, 2007), 8.

12 There are, of course, some who maintain that there is something inherently wrong about selecting the genetic make-up of your children irrespective of how well-intentioned. See, for example, Leon R Kass, 'Triumph or Tragedy? The Moral Meaning of Genetic Technology' (2000) 45 *American Journal of Jurisprudence* 1

13 'Doctor Plans UK "Designer Baby" Clinic', *BBC News* (online), 11 December 2001 <http://news.bbc.co.uk/1/hi/health/1702854.stm> (accessed 26 April 2013).

14 There is a wide spectrum of eugenic practices, from 'positive eugenics' such as targeted family allowances, to 'negative eugenics' such as forced sterilisation and genocide. For a discussion of the history of the eugenics movement and its various forms, see Daniel Wikler, 'Can We Learn from Eugenics' (1999) 25 *Journal of Medical Ethics* 183, 184–86.

15 Raanan Gillon, 'Eugenics, Contraception, Abortion and Ethics' (1998) 24 *Journal of Medical Ethics* 219, 219.

16 Attributed to Galton in Wikler, above n 14, 184.

17 John Gillott, 'Screening for Disability: A Eugenic Pursuit?' (2001) 27 *Journal of Medical Ethics*, Supp No 2, ii21, ii21.

18 In the context of assisted reproduction, Gavaghan suggests it is 'ironic to hear the fear of eugenics used in arguments for more limitations on reproductive autonomy' given that the worst eugenics abuses were state controlled: Gavaghan, above n 11, 3. Gregory Pence describes those who conflate reproductive choice with eugenics as 'Alarmists': Gregory E Pence, *How to Build a Better Human: An Ethical Blueprint* (Rowman & Littlefield, 2012), 16.

19 STC Report, above n 6, [116].

20 The same charge is also levelled at prenatal diagnosis combined with selective termination.

21 Karpin and Savell, above n 2, 3.

22 Julian Savulescu and Guy Kahane, 'The Moral Obligation to Create Children with the Best Chance of the Best Life' (2009) 23 *Bioethics* 274. See also Janet Malek, 'Use or Refuse Reproductive Genetic Technologies: Which Would a "Good Parent" Do?' (2013) 27 *Bioethics* 59.

23 Tyler Greer, 'Medical Ethicist Examines How to Build a Better Human' *UAB Reporter* (Birmingham), 30 August 2012, <http://www.uab.edu/news/reporter/people/item/2697-medical-ethicist-examines-how-to-build-a-better-human> (accessed 26 April 2013).

24 STC Report, above n 6, [114].

25 See, for example, Tom Shakespeare, *Disability Rights and Wrongs* (Routledge, 2006).

26 For a detailed discussion of these objections and their limitations, see Gavaghan, above n 11, 103–23; Stephen Wilkinson, *Choosing Tomorrow's Children: The Ethics of Selective Reproduction* (Clarendon Press, 2010), 166–85.

27 Some commentators have suggested that decreasing the number of people with a disability may in fact benefit people with disabilities by decreasing the number of people competing for resources: Gavaghan, above n 11, 105; Lynn Gillam, 'Prenatal Diagnosis and Discrimination Against the Disabled' (1999) 25 *Journal of Medical Ethics* 163, 164. Furthermore, the majority of disabilities are caused by injury or illness rather than genetics: D C Wertz and J C Fletcher, 'Feminist Criticism of Prenatal Diagnosis: A Response' (1993) 36 *Clinical Obstetrics and Gynaecology* 541, 551.

28 Common prenatal tests include nuchal translucency scans, amniocentesis and chorionic villus sampling.

29 In 1996 in the US, Candy McCullough and Sharon Duchesneau sought a congenitally deaf sperm donor to increase their chances of conceiving a deaf child: Julian Savulescu,

'Deaf Lesbians, "Designer Disability", and the Future of Medicine' (2002) 325 *British Medical Journal* 771. The couple viewed deafness as a 'cultural identity' rather than a disability, which reflects the complexity surrounding the notion of 'disability'. For a detailed discussion of the debate about whether disability is a medical or social phenomenon and its implications for PGD, see Isabel Karpin, Choosing Disability: Preimplantation Genetic Diagnosis and Negative Enhancement' (2007) 15 *Journal of Law and Medicine* 89.

30 Robert J Boyle and Julian Savulescu, 'Ethics of Using Preimplantation Genetic Diagnosis to Select a Stem Cell Donor for an Existing Person' (2001) 323 *British Medical Journal* 1240, 1242. By way of contrast, Michael Sandel condemns this idea of 'liberal eugenics' by arguing that 'removing the coercion does not vindicate eugenics': Michael J Sandel, 'The Case Against Perfection: What's Wrong with Designer Children, Bionic Athletes, and Genetic Engineering' (2004) 292 *The Atlantic Monthly* 50, 60.

31 Rosamund Scott, 'Choosing between Possible Lives: Legal and Ethical Issues in Preimplantation Genetic Diagnosis' (2006) 26 *Oxford Journal of Legal Studies* 153, 163.

32 For example, 'Tay-Sachs children lose motor skills and mental functions. Over time, the child becomes blind, deaf, mentally retarded, paralyzed and non responsive to the environment. Tay-Sachs children usually die by age five', National Tay-Sachs & Allied Diseases Association of Delaware Valley, *Tay-Sachs Disease* (n.d.), <http://www.tay-sachs.org/tay-sachs_disease.php> (accessed 23 April 2013). Even some disability activists support this position. See, for example, Tom Shakespeare, 'Choices and Rights: Eugenics, Genetics and Disability Equality' (1998) 13 *Disability and Society* 665, 670.

33 Scott, above n 31, 164.

34 *R (on the application of Quintavalle) v Human Fertilisation and Embryology Authority* [2003] EWCA Civ 667, [2004] QB 168, [134] (Court of Appeal).

35 Human Fertilisation and Embryology Authority (HFEA) and Human Genetics Commission Joint Working Party, *Outcome of the Public Consultation on Preimplantation Genetic Diagnosis* (November 2001), [25].

36 Aldous Huxley, *Brave New World* (Vintage, first published 1932, 2007 edn).

37 See, for example, Sarah Boseley, 'Green Light for "Designer Babies" to Save Siblings', *The Guardian* (online), 22 July 2004, <http://www.guardian.co.uk/science/2004/jul/22/sciencenews.health3?INTCMP=SRCH> (accessed 26 April 2013).

38 Ram suggests that saviour sibling selection is 'less slippery' because it is aimed at curing a particular disease rather than eradicating it from the gene pool: N R Ram, 'Britain's New Preimplantation Tissue Typing Policy: An Ethical Defence' (2006) 32 *Journal of Medical Ethics* 278, 281.

39 Jodi Picoult, *My Sister's Keeper* (Allen & Unwin, 2005), 103.

40 HFEA, *Sex Selection: Options for Regulation: A Report on the HFEA's 2002–03 Review of Sex Selection Including a Discussion of Legislative and Regulatory Options* (2003), [45].

41 See, for example, Giuseppe Benagiano and Paola Bianchi, 'Sex Preselection: An Aid to Couples or a Threat to Humanity?' (1999) 14 *Human Reproduction* 868. Gender imbalances in favour of males in India and China are frequently cited as examples of the dangers of social sex selection.

42 For a discussion of this feminist opposition to social sex selection, see Adrienne Asch and Gail Geller, 'Feminism, Bioethics, and Genetics' in Susan M Wolf (ed), *Feminism & Bioethics: Beyond Reproduction* (Oxford University Press, 1996), 318, 336.

43 Although there appears to be a clear preference in some cultures for male babies, there is no evidence to suggest that the availability of PGD for social sex selection in all countries would lead to an imbalance in the number of boys over girls. For instance, studies on gender preferences in Germany and the UK revealed that, of those respondents who had an interest in the sex of their children, the vast majority wanted an equal number of boys and girls: E Dahl *et al*, 'Preconception Sex Selection for Non-Medical Reasons: A Representative Survey from Germany' (2003) 18 *Human Reproduction* 2231; E Dahl *et al*, 'Preconception Sex Selection for Non-Medical Reasons: A Representative Survey from the

UK' (2003) 18 *Human Reproduction* 2238. Some commentators argue that, in any event, an imbalance in sex ratios in favour of men might even benefit women: Claude Sureau, 'Gender Selection: A Crime Against Humanity or the Exercise of a Fundamental Right?' (1999) 14 *Human Reproduction* 867.

44 The phrase 'family balancing' is, however, open to interpretation: Wilkinson, above n 26, 217–18.

45 STC Report, above n 6, [142]; Department of Health (UK), *Review of the Human Fertilisation and Embryology Act: Proposals for Revised Legislation (Including Establishment of the Regulatory Authority for Tissue and Embryos)*, Cm 6989 (2006).

46 The NHMRC is established under the National Health and Medical Research Council Act 1992 (Cth).

47 NHMRC, *Assisted Reproductive Technology (ART)* (2012) <http://www.nhmrc.gov.au/health-ethics/australian-health-ethics-committee-ahec/assisted-reproductive-technology-art/assisted-> (accessed 26 April 2013).

48 *JS and LS* [2011] VCAT 856, above n 8, [29]. In the UK, the STC emphasised the need for further empirical research into demographic implications and psychosocial harms associated with social sex selection: STC Report, above n 6, [136], [139].

49 Sandel, above n 30, 52.

50 Roger Brownsword describes the 'dignitarian alliance' as a third perspective to utilitarian and human rights perspective in bioethics. The 'dignitarian alliance' relies on human dignity as a basis for constraint in biotechnology: Roger Brownsword, 'Bioethics Today, Bioethics Tomorrow: Stem Cell Research and the "Dignitarian Alliance"' (2003) 17 *Notre Dame Journal of Law, Ethics & Public Policy* 15, 18.

51 The President's Council on Bioethics, *Human Cloning and Human Dignity: An Ethical Inquiry* (Washington), July 2002, xxix.

52 Michael J Sandel, *The Case Against Perfection: Ethics in the Age of Genetic Engineering* (Harvard University Press, 2007), 46 and 49.

53 See, for example, Wilkinson, above n 26, 21–41; John Davis, 'Selecting Potential Children and Unconditional Parental Love' (2008) 22 *Bioethics* 258.

54 Scott, above n 31, 166.

55 Tonti Filippini, for example, has expressed concerns about acceptance of a child being conditional on gender: *JS and LS* [2011] VCAT 856, above n 8, [36].

56 For a detailed discussion of parental duties and virtues in the context of selective reproduction, see Wilkinson, above n 26, Chapter 2.

57 Immanuel Kant, *Groundwork of the Metaphysics of Morals* (Cambridge University Press, first published 1785, 2005 edn), [4.429].

58 For a discussion of the complex philosophical debate about the difference between wronging and harming, see Rahul Kumar, 'Who Can Be Wronged?' (2003) 31 *Philosophy & Public Affairs* 99.

59 Gavaghan, above n 11, 157.

60 HFEA Ethics & Law Committee, *Ethical Issues in the Creation and Selection of Preimplantation Embryos to Produce Tissue Donors* (22 November 2001), [2.9].

61 Infertility Treatment Authority (ITA), *Report on the Outcome of Consultation with Members of the Infertility Treatment Authority Ethics Panel* (February 2002) (document provided to the author by Tracey Petrillo (Policy Officer, VARTA) in July 2009) (ITA Report).

62 NHMRC ART Guidelines, above n 1, [12.3.1].

63 Tom L Beauchamp and James F Childress, *Principles of Biomedical Ethics* (Oxford University Press, 5th edn, 2001), 351.

64 Gavaghan, above n 11, 156. As Gavaghan points out, everyday transactions between customer and vendor, employer and employee and client and service provider all involve treating someone as a means to an end and are not considered morally objectionable.

65 The principle of nonmaleficence is also one of Beachamp and Childress' four core ethical principles in medical ethics: Beauchamp and Childress, above n 63.

66 Beachamp and Childress note 'that the obligation not to inflict harm on others' is '[o]ften proclaimed the fundamental principle in the Hippocratic tradition of medical ethics' although its precise origins are unclear: Beauchamp and Childress, above n 63, 113.

67 Victorian Law Reform Commission (VLRC), *Assisted Reproductive Technology & Adoption, Final Report* (2007) (VLRC Report), 46.

68 This approach is based on John Stuart Mill's harm principle: John Stuart Mill, 'On Liberty' in Mary Warnock (ed), *Utilitarianism and On Liberty* (Blackwell Publishing, 2nd edn, 2003), 88.

69 This is in accordance with the 'minimum threshold principle' and is consistent with the STC's recommendation: HFEA, *Tomorrow's Children: A Consultation on Guidance to Licensed Fertility Clinics on Taking in Account the Welfare of Children to be Born of Assisted Conception Treatment* (January 2005), [2.4]; STC Report, above n 6, [107].

70 HFEA, *Tomorrow's Children: Report of the Policy Review of Welfare of the Child Assessments in Licensed Assisted Conception Clinics* (January 2005), 1.

71 HFEA, *Code of Practice* (8th edn, first published 2009, revised October 2011) <http://www.hfea.gov.uk/docs/8th_Code_of_Practice.pdf> (accessed 26 April 2013) (HFEA Code of Practice), [8.10].

72 HFEA Code of Practice, ibid, [8.15].

73 The VLRC stated in its report on assisted reproduction that the 'best interests of the child is central to ART legislation in Victoria, South Australia and Western Australia': VLRC Report, above n 67, 46. The NHMRC ART Guidelines also state that '[c]linical decisions must respect, primarily, the interests and welfare of the persons who may be born': NHMRC ART Guidelines, above n 1, [5.1].

74 The elusive nature of the 'best interests' approach is acknowledged by the VLRC in its report on assisted reproduction: VLRC Report, above n 67, 47. I discuss a 'best interests' approach to the welfare of the child in more detail in Chapter 3.

75 Ruth McNair, *Outcomes for Children Born of ART in a Diverse Range of Families* (Victorian Law Reform Commission Occasional Paper), August 2004. ART may involve various procedures, including IVF, intracytoplasmic sperm injection (ICSI) and donor insemination (DI).

76 M Hansen, *et al*, 'Twins Born Following Assisted Reproductive Technology: Perinatal Outcome and Admission to Hospital' (2009) 24 *Human Reproduction* 2321.

77 K Wisborg, H J Ingerslev and T B Henriksen, 'IVF and Stillbirth: a Prospective Follow-Up Study' (2010) 25 *Human Reproduction* 1312.

78 T Savage, *et al*, 'Childhood Outcomes of Assisted Reproductive Technology' (2011) 26 *Human Reproduction* 2392.

79 G Viot, S Epelboin and F Olivennes, 'Is there an Increased Risk of Congenital Malformations after Assisted Reproductive Technologies (ART)? Results of a French Cohort Composed of 15 162 Children' (2010) 25 *Human Reproduction* 154.

80 M Hansen, *et al*, 'The risk of major birth defects after intracytoplasmic sperm injection and in vitro fertilisation' (2002) 346 *New England Journal of Medicine* 725.

81 M Hansen, *et al*, 'Assisted Reproductive Technology and Major Birth Defects in Western Australia' (2012) 120 *Obstetrics & Gynecology* 852.

82 B Källén, *et al*, 'Cancer risk in children and young adults conceived by in vitro fertilisation' (2010) 126 *Pediatrics* e270.

83 S Katari, 'DNA methylation and gene expression differences in children conceived in vitro or in vivo' (2009) 18 *Human Molecular Genetics* 3769.

84 Human Genetics Commission, *Making Babies: Reproductive Decisions and Genetic Technologies* (January 2006), [4.13].

85 Y Yang, *et al*, 'Evaluation of blastomere biopsy using a mouse model indicates the potential high risk of neurodegenerative disorders in the offspring' (2009) 8 *Molecular & Cellular Proteomics* 1490.

86 In the UK, see Human Fertilisation and Embryology Act 1990 (UK), ss 3, 11 and Schedule 2. See also Human Fertilisation and Embryology (Research Purposes)

Regulations 2001 (SI 2001/188) (UK), and HFEA, *Code of Practice*, above n 71, Guidance Note 17. In Australia, see NHMRC ART Guidelines, above n 1, parts 7, 8 and 17. For the definition of 'excess ART embryo' in Australia, see Research Involving Human Embryos Act 2002 (Cth), s 9 (*Research Involving Human Embryos Act*).

87 Gavaghan, above n 11, 156.

88 For example, Catholicism views the embryo as a human life entitled to full human rights. Accordingly, the embryo would be considered to be harmed by its destruction.

89 In contrast to an absolutist or 'pro-life' approach, which affords full human rights to the embryo, the gradualist view provides that the development of personhood is a gradual process but the embryo is entitled to some protection.

90 Many naturally conceived children are also subject to parental expectations, perhaps in relation to sporting or academic achievement. The pressure of parental expectation may, however, be more pronounced where the child's very existence and genetic make-up are directly related to the expectations of the child's parents. For a discussion of the oppressive nature of 'genetic programming', see Jürgen Habermas, *The Future of Human Nature* (Polity, 2003), 92; Bill McKibben, above n 10, 58.

91 In the past, the term 'disability' has been used to describe specific physical or psychiatric impairments, such as deafness, blindness or depression. This medical model of disability has been widely challenged for neglecting the influence of society on the notion of disability. For a detailed discussion of the medical, social and (more recent) postmodern models of 'disability', see Karpin and Savell, above n 2, 15–21. The broad definition of 'disability' I adopt in this book does not align itself with a particular model but attempts to accommodate both medical and social aspects of disability: above n 2.

92 Human Fertilisation and Embryology Act 1990 (UK), s 14(4); NHMRC ART Guidelines, above n 1, [12.2].

93 STC Report, above n 6, [145]; NHMRC ART Guidelines, above n 1, [12.2].

94 'Couple "Choose" to Have a Deaf Baby', *BBC News* (online), 8 April 2002, <http://news.bbc.co.uk/2/hi/health/1916462.stm> (accessed 23 April 2013). For a detailed discussion of the importance of context in defining, see Karpin, above n 29, 94–95.

95 Glover, above n 2, 9.

96 Savulescu, above n 29, 772.

97 See, for example, Boyle and Savulescu, above n 30, 1242; Sally Sheldon and Stephen Wilkinson, 'Hashmi and Whitaker: An Unjustifiable and Misguided Distinction?' (2004) 12 *Medical Law Review* 137, 152–53; J J Harris, 'The Welfare of the Child' (2000) 8 *Health Care Analysis* 27, 29.

98 Joel Feinberg, 'Wrongful Life and the Counterfactual Element in Harming' (1986) 4 *Social Philosophy and Policy* 145. Wrongful life claims are claims made by children born with foreseeable impairments who seek compensation for being brought into the world on the basis that they would have been better off not being born. In the US, damages have been awarded to a child on the basis of a wrongful life claim: *Turpin v Sortini*, 31 Cal 3d 220 (1982), whereas courts in the UK and Australia have rejected wrongful life claims because of the impossibility of assessing damages for the harm caused: *Harriton v Stephens* (2006) 226 CLR 52; *McKay v Essex Area Health Authority* [1982] QB 1166.

99 Derek Parfit, *Reasons and Persons* (Clarendon Press, 1984), 358–61.

100 Sheldon and Wilkinson, above n 97, 152.

101 Gavaghan, above n 11, 154.

102 Harris, above n 97, 33.

103 Boyle and Savulescu, above n 30, 1242.

104 Jonathan Glover and European Commission of Human Rights, *Fertility and the Family: the Glover Report on Reproductive Technologies to the European Commission* (Fourth Estate, 1989), 129.

105 John A Robertson, *Children of Choice: Freedom and the New Reproductive Technologies* (Princeton University Press, 1994), 85.

106 Feinberg, above n 98, 159.

107 Gavaghan, above n 11, 92.

108 Gavaghan, above n 11, 92.

109 *Re B (A Minor) (Wardship: Medical Treatment)* [1990] 3 All ER 927, per Lord Templeman, 929. See also, *Re J (A Minor) (Wardship: Medical Treatment)* [1990] 3 All ER 930.

110 Margaret Coady, 'Families and Future Children: The Role of Rights and Interests in Determining Ethical Policy for Regulating Families' (2002) 9 *Journal of Law and Medicine* 449, 455.

111 In practice, it should be possible to safeguard against this possibility if people convicted of child abuse are prohibited access to ART and/or if government social services took appropriate action to protect any child at risk under child protection laws.

112 S Sheldon and S Wilkinson, 'Should Selecting Saviour Siblings Be Banned?' (2004) 30 *Journal of Medical Ethics* 533, 536.

113 James Rachels, 'When Philosophers Shoot From the Hip' (1991) 5 *Bioethics* 67, 69.

114 Feinberg, above n 98, 161–62.

115 Feinberg, above n 98, 177.

116 David Benatar, *Better Never to Have Been: The Harm of Coming into Existence* (Clarendon Press, 2006) 23.

117 Cynthia Cohen, 'Give Me Children or I Shall Die!' New Reproductive Technologies and Harm to Children' (1996) 26 *Hastings Center Report* 19, 22. Christine Overall argues that '[p]rior to conception, there is no being who can be benefited or harmed by coming into existence': Christine Overall, *Why Have Children? The Ethical Debate* (The MIT Press, 2012) 116.

118 American Academy of Pediatrics (AAP), 'Policy Statement – Children as Hematopoietic Stem Cell Donors' (2010) 125 *Pediatrics* 392, 392.

119 AAP, ibid.

120 AAP, above n 118. HSC transplantation is used to treat a variety of diseases in children and adults, including selected hematologic malignancies, immunodeficiences, hemaglobinpathies, bone marrow failure syndromes and congenital metabolic disorders.

121 The likelihood of success of any HSC transplant varies according to the type of disease being treated and the stage of the disease. For example, the success rate of HSC transplants 'ranges from 50% to 70% in more favourable cases and from 10% to 25% for patients with less favourable conditions or advanced disease': Kendra D MacLeod, *et al*, 'Pediatric Sibling Donors of Successful and Unsuccessful Hematopoietic Stem Cell Transplants (HSCT): A Qualitative Study of Their Psychosocial Experience' (2003) 28 *Journal of Pediatric Psychology* 223, 223.

122 In 1991, Marissa Ayala featured on the cover of *Time Magazine* as a naturally conceived donor for her sister Anissa, who was suffering from leukaemia: Lance Morrow, 'When One Body Can Save Another' (1991) 137 *Time Magazine* 54.

123 AAP, above n 118, 392–93.

124 AAP, above n 118, 393. Cord blood stem cells need not be as perfectly matched to the recipient as conventional bone marrow transplants because cord blood stem cells are less likely to trigger immune rejection: at 395. However, due to the smaller number of stem cells in a unit of cord blood, transplants using cord blood stem cells engraft more slowly than stem cells from peripheral blood or bone marrow. Because transplant patients are at risk of developing life-threatening infections until engraftment occurs, cord blood recipients have a higher risk of infection than peripheral blood or bone marrow recipients: The Leukemia and Lymphoma Society, 'Cord Blood Stem Cell Transplantation' (Fact Sheet No 2, August 2007), <http://www.lls.org/resourcecenter/freeeducationmaterials/treatment/cordblood> (accessed 24 April 2013).

125 G N Samuel, *et al*, 'Ethnicity, Equity and Public Benefit: A Critical Evaluation of Public Umbilical Cord Banking in Australia' (2007) 40 *Bone Marrow Transplantation* 729, 731–32.

126 Samuel, *et al*, ibid.

127 AAP, above n 118, 392.

128 Using PGD to select a particular embryo may be forbidden either expressly or implicitly by prohibitive legislation. In Ireland, Article 40.3.3 of the Irish Constitution expressly protects the right to life of the unborn. In Italy, preimplantation testing is permitted, but all embryos must be implanted so selecting embryos for implantation is forbidden. Article 13 of law 40/2004 only allows diagnostic and therapeutic interventions on the embryo aiming to protect its health and development. However, several recent court and tribunal rulings in Italy have held that couples have a constitutional right to PGD to screen for genetic disease. For a discussion of these cases, see E Turillazzi and V Fineschi, 'Preimplantation Genetic Diagnosis: A Step by Step Guide to Recent Italian Ethical and Legislative Troubles' (2008) 34 *Journal of Medical Ethics* e21, 1. More recently, the European Court of Human Rights ruled that an Italian couple had an international human right to access PGD to screen for cystic fibrosis: *Costa v Italy* (European Court of Human Rights, Chamber, Application No 54270/10, 28 August 2012).

129 There is no federal regulation of ART in the US. Although some US states have legislated in relation to ART generally, there are no laws that explicitly address saviour sibling selection.

130 In Australia, the regulatory framework varies from state to state as a result of federalism. Victorian legislation establishes a more restrictive regime with criminal sanctions, whereas SA, WA and NSW have more permissive legislative schemes.

131 In the UK, see Human Fertilisation and Embryology Act 1990 (UK), s 13(5). In Australia, see NHMRC ART Guidelines, above n 1, [12.3.1]. State legislation also emphasises the welfare of the child to be born. See, for example, Assisted Reproductive Treatment Act 2008 (Vic), s 5.

132 HFEA, *Code of Practice*, above n 71, [10.17]–[10.24].

133 NHMRC ART Guidelines, above n 1, [12.3].

134 Human Fertilisation and Embryology Act 1990 (UK), ss 11–13, 25.

135 Ibid, s 13(5).

136 Department of Health (UK), *Review of the Human Fertilisation and Embryology Act: A Public Consultation* (2005) (Department of Health Public Consultation), [3.1].

137 Iain McDonald, Rachel Anne Fenton and Fiona Dabell, 'Treatment Provisions: Proposals for Reform of the Human Fertilisation and Embryology Act 1990' (2007) 29 *Journal of Social Welfare and Family Law* 293, 295.

138 *R (on the application of Quintavalle) v Human Fertilisation and Embryology Authority* [2002] EWHC 3000 (Admin), [2003] 2 All ER 105 (High Court).

139 *Quintavalle* [2003] EWCA Civ 667, [2004] QB 168, above n 34; *Quintavalle (on behalf of Comment on Reproductive Ethics) v Human Fertilisation and Embryology Authority* [2005] UKHL 28, [2005] 2 AC 561 (House of Lords).

140 Human Fertilisation and Embryology Act 1990 (UK), Schedule 2, para 1ZA(1)(d).

141 Other non-inherited conditions (for which couples have sought PGD solely for tissue typing) are acute lymphoid leukaemia and acute myeloid leukaemia: Jess Buxton, 'Unforeseen Uses of Preimplantation Genetic Diagnosis – Ethical and Legal Issues' in Kirsty Horsey and Hazel Biggs (eds), *Human Fertilisation and Embryology: Reproducing Regulation* (Routledge-Cavendish, 2007) 109, 116.

142 This is contrary to the advice given by the HFEA Ethics & Law Committee on 22 November 2001, which recommended that the HFEA licence PGD for tissue typing alone as well as in conjunction with screening for genetic disease: HFEA Ethics & Law Committee, above n 60, [3.14].

143 See, for example, Sheldon and Wilkinson, above n 97; Ram, above n 38; Gavaghan, above n 11, 162–65.

144 Sheldon and Wilkinson, above n 97, 156.

145 STC Report, above n 6, [251].

146 HFEA, *Minutes of the 139th Open Authority Committee Meeting (Part 2 – Open Meeting)* (21 July 2004), <http://www.hfea.gov.uk/docs/AM_Minutes_Jul04.pdf> (accessed 26

April 2013). The HFEA announced New Guidance on PGD for tissue typing on 4 August 2004.

147 HFEA, *Code of Practice*, above n 71, Guidance Note 10.

148 HFEA, *Code of Practice*, above n 71, [10.18].

149 HFEA, *Code of Practice*, above n 71, [10.19]–[10.21].

150 HFEA, *Code of Practice*, above n 71, [10.22].

151 HFEA, *Code of Practice*, above n 71, [10.24].

152 HFEA, *Minutes of Authority Meeting* (20 January 2010) (HFEA Minutes), [10.13].

153 David King, 'The Case for Case-by-Case Regulation of PGD' (2010) 541 *BioNews*, <http://www.bionews.org.uk/page_53438.asp> (accessed 24 April 2013).

154 Helen Szoke, 'Australia – A Federated Structure of Statutory Regulation of ART' in Jennifer Gunning and Helen Szoke (eds), *The Regulation of Assisted Reproductive Technology* (Ashgate, 2003) 75, 75.

155 Isabel Karpin and Belinda Bennett, 'Genetic Technologies and the Regulation of Reproductive Decision-Making in Australia' (2006) 14 *Journal of Law and Medicine* 127, 130.

156 In its report on ART, the VLRC stated that the absence of uniform ART regulation in Australia has caused people who are ineligible for treatment in one state travel to less regulated states for treatment: VLRC Report, above n 67, 55.

157 NHMRC ART Guidelines, above n 1, [12.3].

158 Fertility Society of Australia, Reproductive Technology Accreditation Committee, *Code of Practice for Assisted Reproductive Technology Units* (revised October 2010). Accreditation is now mandatory under Commonwealth legislation regulating embryo research and human cloning: Research Involving Human Embryos Act 2002 (Cth), ss 8 and 11.

159 NHMRC ART Guidelines, above n 1, [2.11], [3.1].

160 ART is regulated in Victoria by the Assisted Reproductive Treatment Act 2008 (Vic), in SA by the Assisted Reproductive Treatment Act 1988 (SA), in WA by the Human Reproductive Technology Act 1991 (WA), and in NSW by the Assisted Reproductive Technology Act 2007 (NSW). Northern Territory clinics adhere to South Australian legislation subject to some minor changes.

161 NHMRC ART Guidelines, above n 1, [12.1], [12.3]; Human Fertilisation and Embryology Act 1990 (UK), Sch 2, s 1ZA(1)(d).

162 NHMRC ART Guidelines, above n 1, [12.5], see also [9.1], [9.3]; Human Fertilisation and Embryology Act 1990 (UK), s 13(6), Schedule 3ZA; HFEA Code of Practice, above n 71, [3.1], [10.22].

163 NHMRC ART Guidelines, above n 1, [12.3]. In the UK, clinics must obtain a licence from the HFEA to use PGD on a case-by-case basis.

164 NHMRC ART Guidelines, above n 1, [12.3].

165 NHMRC ART Guidelines, above n 1, [5.3.1].

166 In WA, patients are specifically required to be 'medically infertile': Human Reproductive Technology Act 1991 (WA), s 23(1).

167 See Assisted Reproductive Treatment Act 2008 (Vic), s 10(2)(a); Assisted Reproductive Treatment Act 1988 (SA), s 9(1)(c); Human Reproductive Technology Act 1991 (WA), s 23(1)(a). The NHMRC ART Guidelines further restrict the use of PGD to screening out *serious* genetic conditions: NHMRC ART Guidelines, above n 1, [12.2].

168 Assisted Reproductive Treatment Act 2008 (Vic), s 14(1).

169 Ibid, ss 15, 85(e).

170 Ibid, s 5(a); Assisted Reproductive Treatment Act 1988 (SA), s 4A.

171 Human Reproductive Technology Act 1991 (WA), s 23(1)(e). A Select Committee recommended in 1999 that the Act be amended to reflect and give priority to the paramount welfare of the child in all human reproductive technology procedures: WA Select Committee on the Human Reproductive Technology Act 1991, *Report* (1999), recommendation 3b. However, the recommendation was not adopted.

172 NHMRC ART Guidelines, above n 1, [12.3.1].

173 Szoke, above n 154, 80.

174 Rachel Anne Fenton and Fiona Dabell, 'Time for Change (1)' (2007) 157 *New Law Journal* 848; Emily Jackson, 'Conception and the Irrelevance of the Welfare Principle' (2002) 65 *Modern Law Review* 176; Amel Alghrani and John Harris, 'Reproductive Liberty: Should the Foundation of Families be Regulated?' (2006) 18 *Child and Family Law Quarterly* 191.

175 Onora O'Neill argues that although various forms of contemporary Kantian ethics may be criticised for being overly individualistic and ignoring personal relationships, these criticisms are less apt for Kant's ethics: Onora O'Neill, 'Kantian Ethics' in R E Ashcroft *et al* (eds), *Principles of Health Care Ethics* (Wiley, 2nd edn, 2007), 73, 76. The field of applied ethics and bioethics has not, however, always kept up with the more sophisticated debate in moral and political philosophy.

176 Virginia Held, *The Ethics of Care: Personal, Political, and Global* (Oxford University Press, 2006), 63.

177 Patricia Smith, 'Family Responsibility and the Nature of Obligation', in Diana Tietjens Meyers, Kenneth Kipnis and Cornelius F Murphy (eds), *Kindred Matters: Rethinking the Philosophy of the Family* (Cornell University Press, 1993), 41, 42.

178 Held, above n 176, 63.

179 Smith, above n 177, 49.

180 Alison Jost, 'Familiar? Yes. Flawed? Not Necessarily' (2009) *Bioethics Forum*, <http://www.thehastingscenter.org/Bioethicsforum/Post.aspx?id=3676&blogid=140/> (accessed 24 April 2013).

181 Samantha Brennan, 'Recent Work in Feminist Ethics' (1999) 109 *Ethics* 858, 865. Brennan provides a detailed analysis of various feminist approaches to moral philosophy.

182 See, for example, Mackenzie and Stoljar's account of 'relational autonomy' in Catriona Mackenzie and Natalie Stoljar, *Relational Autonomy: Feminist Perspectives of Autonomy, Agency, and the Social Self* (Oxford University Press, 2000).

183 Held, above n 176. See also Carol Gilligan, *In a Different Voice: Psychological Theory and Women's Development* (Harvard University Press, 1993).

184 Held, above n 176, 46.

185 Held, above n 176, 46.

186 Held, above n 176, 63.

187 See, for example, Nancy Sherman, 'The Virtues of Common Pursuit' (1993) 53 *Philosophical and Phenomenological Research* 277.

188 Robert A Crouch and Carl Elliott, 'Moral Agency and the Family: The Case of Living Related Organ Transplantation' (1999) 8 *Cambridge Quarterly of Healthcare Ethics* 275, 283.

189 Erica Grundell, 'Tissue Typing for Bone Marrow Transplantation: An Ethical Examination of Some Arguments Concerning Harm to the Child' (2003) 22 *Monash Bioethics Review* 45, 49.

190 Cynthia Cohen, 'Wrestling with the Future: Should We Test Children for Adult Onset Genetic Conditions?' (1998) 8 *Kennedy Institute of Ethics Journal* 111.

3 The welfare of the child to be born

3.1 Introduction

The welfare of the child to be born is not only a key issue for saviour sibling selection but also a central tenet in the regulation of assisted reproduction in the UK and Australia. ART regulation is most commonly justified on the basis that the state has a responsibility to protect the welfare and interests of children who are 'incapable of participating in the decision-making process in relation to their own conception'.[1] By highlighting the importance of the welfare of the child to be born, ART regulation can help ensure that the interests of the child to be born are not sacrificed to those of the parents and existing children who are in a position to actively assert their own interests. In this chapter, I analyse the role and nature of the welfare of the child principle in ART regulation and its application to saviour sibling selection.

Despite the strong focus on the welfare of the child to be born in UK and Australian ART regulation, there is no clearly defined ethical approach underlying the welfare of the child principle in assisted reproduction in either jurisdiction. This has left the welfare of the child principle open to interpretation, made it difficult to apply in practice and led to some inconsistent decisions about access to treatment in the UK in the past. To date, the ethical debate about saviour sibling selection has conceptualised the welfare of the child to be born in terms of the child's individual interests in respect and protection from harm. I argue that, whilst these interests provide some valuable insights into the welfare of the child in assisted reproduction, they fail to account for the child within the social context of his/her family.

I begin in section 3.2 by analysing the welfare of the child provisions in ART legislation in the UK and Australia, which appear to have been included for reasons of political expediency rather than based on solid ethical foundations. There has been considerable debate about the role of the welfare of the child provision in ART law in the UK in recent years. Some commentators argue that the welfare of the child provision is meaningless in the context of assisted reproduction,[2] whereas others claim it has important symbolic value.[3] Although there is no clearly articulated ethical approach to the welfare of the child provision in UK legislation, current UK policy reflects a 'harm-based' approach to the welfare of the child in assisted reproduction. In contrast, some commentators in Australia have equated the welfare of the child provision in state ART legislation with the 'best interests' of the child approach found in international human rights law and other domestic laws.[4] One important distinction between assisted reproduction law and other laws involving children is that assisted reproduction involves consideration of a child who does not yet exist. In section 3.3, I argue that, although a child does not in fact have any interests until he/she is born, it is possible to impute certain 'generic' interests to the child to be born. I then draw on the ethical debate about saviour siblings to examine in detail how the welfare of the child to be born has been conceptualised to date.

In sections 3.4 and 3.5, I explore in more detail the ethical concerns about commodification and harm introduced in Chapter 2, in the context of saviour sibling selection. I contend that, although these ethical concerns highlight relevant interests of the child to be born in respect and protection from harm, they reflect a narrow and individualistic account of the welfare of the child, whose interests are treated as largely separate to and distinct from the interests of other family members. I conclude in section 3.6 that the welfare of the child to be born should be conceptualised more broadly to include both the child's individual interests and the collective interests the child shares with his/her family. I explore this broader conception of the welfare of the child in detail in Chapter 4.

3.2 Welfare of the child in ART regulation

As discussed in Chapter 2, the availability of ART in the UK is restricted by the duty to consider the welfare of the child to be born under the HFE Act (UK). In Australia, the welfare of the child is also a key principle and the paramount consideration in ART legislation in Victoria and SA. There is, however, little legislative guidance on the role and nature of the welfare of the child principle in either the UK or Australia. This reflects the minimal ethical debate by Parliament leading up to the inclusion of the welfare principle in the relevant legislation. In the UK, there have been calls by some to abolish the welfare of the child provision, at least in its current form,[5] whereas others have argued that the provision should be strengthened to make the child's welfare the 'paramount' consideration in reproductive decisions, as is the case in Victoria and SA.[6]

In recent years, there have been several major reviews and reforms in ART law and policy in the UK and Victoria. In the UK, both the STC and the Department of Health directly considered the role of the welfare of the child provision in the HFE Act (UK). Ultimately, the UK Government chose to retain the provision but provided little clarification on how the welfare of the child principle should be applied in the context of assisted reproduction. In the meantime, the HFEA reviewed its own policy on the welfare of the child in assisted reproduction in 2004 and provided revised guidance in 2005. By way of contrast, the Victorian review of ART law focused specifically on access, surrogacy and parentage questions, leaving the role and nature of the welfare of the child principle largely unexplored.

3.2.1 Origins of the welfare of the child provision in ART legislation

There is no clear guidance in ART legislation in the UK or Australia on how the welfare of the child principle should be applied in the context of assisted reproduction. This is not surprising, given that the origins of the welfare of the child provision in UK and Australian legislation fail to reveal a clear purpose for the provision. The welfare of the child provision appears to have been included as a pragmatic response to concerns about who should have access to treatment.

Emily Jackson notes that, in the parliamentary debates leading up to the passage of the HFE Act (UK) in the UK, 'the inclusion of the welfare principle was neither challenged nor defended'.[7] The duty to consider the welfare of the child in assisted reproduction arose out of the Warnock Report, which recognised the need to protect the interests of any child to be born as a result of infertility treatment.[8] This issue arose in the context of access to treatment and the relevance of family structures. While the Warnock Committee concluded that access to treatment should not be restricted to married couples, it took the view that 'as a general rule it is better for children to be born into a two-parent family, with both father and mother'.[9] Ultimately, however, it proposed that the responsibility for treatment eligibility decisions be devolved to clinicians, recommending only that where treatment is declined, a patient should always be given a full explanation of the reasons.[10] Despite the Warnock Committee's deliberations on the welfare of the child, neither the 1987 White Paper on Human Fertilisation and Embryology[11] nor the subsequent Human Fertilisation and Embryology Bill mentioned the welfare of the child to be born.

The welfare of the child re-emerged as an issue in parliamentary debate following the second reading of the Human Fertilisation and Embryology Bill, published in 1989.[12] There was disagreement between parliamentarians as to whether, on the one hand, only married couples should be given access to treatment[13] and whether, on the other, there should be any social screening of prospective parents.[14] The majority of parliamentarians ultimately reached a 'compromise position' that the welfare of the child to be born should be taken into consideration before treatment is provided, but that it should not be the paramount consideration.[15] Essentially, the UK Parliament declared that there should be limits to the availability of fertility treatment but left the nature of those limits largely undefined. The inclusion of the welfare of the child provision in the HFE Act (UK) has been described as 'a pragmatic regulatory solution which neatly avoids the ethical dilemma of who should gain access to treatment, by leaving it to clinics' discretion'.[16] As Chapter 2 revealed, the lack of clarity of the welfare of the child provision in the HFE Act (UK) led to the HFEA developing *ad hoc* policy on saviour sibling selection that resulted in legal challenge and public criticism in the Hashmi and Whitaker cases.

In Australia, Victoria was the first state to enact legislation on assisted reproduction. The welfare of the child principle was not expressly included in the original Infertility (Medical Procedures) Act 1984 (Vic). However, in its 1985 report on reproductive technologies, the Family Law Council of Australia recommended that the welfare and interests of the child to be born in assisted reproduction be treated as paramount in all federal, state and territory legislation.[17] The Council stressed that:

> Given that the major purpose of reproductive technology is to create a child who would not otherwise have been conceived, and that a substantial allocation of public resources is required to enable this, it seems clear that the community has a particular responsibility to promote and protect the interests, needs and welfare of the child when born.[18]

The inclusion of the welfare of the child principle in the subsequent Infertility Treatment Act 1995 (Vic) (IT Act (Vic)) was unanimously supported by the Victorian Parliament but with little discussion about what it would mean in practice.[19] The welfare of the child principle is retained in the current Assisted Reproductive Treatment Act 2008 (Vic) (ART Act (Vic)). In its 2008 report on assisted reproduction, the VLRC acknowledged that there is divergence on how the welfare of the child should be protected in the context of access to assisted reproductive treatments.[20]

3.2.2 Review of the welfare of the child provision in the UK

The welfare of the child provision came under considerable attack by the STC in its 2005 review of the HFE Act (UK). The STC was critical of the HFEA's application of the welfare of the child provision in its policy and licensing decisions in the Hashmi and Whitaker cases. However, the STC's criticism extended more generally to the welfare of the child provision itself. The STC recommended that the provision 'be abolished in its current form' as it 'discriminates against the infertile and some sections of society, is impossible to implement and is of questionable practical value in protecting the interests of children born as a result of assisted reproduction'.[21] The STC recommended that, instead of the welfare provision, a 'minimum threshold principle' should apply to prevent the 'risk of unpreventable and significant harm' to a child born using ART.[22]

The UK Government chose not to abolish the welfare of the child provision in the HFE Act (UK) on the basis that it 'is a central tenet of the HFE Act', and one of the key guiding principles which informs the HFEA and its Code of Practice.[23] According to the Government, the welfare provision recognises that the welfare of children cannot always be adequately protected by satisfying the interests of the prospective parents involved and there needs to be a balance between the rights and interests of parents and the welfare of any child who may be born.[24] While recognising the difficulty in framing these considerations in national legislation and policy guidance, the Government opted to retain the provision. It agreed, however, to seek wider public views on how the welfare of the child may best be secured, as part of its review on the HFE Act (UK).

The UK Department of Health conducted a public consultation in 2005 to determine whether the welfare of the child requirement should remain in the HFE Act (UK) as a legal obligation on clinics providing treatment services and, if so, how that requirement should be expressed.[25] The Department also sought views on whether the requirement to take account of 'the need of a child for a father' should be removed from the welfare provision.[26] Following the public consultation, the Department commissioned an independent report on the responses obtained. The report, which is qualitative in nature, covered a broad range of views on the purpose and scope of the welfare of the child provision.[27] The Government took the view in its White Paper that the responses to the public consultation 'generally favoured retention of a "welfare of the child" consideration in some form'.[28] The Government therefore proposed retaining the duty to take account of the welfare of the child in providing fertility treatment but removing reference to 'the need for a father'.[29] Ultimately, the reference to 'the need for a father' was replaced with 'the need for supportive parenting' by amending legislation, following a free vote of both Houses of Parliament.

A Joint Committee of both Houses of Parliament (Joint Committee), which reviewed the Human Tissue and Embryos (Draft) Bill, also supported the retention of the welfare of the child provision, stating that 'the welfare of the child is a key area where consistent, understandable and enforceable legislation is needed'.[30] The Joint Committee considered the debate about whether the welfare of the child to be born should be paramount but supported the current position of 'taking into account' the welfare of the child, rather than treating the welfare of the child 'above all else'.[31] The Joint Committee was, however, critical of the Draft Bill for lacking any 'explicit underpinning ethical framework' which, it claims, led to 'mixed messages' about the welfare of the child.[32] The Joint Committee contended that the Draft Bill 'gives the impression of tinkering with existing legislative provisions rather than going back to first principles and seeking to take an overall view of where to go in the next 15 years or so'.[33] The failure by the UK Parliament to explore the ethical framework on which the HFE Act (UK) is based has meant that the HFEA has had to interpret the welfare of the child principle in the absence of clear ethical guidance from Parliament.

3.2.3 Review of HFEA policy on the welfare of the child

The HFEA is required under the HFE Act (UK) to give guidance on the welfare of the child provision in its Code of Practice.[34] The first HFEA Code of Practice was published in 1991. Initially, the Code required assessment for treatment to be based on a wide range of factors, including the demonstration of a commitment to raising children, age, immediate and family medical histories, the needs of any child who may be born, any risk or harm to the child that might be born, and the effect of a new baby on any existing child.[35] Changes have been made to the Code in a piecemeal fashion and additional factors have been added from time to time. The broad range of factors set out in early versions of the Code allowed for treatment decisions to be made by clinics based on a variety of social reasons. The Code was not properly reviewed until after the sixth edition was published in January 2004.[36] The need for review arose due to substantial criticism that the wide discretion afforded to clinics caused discrimination and that the application of the welfare principle was 'ad hoc, inconsistent and dependent upon each individual clinic's general policy, the attitude of their ethics committees and the views of individual clinicians'.[37]

The HFEA launched a review of existing policy on the welfare of the child principle in April 2004. As part of its review, the HFEA undertook a public consultation on the guidance it gives to fertility clinics on the welfare of the child provision. The consultation document outlined three main approaches to the welfare of the child to be born.[38] According to the first 'maximum welfare' approach, 'one should not knowingly and intentionally bring a child into the world in less than ideal circumstances'.[39] The HFEA stated that this approach 'considers a child's welfare to be of paramount importance'.[40] The second 'reasonable welfare' approach provides that the child to be born must have 'an adequate future, cared for by a "good enough" family'.[41] This approach involves consideration of a patient's social circumstances to ensure they can provide a 'satisfactory level of parenting'.[42] Lastly, the 'minimum threshold' approach only prohibits treatment where the child to be born is at 'high risk of serious harm'.[43] The consultation document also posed options for revising the welfare of the child guidance, including: the factors that should be taken into account in an assessment of the welfare of the child; how those factors should be weighed in the decision to provide or refuse treatment; and what enquiries should be made to gather information.[44]

In its 2005 report on the welfare of the child,[45] the HFEA acknowledged that a balance needs to be struck between patient autonomy and the welfare of the child to be born. It concluded that the existing guidance erred too much towards the latter at the expense of patient choice.[46] The HFEA decided that there should be a general presumption in favour of treatment, 'but that treatment should be refused where clinics conclude that the child to be born, or any existing child of the family, is likely to suffer serious harm'.[47] This 'minimum threshold' approach to the welfare of the child to be born, which focuses on the risk of harm to the child, is consistent with the earlier recommendation by the STC.[48] The HFEA also reviewed the risk factors that should be taken into account in an assessment about the welfare of the child. The HFEA concluded that risk factors should be limited to those that may cause serious physical, psychological or medical harm and not include social factors.[49] Lastly, the HFEA concluded that clinics should make welfare assessments in accordance with their own professional judgement, based on information collected from patients, instead of being obliged to contact their general practitioner.[50]

Current HFEA guidance on the welfare of the child creates a presumption in favour of treatment unless there is a 'risk of significant harm or neglect' to either the child to be born or any existing child of the family.[51] HFEA guidance on saviour sibling selection addresses the specific risks to the welfare of saviour siblings by requiring clinics to consider:

- any possible risks associated with embryo biopsy;
- the likely long-term emotional and psychological implications for the child to be born;
- whether the child is likely to require intrusive surgery in treating the existing child; and
- any complications associated with the tissue type selected.[52]

Clinics are required to make fair and non-discriminatory welfare of the child assessments, based on the wishes of all involved.[53] A medical history should be obtained from the patient and her partner and centres should seek their consent to obtain any further information from third parties.[54] As illustrated by current HFEA guidance, the review by the HFEA of its policy on the welfare of the child in assisted reproduction has provided some much-needed clarity on how the welfare principle should be applied in practice.

3.2.4 *Review of ART regulation in Victoria – a missed opportunity*

Legislation in Australia remains vague on the precise meaning of the welfare of the child to be born. There is no clarification of the terms 'welfare' and 'interests' in any of the relevant state Acts. The VLRC conducted a major review of ART regulation in Victoria from 2002 to 2007. In its Final Report in 2007, the VLRC specifically acknowledged that, although the guiding principles in the IT Act (Vic) expressed 'a theoretical commitment to the welfare and interests of children conceived through assisted reproduction', there were 'no provisions which specify how this should be achieved in practice'.[55] This has led to 'a lack of transparency and accountability' in the way clinics decide who should be given access to assisted reproductive treatment.[56]

Disappointingly, there was ultimately little discussion in the VLRC's Final Report about the role of the welfare principle in ART law. The VLRC explored how ART has, in practice, impacted on the welfare of children born. However, the VLRC's research focused on the psychological and social outcomes for children born as a result of donated gametes or embryos, including children born to same-sex parents, single mothers, or through surrogacy arrangements.[57] The VLRC's Final Report briefly mentions the debate about the applicability of a 'best interests' approach to the welfare of the child in assisted reproduction.[58] However, it concluded that the child's best interests should remain the paramount consideration in ART regulation, without adequately addressing the scope and limitations of the approach in the context of assisted reproduction. The VLRC stated that:

> ... our consultations revealed that almost everyone believes the promotion of the best interests of the child should remain the primary concern in the regulation and provision of ART services, even if they differ on precisely how a child's interests should be protected in the context of access to ART.[59]

Whether or not 'almost everyone believes' that the best interests of the child should be the paramount concern in ART regulation, a 'best interests' approach does not sit easily with saviour sibling selection. This is because using PGD to select a saviour sibling is primarily motivated by the interests of the existing child and his/her parents and has little to do with promoting the interests of the child to be born.

The VLRC briefly discussed saviour sibling selection when it considered eligibility for treatment. It acknowledged that, ' ... the conception of a child to act as a "saviour sibling" is controversial and the particular circumstances of the case would need to be carefully considered to ensure protection of the health and welfare of that child'.[60] The VLRC recommended that a review panel, established under the ART Act (Vic), should be able to approve the use of PGD to select a saviour sibling, provided it is in the 'best interests' of the child to be born.[61] However, there is no further analysis of how the welfare of the child should be applied in this context. The lack of analysis of the welfare of the child principle in the context of ART is reflected in the fact that there are still no definitions in the ART Act (Vic) of the terms 'welfare' and 'interests'.

The lack of guidance on the welfare of the child to be born in Victoria means that assessments about the 'welfare and interests' of the child to be born in Victoria are likely to vary from clinic to clinic. The Honourable Alastair Nicholson, the former Chief Justice of the Family Court of Australia, criticised the previous IT Act (Vic) for 'leaving a void as to what is intended by this phrase'.[62] According to Nicholson, the lack of guidance on the welfare of the child principle in the IT Act (Vic) explains some of the difficulties that have arisen in its interpretation.[63] Although family law courts have applied the welfare of the child principle for many years, 'judicial practice is based on extensive and time consuming investigation of the parties' situations by social workers and, often, evidence from the child'.[64] As Kris Walker points out, this investigative process would be cumbersome and inappropriate in the context of assisted reproduction where the child is not yet born.[65]

Some Australian commentators have interpreted the 'welfare and interests' of the child to be born by reference to the rights of the child enshrined in international convention. For example, in relation to the ART Act (Vic), John Tobin argues that:

> ... the substantive content of what constitutes a child's welfare and interests should be informed by the articles under the [United Nations Convention on the Rights of the Child (UNCRC)] in the same way that the best interests principle is defined by reference to the Convention.[66]

Nicholson has expressed a similar view by stating that he doubts there is any significant difference between the phrase 'welfare and interests' contained in ART legislation and the 'best interests of the child' principle found in the UNCRC.[67] The VLRC has in fact treated the two phrases as interchangeable, by stating that '[t]he principle of best interests of the child is central to ART legislation in Victoria ... albeit using different terminology'.[68] The VLRC also noted that the phrase 'best interests of the child' is used in other domestic laws dealing with family law and child protection.[69] The new ART Act (Vic) reinforces a 'best interests' approach to the welfare of the child by requiring the Patient Review Panel to have regard to whether treatment 'is consistent with the best interests of a child who would be born'.[70]

Although the phrase 'welfare and interests of the child' is often equated with the 'best interests' approach to the welfare of the child found in international and domestic law, a 'best interests' approach is not easily applied in the context of assisted reproduction. There is an important distinction between ART law and other domestic laws involving children. In contrast to family and child protection law, the child to be born as a result of ART is not yet in existence. In the context of assisted reproduction, '[w]hat is ordinarily a child-centred test becomes necessarily centred entirely on the merits of the parents-to-be'.[71] The real question in ART law is whether a child should be brought into existence, not 'what should be done to achieve the best outcome for a living child'.[72] Several commentators object to a 'best interests' approach more generally on the basis that it is indeterminate and speculative.[73] In contrast, Margaret Coady defends the principle insofar as it 'can be used to rule out parents who are obviously unfit' because, for example, they have a history of child abuse.[74] Coady contends, however, that the term 'best' should be avoided in ART law as it may 'suggest that what must be decided is the best possible future of all the possible futures' for the child born as a result of ART.[75] According to Stephen Parker, it is difficult to determine which of a number of choices is in a child's best interests.[76] It is even more difficult when the child is not yet in existence.

3.2.5 Should the welfare of the child principle be retained in ART law?

Given the problems in applying the welfare of the child principle in the context of assisted reproduction, it is worthwhile considering whether the principle serves any legitimate purpose in ART law. Some critics argue that the welfare of the child provision should be removed from ART regulation altogether.[77] Jackson, a staunch opponent of the 'welfare principle's colonisation of reproductive choice', argues that the welfare of the child to be born should not be relied on as a justification for interfering with an individual's reproductive liberty.[78] According to Jackson, '[e]xtending the "welfare principle" to decisions taken prior to a child's conception is shown to be unjust, meaningless and inconsistent with existing legal principle'.[79]

The criticisms levelled at the incorporation of the welfare of the child principle in ART law refer to principle and practice. As a matter of principle, the welfare principle has been criticised as discriminatory, paternalistic and unnecessary. Some commentators argue that the principle, which is not applied to people who are able to conceive naturally, may result in discrimination against infertile, single or same-sex parents.[80] Jackson argues that the principle is paternalistic because it unjustly 'deprive[s] some citizens of the zone of privacy that surrounds most people's reproductive decision-making'.[81] Lastly, the welfare of the child principle has been criticised as unnecessary because it adds little to 'good medical practice'.[82] The welfare principle has also been criticised in practice for being difficult to apply in the context of ART and ineffective in safeguarding the child's welfare.[83]

Criticisms of the welfare of the child principle relate to its current formulation in legislation, which is vague and imprecise and 'may result in prejudice being dressed up as concern for the welfare of the child'.[84] In Australia, there is no clear guidance on how the welfare principle should be applied in the context of assisted reproduction. As already discussed in this chapter, the 'best interests' approach proposed by some commentators, based on international human rights law, is problematic in the context of assisted reproduction. Saviour sibling selection, in particular, is arguably not in the best interests of the child to be born but appears to be justified based on the interests of other family members. The fact that the NHMRC and the Victorian Parliament have contemplated saviour sibling selection as a legitimate application of PGD in Australia suggests that, despite the strong focus on the interests of the child to be born, the interests of other family members are also relevant to reproductive treatment decisions.

In the UK, the HFEA's current detailed policy on the welfare of the child addresses many of the criticisms raised against the welfare of the child principle. HFEA policy reflects a 'harm-based' approach to the welfare of the child by imposing a presumption in favour of treatment in the absence of a significant risk of harm or neglect to either the child to be born or any existing child. This approach establishes clear parameters for clinics to work within. It should also minimise discrimination by clinics based on sexuality or marital status under the guise of the welfare of the child provision. A recent empirical study of 'welfare of the child' assessments by ART clinics in the UK under the current regime suggests that there is now a 'strong awareness' within clinics of the need to provide non-discriminatory treatment.[85] Both the HFE Act (UK) and HFEA policy extend consideration to the welfare of *any* existing child but do not specify how this should be balanced against the welfare of the child to be born.[86] It is therefore possible that either a utilitarian or relational approach might be adopted in relation to other family interests.

There is also some tension between ART legislation and policy in the UK that is symptomatic of the UK Parliament's failure to establish a clear ethical approach to the welfare of the child. This tension is evident in the context of access to PGD for saviour sibling selection. The 'harm-based' approach to the welfare of the child in HFEA policy suggests that access to treatment should only be restricted where the child to be born is likely to suffer *serious harm or neglect*. There are, however, several restrictions under the HFE Act (UK) that are at odds with the approach of the HFEA.

First, the requirement in the welfare of the child provision of the HFE Act (UK) to consider 'the need for supportive parenting' seems to reflect more of a 'reasonable welfare' approach insofar it requires consideration of a patient's social circumstances to ensure that she is able to provide 'a satisfactory level of parenting'.[87] Second, the HFE Act (UK) allows PGD for tissue typing to enable donation to siblings but not parents,[88] despite a lack of empirical evidence to suggest that the latter situation is any more likely than the former to result in serious harm or neglect to the child to be born. Third, the HFE Act (UK) limits saviour sibling selection to cases where the existing sibling is suffering from a 'serious medical condition'.[89] Again, the seriousness of the existing sibling's condition is unlikely to impact on the risk of harm to the child who is born. Instead of focusing on the harm to the child to be born, this third restriction appears to be based on a utilitarian approach that balances risk to the child to be born against benefits to the existing child. This may be a valid ethical approach in many contexts. However, as discussed in Chapter 2, the risk in applying a utilitarian approach to the welfare of the child is that the interests of the child to be born may be sacrificed in order to achieve the greatest good. The tension between law and policy in the UK suggests that a clear ethical approach to the welfare of the child is needed to better address the various interests at stake in assisted reproduction. Greater clarity will ensure greater transparency and accuracy in the regulation of saviour siblings.

In Chapter 6, I argue that a clear ethical approach to the welfare of the child in ART regulation can both protect the child to be born and assist prospective parents and clinicians in making ethically complex and emotionally charged reproductive treatment decisions. The welfare of the child principle has 'important symbolic and moral value' as it reminds us that 'children must be protected from harm and given every opportunity to become healthy, well-developed adults'.[90] However, if the welfare of the child principle is to be meaningful in the context of assisted reproduction, the welfare and interests of the child to be born must be clearly defined to ensure that the principle is consistently and effectively applied in all cases. The relational approach proposed in this book aims to provide a comprehensive account of the welfare of the child to be born, by highlighting the child's individual and collective interests.

In the remainder of this chapter, I examine the individual interests of the child to be born in being treated with respect and protected from harm, which are explored in detail in the ethical debate about saviour siblings. These interests are reflected to varying degrees in ART regulation in the UK and Australia. A threshold question in defining the interests of the child to be born in assisted reproduction is whether a child who is not yet born can in fact have any interests. While it may be conceptually difficult to attribute interests to a future or 'hypothetical' child, I argue that the problem is not insurmountable. It is possible to contemplate the likely foreseeable or generic interests of the child to be born.

3.3 Interests of future persons

3.3.1 The future child as a 'hypothetical person'

There are obvious conceptual difficulties in attributing interests to a child who does not yet exist. Colin Gavaghan notes that, given that the child to be born only has a 'hypothetical existence' at the time of the decision to use PGD, he/she does not possess any interests.[91] Andrew Dutney contrasts the application of the welfare principle in the family law context, where the child is in existence and it is therefore possible to ascertain the nature of his/her interests.[92] In assisted reproduction the child's interests do not exist until all the crucial decisions have been made and a child is born.

It may seem artificial to attribute interests to the child to be born as a result of assisted reproduction. As I argued in Chapter 2, a child does not in fact have any interests before he/she comes into existence. Furthermore, it is impossible to predict what the specific interests of any particular child will be. A child who does not yet exist does not have an identity and therefore cannot have any individual preferences. This is because in the context of assisted reproduction, the decision-making itself is 'identity-affecting'.[93] It is possible, however, to impute certain 'generic' interests to the child to be born as a result of assisted reproduction. Gavaghan suggests that the welfare principle may require the 'likely foreseeable interests' of the child to be born to be taken into account.[94]

Coady argues that '[h]owever puzzling it may be to attribute interests to those who do not yet exist, it is clear that we do this intelligibly … in all sorts of fields'.[95] For example, governments consider the interests of those who do not yet exist when they frame present environmental policies for future generations. The fact that a child does not in fact have any interests at the critical time of decision-making in assisted reproduction does not prevent others from imputing certain basic interests to the child to be born. This type of 'surrogate decision making' is well established for those who may not be conscious or rational, including minors, unconscious persons and the psychiatrically disturbed.

In the context of assisted reproduction, certain universal interests of the future child should be protected. Drawing on the language of Gavaghan, we can contemplate the 'likely foreseeable interests that the child will possess if it is brought into existence'.[96] Bringing a child into existence entails a level of responsibility in respect of that child's future. If there are reasonably foreseeable risks to that potential child, responsible regulation should address those risks.

3.3.2 *Likely foreseeable or generic interests of the future child*

If we accept that we should promote certain universal or generic interests of the child to be born, a question arises as to what type of interests we can expect future children to have. Several commentators have addressed the interests of the future child from a practical perspective.[97]

For example, Coady states that we have some general knowledge of what persons need, including food, health, housing and freedom from violence. Assuming that future children will at least in fundamental ways be like existing people, we can assume that they will 'have an interest in being, at a minimum, nourished, sheltered and respected as persons'.[98] Many of these basic interests or needs of children are protected by the UNCRC. As previously discussed, Tobin argues that the nature of a child's interests should be informed by the Articles under the UNCRC.[99] Eric Blyth has similarly relied on the UNCRC to 'flesh out some general expectations' in relation to the interests of the child to be born in ART law.[100] There are several rights of the child that are particularly relevant in the context of assisted reproduction, such as the right to be cared for by his/her parents as far as possible,[101] to an identity,[102] to be protected from harm[103] and to be provided with a safe and secure environment.[104]

Attributing interests to the child to be born based on the universal rights of the child established under international law is a legitimate starting point for ascertaining universal interests of the future child. The two key interests of the child to be born that have been identified in the context of saviour sibling selection (being respected and protected from harm) reflect key human rights found in international law on the rights of the child. As discussed in Chapter 2, these two interests are relevant to decisions about selective reproduction generally.

3.4 Respect

The commodification objection to saviour sibling selection based on the second formulation of Immanuel Kant's categorical imperative is essentially about treating the child to be born with respect. Children conceived as saviour siblings clearly have an interest in being respected in their own right and not treated as a *mere* source of tissue for an existing child. However, as discussed in Chapter 2, provided parents desire another child in his/her own right, Kant's categorical imperative (to never treat people *solely* as a means) is not contravened by allowing parents to select a saviour sibling. The ethical concern about commodification does, however, raise important questions about parental motivation for using PGD and the nature of parental love. Given the complex nature of procreative motivation in general, I argue in the next section that the state should only intervene in saviour sibling selection in extreme cases where parents clearly have no interest in the child to be born beyond his/her role as a stem cell donor. I then suggest that how the child will be treated once he/she is born is ultimately more important than parental motivation for having the child.

3.4.1 Parental motivation for using PGD

Parental motivation is an important consideration in saviour sibling selection. Regulatory bodies in the UK and Australia have, in the past, grappled with the complex nature of parental motivation for using PGD to select a saviour sibling. In Victoria, previous policy on saviour sibling selection attempted to ascertain parental motivation through counselling. The policy of the former Infertility Treatment Authority (ITA) on saviour sibling selection stated that, 'If this motivation is solely for the purposes of furthering the interest of an existing sibling, then this may raise concerns. However, if the child is wanted for his/her own worth, then this may be justifiable'.[105] The NHMRC Guidelines on ART similarly require an ethics committee to consider parental motivation by ascertaining that the parents desire a child 'as an addition to the family and not merely as a source of tissue'.[106]

Ascertaining why people choose to have a child is a complex matter. The Ethics Panel of the ITA acknowledged the complex nature of parental motivation for procreation. One member stated that 'the urge to have children in natural procreation is multifaceted and not always altruistic'.[107] In the UK, the HFEA Ethics Committee conceded that it may be impossible to ascertain parental motivation for having a child by empirical interrogation.[108] As Katrien Devolder states, 'it is extremely difficult, if not impossible, to separate the reasons that lead to the conception of a child because of a "genuine desire for a child" from those linked to an attempt to save another child'.[109] An additional complicating factor is that 'plans to have children typically change according to the circumstances and experiences of childrearing'.[110]

People have children 'for a variety of reasons', which do not preclude the parents from loving their children in their own right.[111] Some common reasons that people have children include a desire to provide companionship for an existing child, to carry on the family line, to care for parents in their old age, to inherit the family business, to satisfy peer expectation, to save a failing marriage or as a sub-conscious quest 'for some sort of genetic immortality'.[112] In other cases, children are completely unexpected, either because contraception failed or was not used. There is no specific motivation – either good or bad – for conceiving a child in these latter cases. As Belinda Bennett states, although we might not agree with some of the reasons (or lack of reason) on which people base their reproductive choices, '[t]hese reasons are left to the private decision-making of the individuals and couples concerned and generally do not lead to debates over public policy'.[113]

Given that people's motivations for having children are not generally scrutinised, a question arises as to whether the state should examine the parental motivation for seeking PGD at all. As Gavaghan points out, '[i]t is perhaps unlikely that any pregnancies are commenced wholly or predominantly out of beneficence towards the future child'.[114] According to John Harris, 'it's difficult ... to find evidence or even persuasive anecdotes that if people are treated as means, they are necessarily treated as mere means, or exclusively as means or solely as means'.[115] It would be inappropriate to impose an unrealistically high standard of altruism on individuals seeking PGD, considering the multitude of self-interested reasons for which parents have children. Parents seeking PGD to save the life of an existing child are perhaps even acting more altruistically than most parents who decide to have children, as their dedication to saving their ill child demonstrates a high level of commitment to the welfare of at least their existing children.

There are, however, certain reasons for which it would be unacceptable to bring a child into the world. Conceiving a child to act as a 'tissue farm' would clearly contravene Kant's categorical imperative. Although there are laws regulating tissue transplantation involving minors in the UK and Australia,[116] it would be inappropriate for an ART clinic actively to assist parents who intend to use a child merely as a source of tissue (whether or not they are likely to be successful in this pursuit) by giving them access to PGD.[117] Given the potential for a saviour sibling to be commodified by his/her parents, some attempt should be made to at least explore the motivation of parents seeking PGD through counselling. The mere fact that the birth of a child can assist an existing sibling should not, however, be seen as *prima facie* evidence that the child will not also be respected as an end in his/herself. If, on the other hand, counselling revealed that parents seeking PGD to conceive a saviour sibling had no interest in another child and were, for example, proposing adoption of that child following successful stem cell donation, then treatment should arguably be withheld.

The cases in which parents intend to treat a child selected using PGD solely as a commodity are likely to be rare.[118] This fact, in itself, does not mean that regulation is unnecessary. There is another more important reason for parental motivation to be explored through counselling. Helping parents examine their own motivations for wanting another child is likely to assist them in making a genuinely informed decision about selective reproduction. It is important for parents contemplating saviour sibling selection to explore and understand their own motivations thoroughly for wanting another child as they will have to live with the outcome for the rest of their lives. The difficult and sometimes neglectful relationship the mother in Jodi Picoult's novel, *My Sister's Keeper*, has with her daughter, Anna, a saviour sibling, highlights the complex issues faced by families with a seriously ill child. Counselling aimed at helping parents come to terms with their own reasons for seeking PGD should better equip them in dealing with future challenges, including the possibility of further stem cell donations in the case of saviour siblings.

3.4.2 Parental love once the child is born

Lastly, it is important not to lose sight of the real issue raised by Kant's categorical imperative – how the child to be born is treated – by focusing too much on the parents' motivation for having the child. According to Guido Pennings, 'the morally relevant point is the way the child is treated by its parents once it is born rather than their reasons for having it'.[119] Ultimately, what matters is that a child born using PGD 'is loved, nurtured and cherished in ways that we would hope all children would be by their parents'.[120] The fact that prospective parents have a preference for a particular type of child does not prevent them loving the child that is born in his/her own right. Many mothers who have yearned for a daughter find themselves equally spellbound by the birth of a baby boy.

Several commentators have argued that provided parents love the child who is born as a result of PGD, the child is not commodified.[121] Robert Sparrow and David Cram argue that this claim is 'tendentious' because, although the parents may love the child in his/her own right, 'it is in many cases less clear that they would have had this child were it not for the desire to source tissue for transplant'.[122] Sparrow and Cram are effectively applying a 'but for' test to the question of commodification. Their argument seems to suggest that the child to be born is commodified where the parents would not have had the child *but for* the fact that their existing child needed a stem cell transplant. However, as noted above, the reasons people choose to procreate are multi-factorial and may change depending on the circumstances in which people find themselves. The fact that parents may be initially motivated by a desire to save an existing child does not mean that the parents will not also develop a genuine desire to have another child in his/her own right. The impetus for the parents' motivation does not mean that the child to be born is commodified provided the parents genuinely want another child for his/her own sake in addition to helping the existing child.

According to John Davis, selecting a child with particular traits prior to conception is not inconsistent with unconditional parental love for the child who is born.[123] Even where the child's conception is motivated by the parents' desire to save an existing child, the parents are not thereby prevented from becoming loving and devoted parents of the child to be born. As Robertson, Khan and Wagner state:

> The birth of a child creates a powerful bond regardless of the circumstances of conception. Indeed, the fact that the parents are willing to

conceive another child to protect the first suggests that they are highly committed to the well-being of their children, and that they will value the second child for its own sake as well.[124]

A similar sentiment was recently expressed by the first parents of twin saviour siblings, born in the UK in 2009. The parents, Laurence Maguire and Wendy Plant, decided to conceive a saviour sibling to cure their eldest son's aplastic anaemia. Mr Maguire stated that '[o]nce you see your children, any notion that they are spare parts is gone. We wouldn't change anything, they are our children and we love them all'.[125]

Parental motivation for seeking PGD should therefore not be over-scrutinised by the state. As Devolder notes, '[w]e judge people on their attitudes toward children, rather than on their motives for having them'.[126] To put it another way, 'how one is treated by others over the course of one's life is more morally significant than the reasons for causing one to exist'.[127] A key concern about how the child is treated once he/she is born relates to whether or not the child is harmed. The risk of physical, psychological or social harm to the child to be born is the second major concern in the debate about saviour sibling selection.

3.5 Protection from harm

Consequentialist concerns about harm to the child to be born highlight the child's interest in being protected from harm or experiencing a 'balance of benefit over harm'.[128] As discussed in Chapter 2, there is a risk of physical harm associated with ART and the embryo biopsy process used in PGD. Further long-term studies are needed in this area to gain a better insight into the level of risk. There are additional risks that are specific to saviour sibling selection. First, there is a future risk of physical harm associated with peripheral blood and bone marrow donations by the child once he/she is born if the initial cord blood donation is unsuccessful. Second, there is a theoretical risk of psychological or social harm to the child associated with being conceived as a donor for an existing sibling.

3.5.1 *Future donation*

The physical risks for a saviour sibling associated with donation depend on the type of stem cells that are being donated. Cord blood stem cell transplants pose no physical risks to the newborn baby provided the mode of delivery of the baby is not modified.[129] As Pennings, Schots and Liebaers state, 'when treatment is possible with the umbilical cord stem cells, no intervention or risk is imposed on the donor child'.[130] The umbilical cord is generally considered waste material and is ordinarily discarded. Success rates for HSC transplants vary significantly, however, according to the type of disease being treated and the stage of the disease.[131]

Where an initial cord blood stem cell transplant is unsuccessful, a saviour sibling may be called upon to donate peripheral blood or bone marrow at a later date. There are clear physical risks to saviour siblings associated with future stem cell donations. Peripheral blood donors experience short-term physical pain and fatigue but there have been no reported cases of long-term serious adverse physical effects on child donors.[132] The major risk of harm for bone marrow donors are the risks associated with general anaesthesia. Bone marrow donors also experience short-term adverse effects, including fatigue and pain, for which recovery is generally longer than in the case of peripheral blood donation.[133]

There are existing legal protections in the UK and Australia regarding future donations by saviour siblings beyond umbilical cord blood. In the UK, children born as a result of PGD are subject to the same protections under common law that apply to all minors. According to Gavaghan, 'the interests of the child, once born, will adequately be protected by the courts'.[134] In Australia, any future donations by saviour siblings would be covered by legislation regulating tissue donation.[135] While there are variations between the different state and territory Acts regulating tissue donation and transplantation in Australia, children are generally permitted to donate regenerative tissue for the benefit of an immediate family member, subject to certain requirements designed to safeguard the welfare of the child.[136] Donation of non-regenerative tissue by minors is generally prohibited, either expressly[137] or by implication.[138] In addition to legislation, the Family Court of Australia has general jurisdiction to make orders in relation to the welfare of the child.[139]

Despite protections under common law and legislation in the UK and Australia, the potential for future tissue donations by saviour siblings will inevitably be 'imprinted' into the child's destiny and there may be familial pressure on the child to continue to donate, irrespective of legal safeguards. Physical harm from future peripheral blood or bone marrow tissue donation is therefore a distinct possibility for the child who has been specifically selected as a saviour sibling. This may be exacerbated by parental expectation that a saviour sibling will continue to help save the life of the ill sibling, which may or may not be openly expressed. It is therefore important to at least acknowledge the future risk of physical harm associated with tissue donations by saviour siblings at the time decisions about saviour sibling selection are being made.

3.5.2 Psychological and social harm

The psychosocial risks to saviour siblings are more speculative than the physical risks. There is a theoretical risk of psychological or social harm associated with being conceived in order to save the life of another. Given that saviour sibling selection is a relatively new procedure, there is currently no empirical evidence on the longer-term psychosocial impact on children selected as saviour siblings.[140] According to Ram, psychosocial evidence from teenage children is critical to assessing the real harms and benefits of being born, in part, as a tissue donor.[141]

Various sources of potential psychosocial harms to saviour siblings have been raised in the debate about saviour sibling selection. Some commentators have suggested that knowing you were brought into existence to save the life of an existing sibling could have a negative impact on a saviour sibling's sense of self-worth, identity or ongoing relationship with the ill sibling.[142] This potential harm is related to the commodification argument discussed above in that it may be a consequence of a breach of Kant's moral imperative. There is also a possibility that other members of the family might actively stigmatise the donor child for having been brought into existence for instrumental reasons.

Erica Grundell refers to the 'psychological impact of selectivity' on a child who is selected for a particular purpose.[143] Such children may not feel important in and of themselves, but instead feel that they have been selected to serve the purpose of another. A related harm is that the child may lose some sense of unconditional parental love in being born to serve a specific purpose. Other commentators have described a child conceived to be a donor as having a 'closed future'.[144] In this respect, saviour sibling selection is inconsistent with what Feinberg describes as the child's 'right to an open future', pursuant to which the child's future interests or options should be kept open until that child has the capacity of self-determination.[145]

Commentators also refer to the psychological burden on the child to be born, who may suffer guilt if treatment fails or if he/she is reluctant at a later stage to undergo further donation procedures.[146] The potential psychological impact of donation between siblings should not be underestimated, particularly where donation has been unsuccessful. Several studies indicate that some sibling bone marrow donors suffer psychosocial harm and that the risk of harm is increased where there is a negative outcome.[147] For example, in cases where a donation was not successful or the sibling died, feelings of anger, guilt and blame generally overshadowed any positive feelings experienced by the donor child.[148] A significant portion of sibling bone marrow donors have been reported to experience a moderate level of post-traumatic stress.[149]

The trauma experienced by sibling bone marrow donors cannot automatically be transposed to saviour siblings (who may or may not ultimately donate bone marrow) without qualification. The impact of sibling donation will vary considerably according to the circumstances of each individual case. Cordelia Thomas argues that the trauma suffered by sibling bone marrow donors could be largely a result of the distress suffered by a family in which a child is critically ill, compounded by the effects of involvement in medical procedures.[150] Other commentators have pointed out that as the impact of donation depends on the conscious experience of the child, the 'psychosocial effects will have become diluted' when a saviour sibling is able to understand the nature of his/her conception.[151] If an umbilical cord blood transplant is successful in curing the existing child, a saviour sibling is not likely to experience the type of trauma suffered by sibling bone marrow donors. However, if the existing child requires further treatment, then a saviour sibling will inevitably have to deal with the critical illness and possible death of a sibling very early on in life, not to mention the pressure in knowing he/she was brought into existence to save that sibling's life. The potential for trauma to the child to be born should not therefore be ignored.

While many commentators argue against saviour sibling selection on the basis of psychosocial harm, others claim that there are psychological and social benefits for the child to be born as a saviour sibling. This line of argument only serves to highlight the speculative nature of this harm/benefit analysis.

3.5.3 Psychological and social benefits

Some commentators argue that being selected to assist an ill sibling may ultimately benefit the child to be born. In other words, there are psychological and social benefits for saviour siblings that outweigh the potential harms so that the child experiences a 'net benefit' overall. Sally Sheldon and Stephen Wilkinson argue that 'it is far from obvious that consideration of child welfare should count against, rather than for, the practice of saviour sibling selection'.[152] Pennings, Schots and Liebaers argue that knowledge of selectivity may in fact have a positive impact on the child to be born, giving the child a greater sense of self-esteem and self-worth and a feeling of pride about his/her role in attempting to save the life of a sibling.[153] Others suggest that the donor child may be cherished and derive increased self-esteem from his/her saviour status, and have an enhanced relationship with the sibling recipient, who otherwise would have died.[154] As Savulsecu points out, '[n]o child has an interest in living in a family under the shadow of avoidable, premature death'.[155]

Julian Savulescu argues that we should not undervalue the extent to which our well-being is intertwined with those to whom we are strongly attached.[156] Thus, in the case of siblings, the donor child's well-being is indirectly enhanced when he/she is able to help an ill sibling. Even where the bond is potential (as is the case with a child yet to be born) Savulescu claims that donors may in the future enjoy a sense of achievement. The donor may also enjoy the love and gratitude from the sibling who was saved and the rest of the family. Sheldon and Wilkinson have similarly suggested that a saviour sibling may benefit from his/her sibling's company and derive pleasure from knowing that he/she has saved the sibling's life.[157] Other commentators have suggested that, even where a sibling dies, there may be benefit in the knowledge that the family exhausted all possible treatment options.[158] Gavaghan notes that the alternative to using PGD – parents attempting to naturally conceive a tissue-matched child – may also cause significant psychological harm to a child who was conceived as a saviour but failed to be a direct tissue match.[159]

Sibling bone marrow donor studies suggest that, although some donors suffer psychosocial harm, others may experience psychosocial benefits. Some of the reported benefits include an increase in self-esteem and a closer relationship with the recipient sibling.[160] An empirical study on paediatric sibling stem cell donors revealed that successful donation had a positive impact on many aspects of their lives, including relationships and self-worth.[161] There is also anecdotal evidence that a child conceived naturally in order to donate stem cells to an ill sibling can have a positive experience overall. Marissa Ayala was born in 1990 as a result of a concerted attempt by her parents to have a child who could serve as a tissue donor to their ill child, Anissa. Marissa, who is a healthy, happy and loved member of her family, is a 'positive example of the psychological impact of being a "saviour sibling"'.[162] Although Marissa's case does not prove that being born to serve as a donor to an ill sibling will always be a positive experience, it does suggest that the psychological outcome for the saviour sibling is not necessarily a negative one.

The alleged psychosocial benefits to saviour siblings above can be roughly divided into two distinct categories: (a) benefit from altruism; and (b) indirect instrumental benefit. These alleged benefits are, however, speculative and ultimately unconvincing. The first category, which suggests that the child will experience self-worth from donating to a sibling, assumes that the child to be born has altruistic or what Feinberg describes as 'other-regarding interests'.[163] However, a young child does not have the capacity for altruism, let alone a child who is not yet born. So any altruistic benefit is, at best, retrospective but arguably non-existent.

Cara Cheyette warns that imputing psychological benefits from altruistic behaviour to minors who lack the cognitive ability to act altruistically is misleading.[164] In the specific context of organ donation,[165] Cheyette, argues that neither the language nor the imputed benefits reflect the experience of the minor donor:

> While the term 'organ donor' is an efficient catchall phrase for the process by which human organs are obtained for transplantation, in this context, verbal efficiency masks meaningful differences between the affirmative act of giving and the passive experience of having something taken away.[166]

Robert Crouch and Carl Elliott have also criticised imputing other-regarding interests to a minor.[167] Other-regarding interests are the interests that an agent has for the well-being of another person. Sibling rivalry, which is common in most families, suggests such altruistic tendencies (at least towards a sibling) are beyond the capacity of most children. Crouch and Elliott argue that this picture of human agency does not apply to minors who are not yet mature or sufficiently mentally developed to have an other-regarding interest in a sibling. In such a case, the donor may not receive any direct psychological benefits from donation.

The second category of psychosocial benefit suggests that the child to be born will experience indirect benefit because the family into which the child is born will be better off as a result of the donation. This argument suggests that, assuming stem cell donation is successful, the parents and sibling will be grateful to the donor child, the donor child will have the company of a healthy sibling, and the ability of the parents to care for the donor child will not be compromised by the trauma of having suffered the death of a child.[168] Although the discussion of indirect psychosocial benefits recognises the relational element of interests within a family, these benefits are ultimately framed as individual interests of the child to be born. The psychosocial benefits for saviour siblings are, however, largely speculative. Furthermore, the empirical studies of bone marrow sibling donors suggest that where donation is unsuccessful, the psychosocial benefits to the donor child are outweighed by the psychosocial harms.

Given that the primary motivation for conceiving a saviour sibling is to save the life of an existing child, the alleged benefits to the child to be born appear more like rationalisations for a procedure that is really about benefiting the ill sibling.[169] Saviour sibling selection is arguably not justified on the basis that it promotes the individual interests of the child to be born. It is difficult to prove that the child to be born will experience any individual net benefit. As Sarah Elliston has pointed out in the context of sibling donations generally, '[T]he fact remains that in any donation scenario the primary motivation is to provide benefit to the recipient and any benefits to the donor child are incidental and uncertain'.[170]

If there is no individual net benefit to the child to be born, a threshold question arises as to whether saviour sibling selection is ever consistent with the welfare of the child to be born. Several commentators have suggested that a broader approach to the welfare of the child is needed in the context of sibling donation generally. Aside from the speculative nature of weighing potential harms and benefits to the donor child, Crouch and Elliott suggest that this equation is inadequate to deal with deeper questions in family medical decision-making and has resulted in an artificial conception of what is in the 'best interests' of the child to be born.[171] Pennings, Schots and Liebaers suggest it is better to accept that the individual interests of the child to be born are not really being served by saviour sibling selection and apply a different standard altogether.[172]

Most people would agree that saving the life of an ill child is a worthwhile pursuit. Saviour sibling selection may be justified if we look beyond the individual interests of the child to be born to the other interests within the family that are at stake. As discussed in Chapter 2, a utilitarian approach is one way of taking into account all relevant interests at stake. However, given the vulnerability of the child to be born, a utilitarian approach may not adequately protect his/her welfare. In Chapter 4, I argue that family interests should be viewed in a way that reflects the interconnectedness of family members and does not sacrifice the members of any individual person to promote the 'greatest good'. I propose a more nuanced approach to the welfare of the child to be born – one that views the child as both an individual and a member of a family. An approach to the welfare of the child that simply balances harms and benefits to the individual child cannot do this.

3.6 Conclusion

There are strong reasons for retaining the welfare of the child provision in ART legislation. The provision has symbolic importance, highlighting the future interests of those who are not yet in a position to assert those interests. Without this protection, there is a risk that decisions about selective reproduction might focus on the interests of prospective parents and any existing children, who are able to communicate their own needs, at the expense of the child to be born. The welfare of the child to be born must, however, be clearly articulated if the welfare provision is to be consistently and meaningfully applied. A clear ethical approach to the welfare of the child in assisted reproduction is needed in order to flesh out the welfare and interests of the child to be born and to evaluate those interests alongside the interests of the parents and any existing children.

Legislation in the UK and Australia provides little guidance on how the welfare of the child should be evaluated in the context of assisted reproduction. Different ethical approaches appear to underlie the welfare of the child provision in ART regulation in these two jurisdictions, although the approaches are not expressly articulated. The essentially 'harm-based' approach in HFEA policy in the UK is arguably more appropriate than the 'best interests' approach in Victoria, particularly in the context of saviour sibling selection where the interests of other family members are clearly important. Some tension remains, however, between legislation and policy in the UK, highlighting the need for the UK Parliament to articulate a clear ethical approach to the welfare of the child to ensure greater transparency and accuracy in the law.

The ethical debate about saviour sibling selection provides some valuable insights into the impact selective reproduction might have on the welfare of the child to be born. In particular, the ethical concerns about commodification and harm highlight the future child's interests in respect and protection from harm. These individual interests of the child to be born are relevant to decisions about selective reproduction generally and raise important considerations about how PGD should be regulated. For instance, the child's interests in being treated with respect should be safeguarded through appropriate counselling of individuals seeking selective reproduction, to ensure that they want the child in his/her own right and plan to care for the child as they would any other child. The current speculative nature of harm to the child to be born also highlights the need for further empirical research into the long- and short-term impacts of selection on saviour siblings.

Given the risks of physical and psychosocial harm to saviour siblings, it is difficult to understand how saviour sibling selection is in the individual interests of the child to be born. Some commentators have argued that a child born as a saviour sibling receives a net benefit overall. In this chapter, I have argued that a child will not necessarily experience an individual net benefit from being selected as a saviour sibling. A saviour sibling may, however, share the collective benefit of his/her family in saving the life of a family member. The nature of this collective benefit requires a more holistic view of the human agent within the family, one that goes beyond notions of retrospective altruism and indirect instrumental benefit to the child to be born. Instead, the child's welfare is conceived as being 'inextricably intertwined'[173] with the interests of the family as a whole.

In Chapter 4, I propose a relational approach to the welfare of the child, which highlights the collective interests that the child shares with his/her family. I draw on relational feminist and communitarian ethical theories to explain the instrumental and inherent value of families to the children within them. My relational approach acknowledges the interdependence between family members and situates the child within the social context of his/her family. In particular, I argue that a child has both individual interests and collective interests that the child shares with other family members. Although saviour sibling selection may not be in the individual interests of the child to be born, I argue that the procedure enhances the collective interests the child shares with his/her family.

Notes

1 Victorian Law Reform Commission (VLRC), *Assisted Reproductive Technology & Adoption*, Final Report (2007) (VLRC Report), 46.
2 See, for example, Emily Jackson, 'Conception and the Irrelevance of the Welfare Principle' (2002) 65 *Modern Law Review* 176.
3 See, for example, S E Mumford, E Corrigan and M G R Hull, 'Access to Assisted Conception: A Framework of Regulation' (1998) 13 *Human Reproduction* 2349, 2353.
4 See, for example, John Tobin, *The Convention on the Rights of the Child: The Rights and Best Interests of Children Conceived Through Assisted Reproduction*, VLRC Occasional Paper, August 2004, 6.
5 House of Commons Science and Technology Committee (STC), *Fifth Report of Session 2004–5, Human Reproductive Technologies and the Law*, HC7-1 (24 March 2005) (STC Report), [107]; Jackson, above n 2; People, Science & Policy Ltd, *Report on the Consultation on the Review of the Human Fertilisation & Embryology Act 1990* (March 2006) (Independent Report on HFE Act Review), [3.2].
6 Joint Committee on the Human Tissue and Embryos, (Draft) Bill Session 2006–7, *Human Tissues and Embryos (Draft) Bill*, HL 169/HC 630-I and II (August 2007) (Joint Committee Report), [221]; STC Report, above n 5, [93].
7 Emily Jackson, 'Rethinking the Pre-Conception Welfare Principle' in Kirsty Horsey and Hazel Biggs (eds), *Human Fertilisation and Embryology: Reproducing Regulation* (Routledge-Cavendish, 2007), 47, 47.
8 United Kingdom, Committee of Inquiry into Human Fertilisation and Embryology, *Report of the Committee of Inquiry into Human Fertilisation and Embryology*, Cmnd 9314 (1984) (Warnock Report), [2.5].

9 Warnock Report, ibid, [2.11].

10 Warnock Report, above n 8, [2.13], Recommendation 24.

11 United Kingdom, Department of Health and Social Security, *Human Fertilisation and Embryology: A Framework for Legislation*, Cm 259 (1987).

12 United Kingdom, *Parliamentary Debates*, House of Lords, 7 December 1989, vol 513, col 1002 (Second Reading Speech).

13 See, for example, United Kingdom, *Parliamentary Debates*, House of Lords, 6 February 1990, vol 515, cols 787–89 (The Lord Chancellor and The Earl of Halsbury).

14 See, for example, United Kingdom, *Parliamentary Debates*, ibid, cols 789–90 (Lord Ennals).

15 Human Fertilisation and Embryology Authority (HFEA), *Tomorrow's Children: A Consultation on Guidance to Licensed Fertility Clinics on Taking in Account the Welfare of Children to Be Born of Assisted Conception Treatment* (January 2005) (*Tomorrow's Children* Consultation), [2.1].

16 Rachel Ann Fenton and Fiona Dabell, 'Time for Change (1)' (2007) 157 *New Law Journal* 848, 848.

17 Family Law Council, *Creating Children. A Uniform Approach to the Law and Practice of Reproductive Technology in Australia*, 1985, [6.1.9].

18 Family Law Council, ibid, [6.1.2].

19 Victoria, *Parliamentary Debates*, Legislative Assembly, 4 May 1995, 1244 (Marie Teehan, Minister for Health); Victoria, *Parliamentary Debates*, Legislative Assembly, 30 May 1995, 1919, 1925, 1928 (John Thwaites); Victoria, *Parliamentary Debates*, Legislative Assembly, 1 June 1995, 2104 (Robert Doyle). See also Victoria, *Parliamentary Debates*, Legislative Council, 6 June 1995, 1214 (Robert Knowles).

20 VLRC Report, above n 1, 47.

21 STC Report, above n 5, [107] (Recommendation 24).

22 STC Report, above n 5, [107] (Recommendation 24). As mentioned above, this 'harm-based' approach is reflected in current HFEA policy.

23 United Kingdom, *Human Reproductive Technologies and the Law: Government Response to the Report from the House of Commons Science and Technology Committee*, Cm 6641 (2005) (Government Response to STC Report), [37].

24 Government Response to STC Report, ibid, [37], [38].

25 Department of Health (UK), *Review of the Human Fertilisation and Embryology Act: A Public Consultation* (2005) (Department of Health Public Consultation), [3.23]–[3.26].

26 Department of Health (UK), ibid, [3.32].

27 Independent Report on HFE Act Review, above n 5.

28 Department of Health (UK), *Review of the Human Fertilisation and Embryology Act: Proposals for Revised Legislation (Including Establishment of the Regulatory Authority for Tissue and Embryos)*, Cm 6989 (December 2006) (White Paper), [1.11].

29 White Paper, ibid, [2.23]–[2.26].

30 Joint Committee Report, above n 6, [241].

31 Joint Committee Report, above n 6, [221]. In support of its position, the Joint Committee quoted Professor Raanan Gillon, Emeritus Professor of Medical Ethics at Imperial College London who told the Committee, 'It seems to me that one needs to be very careful about the welfare of the child being paramount, it does not seem to me that this is the normal reason for having a child'.

32 Joint Committee Report, above n 6, [44]. This criticism has been echoed in academic debate. See, for example, Anna Smajdor, 'The Review of the HFE Act: Ethical Expertise or Moral Cowardice?' (2007) 432 *BioNews*, <http://www.bionews.org.uk/page_37959.asp> (accessed 24 April 2013); Iain McDonald, Rachel Anne Fenton and Fiona Dabell, 'Treatment Provisions: Proposals for Reform of the Human Fertilisation and Embryology Act 1990' (2007) 29 *Journal of Social Welfare and Family Law* 293, 304.

33 Joint Committee Report, above n 6, [44].

34 Human Fertilisation and Embryology Act 1990 (UK), s 25(2), (6). See HFEA, *Code of Practice* (8th edn, first published 2009, revised October 2011) (HFEA, *Code of Practice*), Guidance Note 8.

35 HFEA, *Code of Practice* (1st edn) (1991), <http://www.hfea.gov.uk/docs/1st_Edition_Code_of_Practice.pdf> (accessed 26 April 2013), [3.14].

36 HFEA, *Tomorrow's Children* Consultation, above n 15, Chair's Foreword.

37 Dewinder Birk, 'The Reform of the Human Fertilisation and Embryology Act 1990' (2005) 35 *Family Law* 563, 566.

38 HFEA, *Tomorrow's Children* Consultation, above n 15, [2.4]. The three approaches proposed by the HFEA were previously suggested by Pennings in 1999: Guido Pennings, 'Measuring the Welfare of the Child: in Search of the Appropriate Evaluation Principle' (1999) 14 *Human Reproduction* 1146.

39 HFEA, *Tomorrow's Children* Consultation, above n 15, [2.4].

40 HFEA, *Tomorrow's Children* Consultation, above n 15, [2.4].

41 HFEA, *Tomorrow's Children* Consultation, above n 15, [2.4].

42 HFEA, *Tomorrow's Children* Consultation, above n 15, [2.4].

43 HFEA, *Tomorrow's Children* Consultation, above n 15, [2.4].

44 HFEA, *Tomorrow's Children* Consultation, above n 15, [3].

45 HFEA, *Tomorrow's Children: Report of the Policy Review of Welfare of the Child Assessments in Licensed Assisted Conception Clinics* (November 2005) (*Tomorrow's Children* Report).

46 *Tomorrow's Children* Report, ibid, 6.

47 *Tomorrow's Children* Report, above n 45, 6.

48 STC Report, above n 5, [107].

49 HFEA, *Tomorrow's Children* Report, above n 45, 8.

50 HFEA, *Tomorrow's Children* Report, above n 45, 10–11. Previously, clinics were required to routinely contact a patient's general practitioner before making assessments about treatment.

51 HFEA, *Code of Practice*, above n 34, [8.15]. See also [8.2], [8.3].

52 HFEA, *Code of Practice*, above n 34, [10.20].

53 HFEA, *Code of Practice*, above n 34, [8.7].

54 HFEA, *Code of Practice*, above n 34, [8.13].

55 VLRC Report, above n 1, 54.

56 VLRC Report, above n 1.

57 VLRC Report, above n 1, Chapter 2, 30–38. For example, a report by Ruth McNair focused on the welfare of children born as a result of ART in a diverse range of families: Ruth McNair, *Outcomes for Children Born of ART in a Diverse Range of Families*, VLRC Occasional Paper, August 2004.

58 VLRC Report, above n 1, 46–47.

59 VLRC Report, above n 1, 47.

60 VLRC Report, above n 1, 68.

61 VLRC Report, above n 1, 68.

62 Alistair Nicholson, 'Children's Rights in the Context of Infertility Treatment' (Speech delivered at the Infertility Treatment Authority One Day Symposium, Melbourne, 2 November 2006), 8.

63 Nicholson, ibid.

64 Kristen Walker, 'Should There Be Limits On Who May Access Assisted Reproductive Services? A Legal Perspective' in Jennifer Gunning and Helen Szoke (eds), *The Regulation of Assisted Reproductive Technology* (Ashgate, 2003), 123, 132.

65 Walker, ibid.

66 Tobin, above n 4, 6.

67 Nicholson, above n 62, 4.

68 VLRC Report, above n 1, 46.

69 For example, Family Law Act 1975 (Cth), s 60CA requires the Family Law Court to have regard to the best interests of the child as the paramount consideration in making parenting orders. See also Children, Youth and Families Act 2005 (Vic), s 10.

70 Assisted Reproductive Treatment Act 2008 (Vic), s 15(3)(b)(ii).

71 Mumford, Corrigan and Hull, above n 3, 2352.

72 Loane Skene, 'Why Legislate on Assisted Reproduction?' in Ian Freckelton and Kerry Petersen (eds), *Controversies in Health Law* (Federation Press, 1999), 266, 267.

73 See, for example, Robert Mnookin, 'Child-Custody Adjudication: Judicial Functions in the Face of Indeterminacy' (1975) 39 *Law and Contemporary Problems* 226; Stephen Parker, 'The Best Interests of the Child – Principles and Problems' (1994) 8 *International Journal of Law and the Family* 26; Mumford, Corrigan and Hull, above n 3, 2352–53.

74 Margaret Coady, 'Families and Future Children: The Role of Rights and Interests in Determining Ethical Policy for Regulating Families' (2002) 9 *Journal of Law and Medicine* 449, 452.

75 Coady, ibid, 449.

76 Parker, above n 73, 30.

77 See, for example, Jackson, above n 2; Amel Alghrani and John Harris, 'Reproductive Liberty: Should the Foundation of Families be Regulated?' (2006) 18 *Child and Family Law Quarterly* 191.

78 Jackson, above n 2, 176.

79 Jackson, above n 2, 176.

80 Jackson, above n 2, 182; Walker, above n 64, 131.

81 Jackson, above n 2, 178.

82 In the UK, the STC stated that ART physicians should be encouraged to minimise any risks to the child to be born 'through the promotion of good medical practice not legislation': STC Report, above n 5, [107].

83 Walker argues that it is difficult to assess effectively the welfare of a child who is not yet in existence: Walker, above n 64, 130. Jackson similarly contends that the welfare of the child principle fails to provide clinics with the means to realistically assess the future welfare of the child to be born: Jackson, above n 2, 178, 194.

84 Walker, above n 64, 131.

85 Ellie Lee, Jan Macvarish and Sally Sheldon, 'Assessing Child Welfare under the Human Fertilisation and Embryology Act: The New Law: Summary of Findings' (University of Kent, September 2012). The study revealed no evidence of any 'group discrimination' based on sexuality or relationship status.

86 Human Fertilisation and Embryology Act 1990 (UK), s 13(5). See also HFEA, *Code of Practice*, above n 34, [8.2].

87 HFEA, *Tomorrow's Children* Consultation, above n 15, [2.4]. HFEA policy has, however, interpreted this requirement to bring it in line with a 'minimum threshold' approach. For instance, there is a presumption that all prospective parents will be supportive parents, in the absence of any reasonable concern that any child may be at risk of significant harm or neglect: HFEA, *Code of Practice*, above n 34, [8.11].

88 Human Fertilisation and Embryology Act 1990 (UK), Schedule 2, s 1ZA(1)(d).

89 Ibid.

90 Mumford, Corrigan and Hull, above n 3, 2353.

91 Colin Gavaghan, *Defending the Genetic Supermarket: Law and Ethics of Selecting the Next Generation* (Routledge-Cavendish, 2007), 151.

92 Andrew Dutney, 'Hope Takes Risks: Making Sense of the Interests of ART Offspring' (Paper presented at the WA RTC Seminar on 'Assisted Reproduction: Considering the Interests of the Child', WA, 2000), 31–32.

93 Sally Sheldon and Stephen Wilkinson, 'Hashmi and Whitaker: An Unjustifiable and Misguided Distinction?' (2004) 12 *Medical Law Review* 137, 152.

94 Gavaghan, above n 91, 151.

95 Coady, above n 74, 450.

96 Gavaghan, above n 91, 151.

97 See, for example, Gavaghan, above n 91; Coady, above n 74; Tobin, above n 4; Nicholson, above n 62. See also C L Ten, 'A Child's Right to a Father' (2000) 19(4) *Monash Bioethics Review* 33.

98 Coady, above n 74, 451.

99 See discussion at section 3.2.4.

100 Eric Blyth, 'Conceptions of Welfare' in Kirsty Horsey and Hazel Biggs (eds), *Human Fertilisation and Embryology: Reproducing Regulation* (Routledge-Cavendish, 2007), 17, 37.

101 Convention on the Rights of the Child, opened for signature 20 November 1989, [1991] ATS 4 (entered into force 2 September 1990) (UNCRC), Art 7(1).

102 Ibid, Art 8(1).

103 Ibid, Art 19.

104 Ibid, Art 27(2).

105 Infertility Treatment Authority, *Tissue Typing in Conjunction with Preimplantation Genetic Diagnosis* (adopted February 2003, updated January 2004), [2.3].

106 National Health and Medical Research Council (NHMRC), *Ethical Guidelines on the Use of Assisted Reproductive Technology in Clinical Practice and Research 2004 (as revised in 2007 to take into account the changes in legislation)* (June 2007) (NHMRC ART Guidelines), [12.3].

107 Infertility Treatment Authority, *Report on the Outcome of Consultation with Members of the Infertility Treatment Authority Ethics Panel* (February 2002), (document provided to the author by Tracey Petrillo (Policy Officer, VARTA) in July 2009) (ITA Report), 5.

108 HFEA Ethics & Law Committee, *Ethical Issues in the Creation and Selection of Preimplantation Embryos to Produce Tissue Donors* (22 November 2001), [2.11].

109 K Devolder, 'Preimplantation HLA Typing: having children to save our loved ones' (2005) 31 *Journal of Medical Ethics* 582, 584.

110 Devolder, ibid.

111 Jess Buxton, 'Unforseen Uses of Preimplantation Genetic Diagnosis – Ethical and Legal Issues' in Kirsty Horsey and Hazel Biggs (eds), *Human Fertilisation and Embryology: Reproducing Regulation* (Routledge-Cavendish, 2007), 109, 121. See also Julian Savulescu, 'Sex Selection: The Case for' (1999) 171 *Medical Journal of Australia* 373.

112 Gavaghan, above n 91, 161.

113 Belinda Bennett, 'Symbiotic Relationships: Saviour Siblings, Family Rights and Biomedicine' (2005) 19 *Australian Journal of Family Law* 195, 203.

114 Gavaghan, above n 91, 161.

115 John Harris, 'Sex Selection and Regulated Hatred' (2005) 31 *Journal of Medical Ethics* 291, 293.

116 As discussed in section 3.5.1, there are protections in UK and Australian law against organ and excessive tissue donation by minors. However, these legal protections do not protect the child to be born from damaging attitudes by parents who intended to conceive the child purely as a donor. Such parents may not ultimately care for the child as a person in his/her own right.

117 Parents can, of course, always attempt to conceive a donor sibling for an ill child naturally.

118 Commodification may become more of an issue if fears about an increased use of PGD in the future for trivial reasons, such as eye or hair colour, are realised.

119 Guido Pennings, 'Saviour Siblings: Using Preimplantation Genetic Diagnosis for Tissue Typing' (2004) 1266 *International Congress Series* 311, 311.

120 Bennett, above n 113, 203.

121 Pennings, 'Saviour Siblings', above n 119, 313. Robert J Boyle and Julian Savulescu, 'Ethics of Using Preimplantation Genetic Diagnosis to Select a Stem Cell Donor for an Existing Person' (2001) 323 *British Medical Journal* 1240, 1241. Devolder, above n 109, 584.

122 Robert Sparrow and David Cram, 'Saviour Embryos? Preimplantation Genetic Diagnosis as a Therapeutic Technology' (2010) 20 *Reproductive Biomedicine Online* 667, 671.

123 Davis distinguishes between the decision by parents to choose a particular type of child and how a parent relates to a child once it is born: John Davis, 'Selecting Potential Children and Unconditional Parental Love' (2008) 22 *Bioethics* 258, 261–63. As Pennings points out, the postnatal attitude of parents toward a child does not depend on the pre-conceptional desire for a child. If this were the case, then most children conceived 'by

accident' would not be the recipients of unconditional parental love. See Pennings, above n 119, 313.

124 J A Robertson, J P Khan and J E Wagner, 'Conception to Obtain Hematopoietic Stem Cells' (2002) 32 *Hastings Center Report* 34.

125 Rebecca Smith, 'Britain's Only Saviour Sibling Twins', *The Daily Telegraph* (online), 9 August 2009, <http://www.telegraph.co.uk/health/children_shealth/5998991/Britains-only-saviour-sibling-twins.html> (accessed 24 April 2013).

126 Devolder, above n 109, 584.

127 Walter Glannon, *Genes and Future People: Philosophical Issues in Human Genetics* (Westview Press, 2001), 120.

128 Gavaghan, above n 91, 151.

129 American Academy of Pediatrics (AAP), 'Policy Statement – Children as Hematopoietic Stem Cell Donors' (2010) 125 *Pediatrics*, 392, 395. New research suggests, however, that delaying clamping of the umbilical cord after birth by several minutes brings statistically significant benefits to babies: Jose N Tolosa, *et al*, 'Mankind's First Natural Stem Cell Transplant' (2010) 14 *Journal of Cellular and Molecular Medicine* 488. Delaying clamping of the umbilical cord is likely to reduce the number of stem cells collected for transplant.

130 G Pennings, R Schots and I Liebaers, 'Ethical Considerations on Preimplantation Genetic Diagnosis for HLA Typing to Match a Future Child as a Donor of Haematopoietic Stem Cells to a Sibling' (2002) 17 *Human Reproduction* 534, 537.

131 See Chapter 2, section 2.5.1, esp n 121.

132 AAP, above n 129, 394.

133 AAP, above n 129, 394.

134 Gavaghan, above n 91, 154.

135 See, for example, Human Tissue Act 1982 (Vic). For a summary of the legislation regulating human tissue donation in Australia, see Bennett, above n 113, 205–7.

136 See, for example, Human Tissue Act 1982 (Vic), s 15(1). Regenerative tissue is tissue that the human body can replace, once removed, by natural processes of growth or repair.

137 This is the case in Victoria, SA and WA. See, for example, ibid, s 14(1).

138 The legislation is silent on this issue in NSW, Queensland, Tasmania and the Northern Territory. The Australian Capital Territory is the exception, in that it expressly permits the donation of non-regenerative tissue from minors under very strict conditions: Transplantation and Anatomy Act 1978 (ACT), s 14.

139 Family Law Act 1975, s 67ZC(1).

140 Human Genetics Commission (HGC), *Making Babies: Reproductive Decisions and Genetic Technologies* (January 2006) (*Making Babies* Report), [4.21], [4.22].

141 N R Ram, 'Britain's New Preimplantation Tissue Typing Policy: an Ethical Defence' (2006) 32 *Journal of Medical Ethics* 278, 280. Saviour sibling selection using PGD has only been available since 2000 so the oldest saviour siblings have only just reached adolescence, at which point they become psychologically independent from their family and seek their own identity. See also, J A Daniels, 'Adolescent separation-individuation and family transitions' (1990) 25 *Adolescence* 105.

142 See, for example, Cordelia Thomas, 'Pre-Implantation Testing and the Protection of the "Saviour Sibling"' (2004) 9 *Deakin Law Review* 119, 123.

143 Erica Grundell, 'Tissue Typing for Bone Marrow Transplantation: An Ethical Examination of Some Arguments Concerning Harm to the Child' (2003) *Monash Bioethics Review* 22 45, 48.

144 M Spriggs and J Savulescu, 'Saviour Siblings' (2002) 28 *Journal of Medical Ethics* 289. See also comments by Australian bioethicist, Nicholas Tonti-Filippini, reported by A Keenan and S Stock in '"Closed Future" for Saviour Siblings', *The Australian*, 17 April 2002, 3.

145 Joel Feinberg, 'The Child's Right to an Open Future' in William Aiken and Hugh LaFollette (eds), *Whose Child? Children's Rights, Parental Authority, and State Power* (Rowman and Littlefield, 1980), 124. The notion of a child's right to an open future has, however, been criticised as 'self-contradictory' and 'problematic': Lainie Friedman Ross,

Children, Families, and Health Care Decision Making (Clarendon Press, 1998); Stephen Wilkinson, *Choosing Tomorrow's Children: The Ethics of Selective Reproduction* (Clarendon Press, 2010), 500.

146 See, for example, Grundell, above n 143, 47–48; Pennings, Schots and Liebaers, above n 130, 537.

147 See for example, W L Packman, 'Psychosocial Impact of Pediatric BMT on Siblings' (1999) 24 *Bone Marrow Transplantation* 701. For a qualitative study of the impact on siblings of unsuccessful donation, see Kendra D MacLeod, *et al*, 'Pediatric Sibling Donors of Successful and Unsuccessful Hematopoietic Stem Cell Transplants (HSCT): A Qualitative Study of their Psychosocial Experience' (2003) 28 *Journal of Pediatric Psychology* 223.

148 Packman, ibid.

149 Packman, above n 147.

150 Thomas, above n 142, 138. If stem cells harvested from the placenta successfully cure the ill sibling, then the saviour sibling will not need to undergo any invasive medical procedures.

151 Pennings, Schots and Liebaers, above n 130, 537.

152 S Sheldon and S Wilkinson, 'Should Selecting Saviour Siblings Be Banned?' (2004) 30 *Journal of Medical Ethics* 533, 536.

153 Pennings, Schots and Liebaers, above n 130, 537.

154 See, for example, Thomas, above n 142, 123, 138; Sheldon and Wilkinson, above n 152, 536; Julian Savulescu, 'Substantial Harm but Substantial Benefit' (1996) 312 *British Medical Journal* 241.

155 Savulescu, above n 154.

156 Savulescu, above n 154.

157 Sheldon and Wilkinson, above n 152, 536.

158 See, for example, Peter Browett and Stephen Palmer, 'Legal Barriers Might Have Catastrophic Effects' (1996) 312 *British Medical Journal* 242, 243; Robert A Crouch and Carl Elliott, 'Moral Agency and the Family: The Case of Living Related Organ Transplantation' (1999) 8 *Cambridge Quarterly of Healthcare Ethics* 275, 282; Grundell, above n 143, 48.

159 Gavaghan, above n 91, 155. See also Sheldon and Wilkinson, above n XXXX, 152.

160 B L Freund and K Siegel, 'Problems in Transition Following Bone Marrow Transplantation: Psychosocial Aspects' (1986) 56 *American Journal of Orthopsychiatry* 244.

161 MacLeod, *et al*, above n 147.

162 Ram, above n 141, 280.

163 Joel Feinberg, *Harm to Others. Volume 1: The Moral Limits of the Criminal Law* (Oxford University Press, 1984), 70–79.

164 Cara Cheyette, 'Organ Harvests from the Legally Incompetent: An Argument Against Compelled Altruism' (2000) 41 *Boston College Law Review* 465, 508.

165 As discussed in Chapter 2, saviour sibling selection is not permitted for the purposes of organ donation in the UK and Australia. Cheyette's argument can, however, be extended to the donation of non-regenerative tissue such as bone marrow, bearing in mind that the impact of the removal of regenerative tissue is likely to be less significant than it is for the removal of non-regenerative tissue.

166 Cheyette, above n 164, 506.

167 Crouch and Elliott, above n 158, 280–83.

168 The last-mentioned instrumental benefit is not in fact a 'benefit' to the child to be born because the alternative to saviour sibling selection for that child is not to grow up in a family traumatised by the death of a child but to not exist at all. The 'benefit' for the child to be born could only be that it gets born. However, as I argue in Chapter 2, the argument that it is 'better to be born than not' is problematic in the context of selective reproduction.

169 A similar complaint has been made about justifying organ or bone marrow donation on the basis of psychological or social benefits for the donor: Pennings, Schots and Liebaers,

above n 130, 536. See also James Dwyer and Elizabeth Vig, 'Rethinking Transplantation Between Siblings' (1995) 25 *Hastings Center Report* 7, 12; Crouch and Elliott, above n 158.

170 Sarah Elliston, *The Best Interests of the Child in Healthcare* (Routledge-Cavendish, 2007), 258.

171 Crouch and Elliott, above n 158, 275.

172 Pennings, Schots and Liebaers, above n 130, 536.

173 Crouch and Elliott, above n 158, 284.

4 A relational approach to the welfare of the child

4.1 Introduction

The welfare of a child is inextricably linked to the welfare of the family in which he/she will be raised. It is therefore unsatisfactory to focus solely on the individual interests of the child to be born in assisted reproduction. A more holistic approach to the welfare of the child – one that recognises the importance of connection and interdependence within a family – is needed in order to protect not only the child to be born but also the family that will enable the child to flourish. A comprehensive account of the welfare of the child to be born must therefore include the individual interests of the future child as well as the collective interests the child will share with his/her family. In this chapter, I propose a relational approach to the welfare of the child based on the notion of human flourishing. My relational approach acknowledges that, in order to flourish, a child needs not only to be treated with respect and protected from harm but also requires the intimacy, love and meaning that comes from being involved in the collective endeavour of family.

I begin section 4.2 of this chapter by exploring the welfare of the child to be born in the broader social context of his/her family. In particular, I examine the role of intimate families in promoting human flourishing. I use the term 'intimate family' to encompass a diverse range of family structures in which members are closely connected. Drawing from relational feminist and communitarian ethics, I argue that intimate families are not only instrumentally valuable to the children they rear, but also inherently valuable as they provide opportunities for the type of collective endeavour that is integral to a meaningful life. The welfare of the child is therefore inextricably tied up with the collective interests of his/her family. I explore the specific nature of collective interests in the context of saviour sibling selection in section 4.3. I argue that it is particularly important to consider the welfare of the family as a whole in relation to saviour sibling selection because the procedure affects all family members, in particular the interests of the parents and the existing ill child. Moreover, I explain how promoting the welfare of the family as a whole enhances the welfare of a saviour sibling.

Recognising that the welfare of the child to be born is not necessarily synonymous with the welfare of his/her family, in section 4.4 I examine the role of familial duty as a justification for compromising some of the individual interests of the child to be born in favour of the collective interests of the family as a whole. I also argue that the compromise entailed by familial duty need not necessarily be voluntary or based on constructive consent. Instead, I contend that membership alone provides the foundation for moral responsibility to the family. Lastly, I argue that the duty owed by family members to one another is greater than the duty owed to strangers because intimate relationships involve a higher level of mutual obligation and reliance than non-intimate relationships. Accordingly, a different range of principles and objectives apply to obligations of family membership than the universal moral obligations grounded in modern liberal theory. This is not to suggest that there are not some universal moral constraints that operate within families to protect children from exploitation, abuse or neglect. I discuss the point at which acceptable compromise becomes unacceptable sacrifice in detail in Chapter 5.

4.2 Families and human flourishing

A child has certain basic interests, which ought to be protected. The debate about saviour sibling selection has focused on two key individual interests of the child to be born, namely respect and protection from harm. However, a child's welfare is also intimately and inextricably connected with the collective welfare of his/her family. The collective interests that are shared by intimate family members are integral to human flourishing. We therefore need to view the child to be born as a human agent within his/her family and understand the welfare of the child from this perspective. It is important to stress that this conception of the welfare of the child is not merely one where the child's *individual interests* are *indirectly enhanced* by the welfare of his/her family as a whole, but one where the *child's welfare as a member of an intimate collective* is *directly enhanced*. I begin my discussion in the next section by clarifying what I mean by the phrase 'intimate family'.

4.2.1 Nature of intimate family

The family is a complex social unit and no two families are the same. Families come in all shapes and sizes. The development of ART has increased the diversity of family structures. The term 'family' is not confined to biological heterosexual two-parent nuclear families. It includes adoptive families, foster families, step-families, blended families,[1] extended families and families whose parents have separated or divorced. It also includes families created through assisted reproduction, which may consist of households with a single parent, same sex parents or with children created through gamete donation or surrogacy arrangements.

4.2.1.1 Diverse and dynamic nature of family

The fact that families take various forms is reflected in the multiple definitions that are available for the term 'family'.[2] For example, the *Macquarie Dictionary* defines family in various ways, including: 'parents and their children, whether dwelling together or not'; 'any group of persons closely related by blood, as parents, children, uncles, aunts, and cousins'; or 'a group of persons who form a household and who regard themselves as having familial ties'.[3] Elsewhere, 'family' is defined as 'a fundamental social group in society typically consisting of one or two parents and their children' and 'two or more people who share goals and values, have long-term commitments to one another, and reside usually in the same dwelling place'.[4] These definitions of 'family' clearly extend beyond biological connection to include, at the broadest level, a group of persons in a household who regard themselves as family.

Not only are family structures diverse, they also change and evolve over time. Individual family structures are never static. Children grow up and move out of home and many begin their own families. Family members pass away or become estranged. Not uncommonly, parents separate due to irreconcilable differences and children either live with one parent or according to shared-parenting arrangements. Despite the dynamic and changing nature of family, an individual's identity is continually shaped by the ongoing narrative of his/her family. As Hilde and James Lindemann Nelson point out, a 'family reconfigures as the people within it grow, but the story that is lived out within the successive configurations preserves its continuity'.[5]

4.2.1.2 What makes a family intimate?

For the purpose of the following discussion, I shall focus on a particular type of family, which I describe as 'intimate family'. Not all family members are sufficiently close to one another to be classified as 'intimate'. The important feature of an intimate family is not the particular structure of the family but the closeness of its members.[6] To be 'intimate' with someone is to be 'associated in close personal relations' with that person.[7] According to Kuczewski, describing the family in terms of 'closeness' as opposed to biology is 'commonplace in medical ethics'.[8] The importance of function over form within families was highlighted recently in a report commissioned by the VLRC and written by Ruth McNair, which explores the outcomes of children born of assisted reproduction in a diverse range of families.[9] McNair reported that, overall, family functioning or processes were more important than family structure to children's outcomes.[10] The one element of structure that McNair found did influence outcomes directly is consistency of family structure, which impacts on a child's feeling of security.[11]

Like other forms of intimate groupings, intimate families involve 'enduring relationships in which people's interests are complexly entwined, and in which people care deeply about one another'.[12] It is the interconnectedness between family members that makes them intimate, rather than the specific structure of the family itself. Families are not the only examples of close personal relationships. Longstanding friendships also provide opportunities for intimacy.[13] Much of what I discuss in the next section about the value of intimacy is also pertinent to these other types of intimate relationships. One way in which we can distinguish families from other intimate relationships is by acknowledging their role in child-rearing. Selective reproduction involves families that are, or wish to become, actively engaged in child-rearing. Parents have specific functions in relation to raising children, which include protecting the child from harm, nurturing and socialising the child.[14]

4.2.1.3 When families become dysfunctional

Intimate family members generally love, care for and support one another within a relationship of mutual interdependence. However, no family is perfect and, as with all relationships of intimacy, family members have the ability to damage as well as benefit one another. I do not use the term 'intimate family' to invoke a romantic notion of a perfectly functioning family, in which the members are always kind, thoughtful and caring towards one another. While many parents may strive to emulate a perfectly functioning family unit, it is doubtful that such a family exists in reality. Parents and children will inevitably argue, parents will at times treat children unfairly because they are tired or stressed, and children will continue to aggravate their parents and each other as they learn the boundaries of what is acceptable behaviour. This is what makes us human and it is why families are important social units.

Unlike in other relationships, family members cannot easily disassociate from one another. According to Nelson and Nelson, 'seeing families as composed of replaceable parts is inconsistent with our understanding of what an intimate relationship is, and with the ability of such relationships to convey the special goods of intimacy'.[15] We may not always like our family members but we need to learn how to 'get along' with one another. As Jeffrey Blustein points out, 'the family is the center of most people's lives, for better or for worse'.[16] Conflict and reconciliation are an integral part of intimacy. Bearing in mind that individuals within families will differ in their needs and preferences, it is the 'business of families' to maintain a constant tension between fusion and individuation for their members.[17]

In some cases, families are unable to accommodate the basic needs of their members to the extent that they become dysfunctional and lose their value as intimate collectives. Irresolvable conflict, oppression, exploitation, neglect and abuse within families are all extremely damaging, particularly because they occur inside a relationship of trust.[18] Vulnerable family members, in particular children, need protection from dysfunctional families. In Chapter 5, I discuss in detail the point at which families become dysfunctional to a level at which state intervention is justified. This is not, however, an issue specific to families involved in selective reproduction and I argue that these families are no more likely to be dysfunctional than any other family. It is also important to bear in mind that the value of intimate family relationships is not negated by the existence of dysfunctional families. As Patricia Smith points out:

> ... *bad families are not counterexamples to the value of good families.* It is clear that human beings cannot survive in isolation, and institutional child-rearing seems most successful when (familylike) arrangements allow personal relationships to grow and flourish ... Family living (at least in the sense of small group living) is a fundamental value for humanity as a whole and for every human being individually.'[19] (emphasis added)

In the next section, I draw on relational feminist and communitarian theories to argue that intimate families are both instrumentally and inherently valuable. Intimate families are instrumentally valuable as they enable human beings to thrive. They are also inherently valuable as a primary source of collective endeavour, which is essential to a meaningful life. Thus, whether we view families through a romantic lens or as a 'necessary evil', they play a profound role in human flourishing. The welfare of a child is therefore inextricably connected to the welfare of the intimate collective that is his/her family.

4.2.2 Role of families in promoting human flourishing

4.2.2.1 Instrumental value of family

Children require more than nourishment, shelter and protection from harm to flourish or thrive. They also need the less tangible benefits that come from being part of an intimate collective, such as love, intimacy and affection. Virginia Held argues that when children are provided with the necessities 'without the relational human caring' they need, they 'do not develop well, if at all'.[20] There is empirical evidence to suggest that children who are raised in institutions are substantially less likely to thrive physically, cognitively, psychologically and socially than those who are raised within an intimate family.[21]

Intimate families are important for the development of self-esteem and self-understanding as they provide their members with a source of identity, connection, support and love.[22] Parents play a key role in fostering intimate relationships within families by 'providing opportunities for the emergence of meaning, intimacy, identity, and character'.[23] These inner qualities cannot be developed outside intimate relationships. Smith argues that 'family living is very probably a necessity for human existence'.[24] According to Smith, families provide the essential conditions for human beings to thrive, 'These sorts of values, connection, commitment, support, and love can be provided only by a small intimate group founded on assumptions of mutual reliance and communal cooperation. One name for such a group is family'.[25] Nelson and Nelson describe the primary role that families play in forging human identity in the following way:

> When we live in close and affectionate proximity with others, we can be seen and celebrated specially; we can be known more fully than our relationships in the workplace, in civic life, or in casual friendships permit. Being known well – being seen lovingly and particularly, in a way that singles us out from the billions of others who walk in the world – reinforces our understanding of who we are.[26]

Although our identity is also defined by non-intimate relationships, through culture, language, practices and customs of our society, 'the unit of family permits each member to be seen more particularly and specially than is possible, say, in an orphanage or boarding school'.[27] The intensity of family relationships, 'for good or ill, leaves its mark more deeply than the impersonal relationships formed in early life'.[28]

4.2.2.2 Inherent value of family

The value of family goes beyond the benefits it confers on its individual members. In addition to the instrumental value of family as a means of achieving the 'primary goods' of protection, nurturing, socialisation and identity, families are inherently valuable in themselves. The inherent value of intimate families should not be confused with some conservative notion of 'family values' that often undermines women and same-sex relationships. Intimate families, whatever their form, are inherently valuable for the collective endeavour they entail, which gives our life meaning. Interaction between family members 'that shows mutual interest and responsiveness'[29] is valuable, irrespective of the outcome of that interaction. As Nancy Sherman states, 'the value of group dynamic' is 'independent of specific products and activities' that arise out of the interaction.[30]

The value of family goes 'beyond its ability to promote self-respect, or to give people a personal identity, or physical care, or social and moral education'.[31] Ferdinand Schoeman argues that intimate families have value not merely because of their instrumental benefit to the individual children within them. They are also inherently valuable in and of themselves as sources of shared intimacies, which are essential to a meaningful life, 'The point of an intimate relationship is not just to supply some necessary ingredient in a needy child's life. The relationship within a family typically has an inner focus and an independent meaning which results from sharing of life and its intimacies'.[32] Robert Crouch and Carl Elliott also highlight the inherent value of the family by emphasising what is important in family life and to human agency, 'In families, the important factor is that family members cherish each other simply for each other's sake, and that being devoted to "the family" and its members is a source of deep meaning and value in our lives and the lives of those around us'.[33] They describe these shared or collective interests within families as "strongly valued goods", that come (to an extent, at least) from the fact that we are engaged in a shared journey'.[34] In part, 'the sharing in itself is valued',[35] not just the benefits that arise out of the sharing.

Several commentators have identified the importance of sharing intimate connections to human flourishing. In explaining the value of collective endeavour or affiliation, Sherman describes the 'pleasure of mutuality and the expansion of self that comes with it' as 'a part of human flourishing'.[36] Crouch and Elliott add that '[t]he importance of this mutuality runs deeper than an expansion of self' and use the term 'union' to describe the nature of family relationships.[37] Schoeman expresses the idea that human beings flourish through intimate connection within a family in the following way, 'We *share our selves* with those with whom we are intimate and are aware that they do the same with us. Traditional moral boundaries, which give rigid shape to the self, are transparent to this kind of sharing'.[38] Nelson and Nelson also highlight the connection between intimacy and collective identity by stating that 'intimacy changes the very identities of the persons involved, so that to destroy the relationship is to damage the selves within it'.[39]

4.3 Saviour siblings and collective family interests

4.3.1 A shared family journey

The collective interests of intimate family members are particularly relevant in the context of saviour sibling selection, which is by its very nature a shared enterprise. Parents use PGD to select a child who can donate cord blood stem cells to save the life of an existing ill sibling. The role of the child to be born is integral to the survival of the existing sibling and the welfare of the family as a whole. Even more than in other families, families involved in saviour sibling selection are inextricably connected as the members engage in a shared journey to save the life of an ill child.

The decision to use PGD to conceive a saviour sibling is primarily motivated by the interests of existing family members, in particular the parents' interest in saving the life of their ill child and the ill child's own interest in leading a healthy life. From the family's perspective as a whole, it is preferable that selection takes place. However, as I discussed in Chapter 3, saviour sibling selection does not necessarily promote the individual interests of the child to be born. The individual interests of the child to be born should therefore be considered alongside the collective family interests in saving the life of the ill child. Given the importance of family to human flourishing, it is preferable to view the interests of the child to be born *in connection with*, rather than *in opposition to*, the collective interests the child shares with his/her family.

If we accept that family members share collective interests, we can begin to see how the welfare of the child to be born may be enhanced by experiencing the intimacy, devotion and meaning that comes from being part of the shared journey of the child's family to save the life of one of its members. It is not important that the child selected to be a saviour sibling does not have the capacity to realise the nature of his/her involvement at the time of donation because the issue is one of human flourishing, which takes place through the journey itself. Being a donor sibling is one of many shared experiences the child will have with one or more members of his/her family, all of which will contribute to the child's identity and development as a human being with intimate connections. While children who donate tissue to a sibling can experience some physical and/or psychosocial harm, successful donations between siblings have been shown to have a positive impact on sibling relationships.[40] Given that family members have collective interests in maintaining positive intimate relationships, saviour sibling selection potentially promotes the welfare of the family as a whole.

This is not to suggest that the collective interests of a family seeking saviour sibling selection should outweigh the individual interests of the child to be born. As explained in Chapter 3, there are certain individual interests of the child to be born that require protection. In particular, the interests of the child to be born in being respected and protected from harm require careful consideration. But, as Crouch and Elliott point out, we need to, ' ... replace the discrete and separable interests of family members with a more realistic view of the family, one that recognises the conflict, confluence, and confusion of interests characteristic of life within a family'.[41] Jansen similarly states that, although family members 'share interests and concerns, they also have interests and concerns of their own that can and often do come into conflict with the interests and concerns of other family members'.[42] However, in order to have a realistic and comprehensive understanding of the welfare of the child to be born, we need first to recognise the often neglected collective benefit that comes from being part of a shared and intimate enterprise, before we tease out the areas of conflict. Once we have done this, we can then move on to developing an approach which recognises and reconciles the 'conflict, confluence, and confusion of interests' within a family.

4.3.2 Are collective interests legitimate?

Several critics have rejected the notion that a family exists as an intimate group with collective goals and interests. For example, Allen Buchanan and Dan Brock argue that 'to speak of the family as having its own goals and purposes and to speak of the familial perspective and family objectives is to engage in dangerous reification'.[43] They claim that decisions made by the family are, in reality, decisions that the parents impose on the family. Lynn Jansen similarly argues that treating the family as a separate entity 'unnecessarily reifies the family, making it look as if it has purposes and goals of its own that stand over and above the purposes and goals of individuals within it'.[44]

These criticisms are misguided in three respects. First, the claims of reification appear to be based on a misunderstanding of the nature of collective interests within a family. Second, collective interests are not synonymous with parental interests, as Buchanan and Brock suggest. Third, just because we acknowledge the existence of collective interests within families does not mean that those interests should necessarily override the interests of individual members. Rather, it means that we need a strategy for dealing with individual and collective interests when they come into conflict. In the remainder of this section, I clarify the nature of collective interests within a family and argue that collective family interests are not, in fact, synonymous with parental interests. In Chapter 5, I propose a strategy for reconciling individual and collective interests within a family.

4.3.2.1 Distinguishing collective interests from abstract family goals

The argument that attributing collective interests to families constitutes reification is based on a conception of family as an abstract entity, rather than as a group of individuals who share a common purpose. Smith provides a helpful distinction, in the context of family obligation, between the 'family in the abstract' and the 'family as household' or a group of intimates.[45] She uses the phrase, 'family in the abstract' to refer to 'a family name or genetic line, the extended family in the largest sense, whose boundaries or members extend over both space and time'. By contrast, she uses 'family as household' to refer to 'an aggregate or group of actual (living) members, who are closely associated by living arrangement or by commitment, for better or worse'.[46]

Abstract family goals, such as maintaining family traditions, can generally be distinguished from family household goals, which involve promoting the common good of the members by accommodating their special needs.[47] It is this latter notion of family as an intimate group of people or community on which I base my discussion of collective interests. This is not an abstract notion of 'the family' but rather a very real notion of a group of people with interconnected interests. The collective interests I have been discussing are not about abstract group ends, such as 'continuing the family line' or 'upholding the family's good reputation' but are related to the act of sharing or the collective endeavour itself.

Sherman similarly highlights the inherent value of sharing or collective endeavour by distinguishing between the value of abstract group ends and the collective dynamic that promotes them, '[A]part from the particular activities and products that may define a species of community, we value doing things with others. We value creating a shared world, and the mutuality that is defined by our interactions'.[48] My discussion of collective interests within a family is based on the value that human beings derive from being collectively involved with other family members in the common pursuits of a household.

According to Sherman, collective endeavour or 'affiliation' among a group of people is 'an important constituent of good living'.[49] Human beings:

> ... are supported by pleasurable interactions with other people, and depend upon these connections for our sense of self-esteem and self-understanding. It is in the act of relating and being reflected in the opinions and judgments of others whom we respect that we refine our sense of who we are and how worthwhile our lives have been.[50]

The value of saviour sibling selection for the child to be born lies in the child's collective involvement with other family members in the family's shared journey, which includes attempting to save the life of an existing member. It is the child's involvement in this shared journey of the family that is important, irrespective of whether the family goal of saving an ill family member is ultimately achieved. The journey itself becomes a collective endeavour from which the child will develop a sense of 'self-esteem and self-understanding'. The 'shared world' into which the child is born will shape the child's identity as a human being and provide meaning through intimate connections with others.

4.3.2.2 Collective family interests are not synonymous with parental interests

Some commentators are critical of the notion of collective interests within families. Buchanan and Brock argue that decisions by the family as a whole are essentially decisions imposed on other members of the family by the parents, 'Given the very great inequality of power between parents and children, reference to the family's interest or "familial objectives" is all too likely to serve as a cover for the parents' interests precisely in those cases in which the latter conflict with those of the child'.[51] This interpretation disregards, however, the fact that parents can act as both 'agents of themselves' and 'agents of the family as a group'. As Lainie Friedman Ross points out, Buchanan and Brock's statement, ' ... ignores the possibility that within intimate families, one member's well-being is an integral part of the other member's well-being. Intimates take on one another's goals, even as they retain their independent goals and identity'.[52] Schoeman similarly supports a view of parents as 'representing the interests of the family as an integrated whole in addition to representing their own particular interests'.[53]

Furthermore, parents are not the only members of a family that can influence its direction or projects. Clearly, parents have greater input into the direction of the family, particularly when children are still very young and incapable of either understanding or satisfying their own needs. However, children form preferences very early on and have ways to influence those around them. For example, a crying infant has a powerful impact on his/her parents. Margaret Steinfels cites research which 'confirms the experience of many parents that "behaviour control" is by no means exclusively in the hands of the adults of the family'.[54] She argues that infants have 'compelling powers to control behaviour and elicit responses in adults' that can 'effectively establish the *modus vivendi* of family life'.[55] Clearly a child who is not yet conceived has no influence on collective family goals before he/she comes into existence. It is therefore important to ensure that safeguards are in place to protect the basic needs of a child who is not yet born.[56] Once a child is born, however, that child will begin to influence the collective goals of his/her family.

As children grow as individuals within a family, they develop more distinct preferences, become more capable of expressing their independent wishes, and begin to have more influence over the family's projects. The family is not a rigid unit but is in a constant state of evolution as it grows to accommodate the needs and preferences of all its members. Notwithstanding the increasing independence of children within a family, the family will continue to operate as an intimate community with collective goals until the children move out and live independently. Even then there will still be some level at which the family is bound together, despite their different locations. For example, family members may continue to help each other out in times of need, share significant occasions such as birthdays and religious or cultural events, and visit or care for ill or ageing parents. Toward the end of life, it is the children who tend to have a greater influence over family projects, by caring and making decisions for their elderly parents when they are no longer capable of independently caring for themselves.

Clearly there are limits to what parents can require of their children in order to promote collective family interests. A child's interests should not be sacrificed for the welfare of the family as a whole. There is no simple solution to where the limits on parental discretion should lie and how the law should enforce those limits. Limits on parental discretion will also vary according to the context in which the discretion is exercised. For example, it is particularly difficult to draw a line on the types of risks to which parents should be allowed to expose their children in the context of religious or cultural identification, when the decision conflicts with accepted public standards relating to education or bodily integrity.[57]

4.4 Compromise within families

Considering the interests of other family members is not inconsistent with the welfare of the child to be born if we conceptualise the child's welfare in terms of human flourishing. If, as I have argued above, a child's interests are intertwined with those of his/her family, it makes sense to consider the interests of other members of the family as the welfare of the child is interconnected with the welfare of the family as a whole. However, the individual interests of the child will not always be compatible with the collective interests of his/her family. There will be times at which the interests of an individual family member will be in conflict with the collective interests of the family. In some cases, the interests of the individual may need to be compromised to promote the interests of the wider family. The child to be born as a result of PGD is in a vulnerable position and in need of some protection. The question therefore arises as to whether, in considering the collective family interests, it is acceptable for some individual interests of the child to be born to be compromised.

In the next section, I explore the role of familial duty in intimate families. I argue that the individual compromise entailed by familial duty is essential for the continued existence and welfare of intimate families because intimacy necessarily involves compromise. Individual compromise by a child within a family is therefore not only acceptable but also integral to a conception of the welfare of the child based on human flourishing.

4.4.1 Familial duty as a justification for individual compromise

4.4.1.1 Intimacy and compromise – 'taking the good with the bad'

In section 4.2, I discussed the importance of intimacy to human flourishing and the instrumental and inherent value of intimate families. Intimacy does not, however, come without a price. Intimacy necessarily involves compromise. Smith describes the compromise within intimate families as one of the 'shared costs in a communal enterprise'.[58] Compromise is an essential part of being 'bound to one another'.[59] This is partly because intimate groups share basic finite resources that must somehow be divided between members of the group. For example, parents with more than one child may have unlimited love for all their children but they have limited time and financial resources that must be shared amongst the various children.

Compromise is also a natural consequence of living in a shared space where individuals may have conflicting, as well as confluent, interests. For example, if one parent wishes to pursue an attractive job offer in a foreign country but the rest of the family wishes to continue to live in their home country, then, if the family is to live together, compromise is essential. The other parent and the children may be required to compromise their interests in remaining in their own home country in order to accompany the parent who wishes to move to a new country. Alternatively, the parent offered the job may need to compromise his/her own professional interests by passing up the new job in order to accommodate the needs and wishes of the rest of the family. Compromise by one or more members for the benefit of another is an essential part of intimate family life. As John Hardwig suggests:

> Because the lives of those who are close are not separable, to be close is to no longer have a life entirely as you choose. To be part of a family is to be morally required to make decisions on the basis of thinking about what is best for all concerned, not simply what is best for yourself.[60]

This raises the important question of how decisions ought to be made within families, a theme I will return to in Chapter 5.

4.4.1.2 The notion of familial duty

The compromise intimate families require of their members is sometimes described as 'familial duty'. Familial duty or obligation has been described as 'probably the oldest and possibly the least questioned form of obligation that human beings have'.[61] Smith argues that, ' ... the intrinsic value [of family] is the justification of its general obligations of cooperation and support. This, I suggest, is the essence of family obligation and family membership'.[62] Doing things for intimate others enables family members to flourish as humans in a way that can only occur from being part of an intimate collective such as a family. So although the *interests* of an individual member may at times be compromised for the welfare of the family, the *welfare* of the individual member is enhanced if we accept a picture of human agency that recognises the value of intimate relations to human flourishing. There will obviously come a point beyond which individual compromise becomes so great that it will ultimately have a negative impact on a person's welfare or ability to flourish. For instance, parents should not be able to sacrifice the interests of individual members for the sake of the family.

The prospect of a conflict of interests between family members is not a remote possibility for saviour sibling selection. The discussion in Chapter 3 revealed that there is a risk that the child to be born could experience physical and/or psychosocial harm. Given this potential risk, we must consider whether it is acceptable for the individual interests of the donor child to be compromised in favour of the collective interests of the family or one of its members. Crouch and Elliott raise a similar question in the context of sibling organ donation by asking 'whether parents can legitimately expect their children to bear some burdens for the sake of family interests, even interests that the children might not yet endorse'.[63]

The inherent value of intimate family provides a justification for compromising some interests of individual members for the benefit of the family as a whole and underlies the notion of familial duty. This is particularly relevant in the context of saviour sibling selection, where the very nature of the family will change if the ill child dies. One important issue that arises for the child to be born is the fact that the child does not choose to become a part of the intimate family into which he/she will be born. The fact that a child does not choose to be a part of his/her family does not exempt that child from familial duties. This is because membership alone (irrespective of consent) provides the foundation for moral responsibility to the family.

4.4.2 Membership as a foundation for moral responsibility

4.4.2.1 Family duty arises out of membership not consent

Unlike modern legal and social contract models of obligation, which rely on actual or constructive consent as a justification for moral obligation, familial obligation or duty is (at least for children) involuntary. Generally speaking, families are 'nonvoluntary social units that ill fit the social contract model'.[64] Children do not choose to be born into their respective families, nor do they play a significant role in determining their family's particular character or projects, at least in the early years. Many of the duties parents impose on their children, such as assisting with family chores, visiting ailing grandparents and helping out their siblings, are not necessarily sanctioned by the children themselves. Rather they are imposed on them as duties to the family of which they are members. In this section, I argue that familial duty legitimately arises out of family membership.

The idea that membership provides the foundation for moral responsibility has been mooted in the past, most notably by ancient philosophers and some communitarian philosophers.[65] In the specific context of international relations, Haskell Fain has developed a similar notion of political obligation based on the idea of 'communal tasks'.[66] More recently, Smith has drawn from Fain's ideas about what it means to be a member, and how membership creates obligation, in her exploration of familial obligation.[67] She highlights the necessity of sharing common tasks between the members of a common enterprise, 'A household is the epitome of a shared enterprise. Where people not only pool their resources but merge their lives, then a common sharing of burdens – the idea of communal tasks mentioned earlier – is most appropriate'.[68] Membership provides an alternative justification for familial obligation to the predominant social contract theory used by liberal theorists to justify universal moral obligation and the requirements of justice. Unlike social contract theory, which is strongly connected to the individualistic idea of contract based on individual consent, family obligations are not individualistic nor are they necessarily based on voluntary consent.[69] Membership not only provides the source of familial obligation but also defines its nature, '[Familial obligation] is derived from and determined by family connection and commitment. The reason you have this sort of obligation is that you are part of something, you belong to something larger than yourself, with which you are partly identified; you are connected'.[70]

Within intimate families, family members (including siblings) have obligations to one another, by reason of the fact that they are in the same family. We expect more from those with whom we are close because intimate relationships give rise to obligations. As Dwyer and Vig state, 'family relationships have ethical import'.[71] Obligation to intimate family members 'generally refers to the promotion of the common good of the members'.[72] Familial obligations or duties may require individual members to, at times, compromise their own interests for the welfare of the family as a whole. For example, parents have a general duty to provide care and support for their children, which includes a duty to try to save the life of an existing child. Similarly, siblings also have duties to one another, albeit not as extensive as those of parents.[73]

Parents can, and do, expect their children to make compromises for one another or for the family as a whole. Some family duties relate to maintaining the ongoing collective enterprise of family. For instance, many families view simple chores parents impose on children, such as washing the dishes or tidying up their mess, as necessary for the efficient functioning of the family unit. Other duties are grounded in debt or gratitude. For example, parents may require unwilling children to visit their elderly grandparents as a sign of respect and appreciation for the sacrifices they made in their life so that their children and grandchildren could thrive. Many family duties arise out of the immediate needs of individual family members. This is particularly relevant in families with several children, where one child has the capacity to meet the needs of a sibling. Parents often require one child to help out a sibling simply because of the sibling relationship. For example, a parent may request a child to 'look out for' a younger sibling at school or attend a sibling's music concert, even though that child may prefer to keep some distance from his younger sibling at school or stay at home rather than attending the concert. How many parents have exhorted a child to help out a younger sibling, with the only explanation being 'because you're family'?[74]

The familial duties parents impose on children all arise out of family membership rather than by choice. The duties arise as a natural consequence of being bound together with one another in an intimate relationship. Crouch and Elliott describe the nature of familial duty in the following way:

> We do things, and should be expected to do things, for the family and for particular family members that we simply would not do for non-family members. For the most part, such burdens come with the very fact that we are bound to one another within a particular family.[75]

According to Schoeman, 'it is the role as a member of a family unit that defines an individual's responsibilities'.[76] He describes 'the child as having a status within the family by virtue of which certain liabilities and responsibilities accrue'.[77]

I have argued that family members have duties to one another by virtue of membership rather than consent. Applying this reasoning to saviour sibling selection means that the family relationship provides the justification for imposing some risks on the child to be born in order to save the life of an existing child. A question arises as to how far familial duties extend and what risks we should allow families to impose on the child to be born. Clearly some risks would be too high and children need protection from being 'treated as mere conveniences to advance others' ends'.[78] In Chapter 5, I argue that parents should not be able to sacrifice the basic interests of the child to be born for the sake of the family as this would amount to exploitation, abuse and/or neglect. As Nelson and Nelson point out, 'To acknowledge the non-consensual element in families and in other settings of intimacy is not to deny that there are general (universalisable, impartial) moral constraints that operate within them as well'.[79] Abuse of intimates is particularly wrongful as it 'backlights, as it were, the special moral significance of intimate relationships'.[80]

4.4.2.2 Critique of the involuntary nature of family duty

The involuntary nature of familial obligation is not without its critics. In particular, some feminist theorists are sceptical about the role traditional families have played in reinforcing gender inequalities and emphasise the importance of choosing relationships voluntarily.[81] As Samantha Brennan states, it 'has been important for women to say, and be able to say, that they are more than someone's daughter, or someone's wife, to assert that one's identity transcends the roles assigned to women'.[82] Similarly, it is important for children to be able to forge their own identities within their families, as they become independent and develop preferences of their own that may not coincide with those of other family members. The involuntary nature of family duty, when coupled with power imbalances within families, clearly has the potential to become 'a major source of oppression'.[83] It is therefore important to recognise that members of a family are individuals as well as members of a collective and should be given sufficient freedom to choose their path in life.

Recognising individuality and respecting choice does not mean that children, parents and siblings do not have specific responsibilities to one another by virtue of their intimate relationships. In some ways, intimacy has very little to do with choice. Children do not choose to be born into a particular family any more than parents can choose the nature of their children. There are also many who would argue that we do not necessarily choose the person with whom we will fall in love. According to Anne Donchin, 'our most significant social relations will often not actually be voluntary'.[84] Nelson and Nelson point out that 'even where we choose our intimates freely, once the choice is made we are not free to leave at will'.[85] This is because, to a certain degree, intimacy impedes choice. This is what we mean by the term 'commitment', in the sense of being bound emotionally to another person. Emotional commitment is essential to intimacy because 'if you are always free to leave you can't get the good of settled, abiding relationships'.[86]

While intimacy does not require a complete embedding or loss of self, being in an intimate relationship with others entails a sense of union, which inevitably impacts on our sense of self and the choices we make. Clearly there are limitations on the 'moral sacrifices family members can be expected to make for another'.[87] I explore these limitations in more detail in Chapter 5. However, if we accept that intimate families are both instrumentally and inherently valuable, there are good reasons why family members should make compromises for one another for the welfare of the family as a whole. Because these compromises are not necessarily made out of choice, we need a different model to the social contract model found in liberal theory to explain the nature of moral responsibility within families and other intimate relationships. Relational and care-based theories provide a better explanation of the nature of moral responsibility within families.

According to a relational model of moral development, the responsibilities siblings have to one another are important for the child's future development:

> In actual families, children have responsibilities to one another long before they develop capacities to avow them voluntarily. Preparation for autonomous adulthood includes experience in caring for others one cares about and coming to recognise one's own needs by responding to theirs. Adults who lack such grounding are ill-fitted to build enduring relationships with others on a foundation of mutual reciprocity.[88]

This relational approach to moral responsibility has been heavily influenced by the ethics of care and the groundbreaking work on moral psychology by Carol Gilligan.[89] In contrast to liberal theory, the care perspective views people as interconnected and inherently social. Accordingly, the 'moral self is a self-in-relation'.[90] The ethics of care recognises the potential for inequality in intimate relationships but attempts to address the problem from a relational rather than individualistic perspective. According to Diana Tietjens Meyers:

> ... the experiences of self-in-relation are often experiences of inequality – of dependency as a child, of power as a parent, of dependency in old age. ... Thus, the care perspective regards inequality not as a degenerative moral condition, but rather as a central moral reality.[91]

The care perspective responds to this inequality, not through the promotion of individual interests or rights but with 'general injunctions to avoid harm, give care and maintain relationships' and to 'respond sensitively to distinctive needs of individuals in concrete situations'.[92] I draw from relational models and the ethics of care in Chapter 5, when I propose a relational model for selective reproduction. Adopting a relational model does not necessarily entail abandoning all of the protections offered by liberal or rights-based theories, which are based on a more generalised, account of morality. In dealing with the specific context of family, generalised accounts of morality can be helpful for 'making comparative assessments of morally relevant features of specific situations'[93] and drawing limits on what an intimate family can require of individual members. The level of obligation between family members will vary according to their role within the family and the general character of the family. However, generally speaking, the level of duty owed to family members is greater than that owed to strangers by virtue of the intimate relationships that exist within families.

4.4.3 Higher duty to family than strangers

Parents who use PGD to conceive a saviour sibling may call on the child to donate blood or bone marrow in the future if the initial cord blood transplant fails to cure the existing child. Some commentators have expressly argued, in the context of tissue donation between siblings, that '[g]iving bone marrow is a sacrifice that does "not exceed the ordinary sacrifices family members make and expect from one another"'.[94] The duty to help save the life of a family member through donation is a higher level of duty than that which we would expect from a stranger. According to Nancy Jecker, 'family members are governed by stronger ethical responsibilities than strangers, and we expect them to serve each other's welfare to a greater extent'.[95] There is, of course, a natural duty to help others, which is generally accepted by liberal theorists.[96] However, most people would not expect a stranger to donate bone marrow to someone else's child, even if this was the only means of saving that child's life. This raises the question as to why we owe a higher duty to family members than to strangers.

Put simply, the intimacy or 'close relationship' of family members creates a higher level of duty than that imposed on individual members of society in accordance with liberal theory.[97] Liberal theory proposes minimal universal obligations, including obligations not to harm or interfere with another, whereas family obligations or duties are greater than minimal. Many of the most important moral obligations human beings have to family 'are not simply obligations not to harm or interfere, but obligations to cooperate, reciprocate, or even to aid or support'.[98] According to Smith, obligations of family membership are different from the universal moral obligations grounded in liberal theory in two ways. First, they invoke affirmative obligations of cooperation and support that go beyond non-harm and non-interference. Second, familial obligations are collective in that 'all are committed to all'.[99] As Smith notes, 'family obligation is potentially the most burdensome – depending on the nature of the particular family membership – and the most beneficial obligation human beings can have'.[100] It is the beneficial nature of familial duty and the intimacy it promotes that provides a justification for imposing a higher duty on family members. According to Virginia Sharpe, intimacy cannot be sustained without a 'nucleus of well-wishing (benevolence) and well-acting (beneficence)'.[101]

The individual compromise required by familial duty may appear overly burdensome to some proponents of liberal theory.[102] Requiring a higher level of duty from family members seems to contradict fundamental liberal tenets, such as individual autonomy and the rights of the child, which have dominated Western bioethics.[103] However, it would be more accurate to say that the scope of familial duty highlights the inadequacy of liberal theory in dealing with family relations and its inability to capture 'the emotional density of most family ties'.[104] Schoeman argues that, '[w]elfare and autonomy of the child are only part of what should be considered when judging how children may be limited in the range of their discretion. It is also only part of what the parent must keep in mind in making medical decisions for a child'.[105] The difficulty in applying liberal theory to familial relations is that it does not give due regard to the value of intimacy and the intrinsic benefits of collective endeavour that are associated with intimate family. Liberal theory therefore fails to provide a satisfactory justification for the higher level of obligation or duty we expect from family members.

We owe a higher level of duty to family members than to strangers because we generally favour intimates over strangers. Favouritism within families stands in direct contrast with Jeremy Bentham's impartial ideal that 'everybody to count for one, nobody for more than one' underpinning general universal theories of morality.[106] Bernard Williams' famous discussion (of the man who decided to rescue his wife over another) highlights the limitations of impartial principles in explaining family relations. Williams criticises the man for justifying his action by appealing to the impartial moral principle that it is permissible for husbands to save their wives over others. According to Williams, the man has had 'one thought too many'.[107] The favouritism we show to our intimates is based not on some impartial moral principle but on love itself. Favouritism is integral to love. Nelson and Nelson state that '[b]oth letting ourselves be vulnerable to those we love and being prized by our loved ones over others are part of what it means to us to be loved'.[108] Favouritism explains why we would do certain things for family members above and beyond that which we would do for strangers. Meyers claims that the interpersonal ties that give rise to the demands of intimates 'number among the ground projects that are constitutive of our integrity as individuals and that give us vital reasons to live'.[109] According to Bernard Williams, without deep attachments to others, 'there will not be enough substance or conviction in a man's life to compel his allegiance to life itself'.[110]

The family is a very different entity from the state and the requirements of intimacy do not fit neatly within liberal theory. In contrast to the state, which occupies a formal relationship with the child, 'parents occupy an intimate relationship – one in which a different range of principles and objectives applies'.[111] This does not mean that there should not be limits on what parents can expect from their children. Rather, state interference in the distribution of benefits and burdens within families should be limited to preventing abuses of parental discretion. Schoeman highlights the limitations of liberal theory in dealing with intimate arrangements between family members by suggesting that:

> If the family is to be thought of as an intimate arrangement having its own goals and purposes, it is inappropriate to impose upon that arrangement … abstract liberal principles … This is not to say that these liberal principles do not have any moral weight in the context of the family, but that they are not exhaustive of the principles which may legitimately bind people together and structure their relationship.[112]

Similarly, Virginia Sharpe considers it 'inappropriate to speak of "respect for persons" in the context of intimate or filial relationships'.[113] Rather, 'we care for our intimates because they are our intimates and we need not filter our concern through the principle of respect for persons'.[114] It is only when the nucleus of well-being and well-acting essential to intimacy breaks down that 'it is appropriate to revert to the language of strangers'.[115] In the context of saviour sibling selection, the element of utility in the parents' decision to conceive the child to be born does not necessarily cancel out the parents' intention to love and care for that child. Despite some potential risk of psychological harm to the child to be born, the 'nucleus of well-wishing' ordinarily remains intact.[116]

Not all families will impose the same level of duty on their members. The nature and level of obligation of an individual family member within a family will depend on several factors, including the individual's characteristics, level of involvement and the character of relations within the particular family. Smith points out that '[a] tightly knit family may generate extensive particular obligations' whereas 'a more loosely structured family may have few particular obligations'.[117] As discussed at the beginning of this chapter, all families are different, and different family structures and cultural influences will promote different levels of obligation between their members. For instance, a child who is a compatible tissue match for an existing ill sibling would, by virtue of his/her particular genetic characteristics, have a higher duty to save the life of the ill sibling than a non-compatible tissue matched sibling. This does not mean that every family would expose a child to the risks of bone marrow donation or use PGD to bring a child donor into existence, but some would. When dealing with families involved in selective reproduction, we therefore need a decision-making model that recognises the higher duty owed to intimates and can accommodate the variation in levels of obligation between different families. A relational model is well-suited to this task.

4.5 Conclusion

Children require more than nourishment, shelter, protection from harm and respect in order to flourish. The welfare of the child is inextricably connected to the collective interests of his/her family in intimacy, love, affection and the collective endeavour that gives life meaning. These collective interests that are shared by intimate family members are integral to human flourishing. If we reconceptualise the welfare of the child in terms of human flourishing, we must look beyond the individual interests of the child and also consider the collective interests of his/her family. To put it another way, the welfare of the child depends, at least in part, on the welfare of his/her family as a whole.

The birth of a child invokes not only the interests of the individual child but also the collective interests the child will inevitably share with his/her family and which are integral to the child's ability to flourish. It is particularly important to consider the collective interests or welfare of the family as a whole in the context of saviour sibling selection because conceiving a family member to save the life of another is a shared enterprise that affects the whole family. Families who undertake PGD to select a saviour sibling are inextricably connected in a shared journey to save the life of an ill child. The decision to select a saviour sibling is also primarily motivated by the interests of the parents and the existing ill child. It would therefore be disingenuous to ignore the interests of these other family members.

This is not to suggest that the collective interests of the family should override the individual interests of its members. While familial duty requires compromise on behalf of individual family members, there are limits on how far an individual should be expected to compromise to promote the welfare of his/her family as a whole. Given the vulnerability of the child to be born in the context of selective reproduction, safeguards should be in place to protect that child from exploitation, abuse or neglect. In Chapter 5, I propose a relational model for selective reproduction, which promotes both the welfare of the child to be born and the welfare of his/her family. I also recommend guidelines for determining when acceptable compromise becomes unacceptable sacrifice in order to protect the child to be born from exploitation, abuse or neglect.

Notes

1   Blended families are families in which there is a least one biological child from both parents and at least one step-child of either parent: Ruth McNair, *Outcomes for Children Born of ART in a Diverse Range of Families* (Victorian Law Reform Commission Occasional Paper, August 2004), 17.

2   The term 'family' is given 16 separate definitions in the *Macquarie Dictionary*: S Butler (ed), *Macquarie Dictionary* (Macquarie Dictionary Publishers, 5th edn, 2009), and 11 separate definitions in the *Oxford English Dictionary*: J A Simpson and E C Weiner, *The Oxford English Dictionary* (Oxford University Press, 1989).

3   Butler, above n 2, definitions 1, 3 and 6.

4   The *American Heritage Dictionary of the English Language* (Houghton Mifflin Company, 4th edn, 2003) cited in *The Free Dictionary* by Farlex, <http://www.thefreedictionary.com/family> (accessed 24 April 2013), definitions 1a and b.

5   Hilde Lindemann Nelson and James Lindemann Nelson, *The Patient in the Family: An Ethics of Medicine and Families* (Routledge, 1995), 42.

6   It is intimacy rather than mere biological connection that defines family responsibilities. Dwyer and Vig define family relationships as 'a special kind of social relationship rather than a biological relationship': James Dwyer and Elizabeth Vig, 'Rethinking Transplantation Between Siblings' (1995) 25 *Hastings Center Report* 7, 11. Courts in tissue donation cases involving incompetent patients in several countries have focused on social as well as biological relationships to justify tissue donations between family members: Anne Donchin, 'Autonomy and Interdependence: Quandaries in Genetic Decision Making' in Catriona Mackenzie and Natalie Stoljar (eds), *Relational Autonomy: Feminist Perspectives of Autonomy, Agency, and the Social Self* (Oxford University Press, 2000), 236, 242. See, for example, *Strunk v Strunk* 445 S W 2d 145 (Ky 1969) in the US; *Re Y (Mental Incapacity: Bone Marrow Transplant)* [1996] 2 FLR 787 in the UK; and *In the Marriage of GWW and CMW* (1997) 136 FLR 421 in Australia.

7   Butler above n 2, definition 1.

8   Mark G Kuczewski, 'Reconceiving the Family: The Process of Consent in Medical Decisionmaking' (1996) 26 *The Hastings Center Report* 30.

9   McNair, above n 1.

10 McNair, above n 1, 2.

11 McNair, above n 1, 18. This does not necessarily prevent families in which parents are separated or divorced from being intimate. According to McNair, evidence suggests that it is conflict rather than separation or divorce itself, which is most damaging to children.

12 James Lindemann Nelson, 'Taking Families Seriously' (1992) 22 *The Hastings Center Report* 6, 7. A care-based account of families similarly characterises families as 'intersecting webs of people who give care, people who receive care, and, primarily, people who both give and receive care': Matthew M Kavanagh, 'Rewriting the Legal Family' (2004) 16 *Yale Journal of Law and Feminism* 83, 117.

13 See, for example, Marilyn Friedman, *What are Friends For? Feminist Perspectives on Personal Relationships and Moral Theory* (Cornell University Press, 1993).

14 Sara Ruddick describes these tasks as 'maternal work', which is in principle open to either gender: Sara Ruddick, *Maternal Thinking: Toward a Politics of Peace* (Beacon Press, 1989), 17.

15 Nelson and Nelson, above n 5, 76.

16 Jeffrey Blustein, 'The Family in Medical Decisionmaking' (1993) 23 *Hastings Center Report* 6, 12.

17 Nelson and Nelson, above n 5, 34.

18 Research indicates that people who are abused by intimates tend to suffer more deeply than those who have been abused by strangers: Nelson and Nelson, above n 5, 70.

19 Patricia Smith, 'Family Responsibility and the Nature of Obligation' in Diana Tietjens Meyers, Kenneth Kipnis and Cornelius F Murphy (eds), *Kindred Matters: Rethinking the Philosophy of the Family* (Cornell University Press, 1993), 41, 54.

20 Virginia Held, *The Ethics of Care: Personal, Political, and Global* (Oxford University Press, 2006), 71.

21 For a discussion of studies of the negative impacts of children raised in institutions, see S Matthew Liao, 'The Right of Children to Be Loved' (2006) 14 *The Journal of Political Philosophy* 420, 423–24. Liao also compares studies of infant monkeys in laboratories, which show similar results.

22 Liao describes the love that intimate relationships engender as 'an essential primary condition for a good life': ibid, 424.

23 Ferdinand Schoeman, 'Parental Discretion and Children's Rights: Background and Implications for Medical Decision-Making' (1985) 10 *The Journal of Medicine and Philosophy* 45, 48.

24 Smith, above n 19, 54.

25 Smith, above n 19, 56.

26 Nelson and Nelson, above n 5, 36–37.

27 Nelson and Nelson, above n 5, 37.

28 Nelson and Nelson, above n 5, 37.

29 Nancy Sherman, 'The Virtues of Common Pursuit' (1993) 53 *Philosophy and Phenomenological Research* 277, 279.

30 Sherman, ibid, 279.

31 Nelson and Nelson, above n 5, 44.

32 Schoeman, above n 23, 48–49.

33 Robert A Crouch and Carl Elliott, 'Moral Agency and the Family: The Case of Living Related Organ Transplantation' (1999) 8 *Cambridge Quarterly of Healthcare Ethics* 275, 283.

34 Crouch and Elliott, ibid, 284.

35 Crouch and Elliott, above n 33, 283. See also Charles Taylor, 'Hegel's Ambiguous Legacy for Modern Liberalism' (1988–89) 10 *Cardozo Law Review* 857, 861.

36 Sherman, above n 29, 278.

37 Crouch and Elliott, above n 33, 284.

38 Ferdinand Schoeman, 'Rights of Children, Rights of Parents, and the Moral Basis of the Family' (1980) 91 *Ethics* 6, 8.

39 Nelson and Nelson, above n 5, 70.

40 See, for example, B L Freund and K Siegel, 'Problems in Transition Following Bone Marrow Transplantation: Psychosocial Aspects' (1986) 56 *American Journal of Orthopsychiatry* 244; Kendra D MacLeod, *et al*, 'Pediatric Sibling Donors of Successful and Unsuccessful Hematopoietic Stem Cell Transplants (HSCT): A Qualitative Study of Their Psychosocial Experience' (2003) 28 *Journal of Pediatric Psychology* 223.

41 Crouch and Elliott, above n 33, 284.

42 Lynn A Jansen, 'Child Organ Donation, Family Autonomy, and Intimate Attachments' (2004) 13 *Cambridge Quarterly of Healthcare Ethics* 133, 137.

43 Allen Buchanan and Dan Brock, *Deciding For Others: The Ethics of Surrogate Decision Making* (Cambridge University Press, 1989), 236.

44 Jansen, above n 42, 137.

45 Smith, above n 19, 47–51.

46 Smith, above n 19, 47.

47 Smith explains that there may be some overlap between the goals of a household and those of family in the abstract: Smith, above n 19, 49.

48 Sherman, above n 29, 278.

49 Sherman, above n 29, 278.

50 Sherman, above n 29, 278.

51 Buchanan and Brock, above n 43, 237.

52 Lainie Friedman Ross, *Children, Families, and Health Care Decision Making* (Clarendon Press, 1998), 31.

53 Schoeman, above n 38, 19.

54 Margaret O'Brien Steinfels, 'Children's Rights, Parental Rights, Family Privacy and Family Autonomy' in Willard Gaylin and Ruth Macklin (eds), *Who Speaks for the Child: The Problems of Proxy Consent* (Plenum Press, 1982), 253.

55 Steinfels, ibid.

56 I discuss how this may be achieved in Chapter 5.

57 The US Supreme Court upheld the discretion of Amish parents to limit their child's access to secondary education in *Wisconsin v Yoder* 406 US 205 (1972). There is less support for parents exposing their children to physical harm for religious reasons. For example, the United Nations General Assembly's human rights committee recently passed *a resolution* calling for a global ban on female circumcision: United Nations Resolution On Intensifying Global Efforts for the Elimination of Female Genital Mutilations, UN GA/ 11331, 67th Session, UN Doc A/RES/67/146 (20 December, 2012). Female circumcision has been a crime in most Australian states since the late 1990s. See, for example, Crimes Act 1958 (Vic), ss 32, 33. Female circumcision has been specifically prohibited by national legislation in the US since 1996: 18 USC § 116 and in the UK since 1985: Female Genital Mutilation Act 2003 (UK), which replaced the Prohibition of Female Circumcision Act 1985 (UK).

58 Smith, above n 19, 55.

59 Crouch and Elliott, above n 33, 284.

60 John Hardwig, 'What About the Family?' (1990) 20 *The Hastings Center Report* 5, 6.

61 Smith, above n 19, 46.

62 Smith, above n 19, 56.

63 Crouch and Elliott, above n 33, 285.

64 Diana Tietjens Meyers, 'Introduction' in Diana Tietjens Meyers, Kenneth Kipnis and Cornelius F Murphy (eds), *Kindred Matters: Rethinking the Philosophy of the Family* (Cornell University Press, 1993), 13, 14.

65 Smith cites ancient philosophers (Plato and Aristotle) and communitarian philosophers (Alasdair MacIntyre and Michael Sandel): Smith, above n 19, 45.

66 Haskell Fain, *Normative Politics and the Community of Nations* (Temple University Press, 1987).

67 Smith, above n 19, 45. Schoeman also relies on the notion of communal tasks in a shared enterprise, when he states that familial 'responsibilities are aimed at making the family as such a working entity': Schoeman, above n 23, 49.

68 Smith, above n 19, 55.

69 The adage, 'you can choose your friends but not your family' is testament to the involuntary nature of family obligation.

70 Smith, above n 19, 50.

71 Dwyer and Vig, above n 6, 11.

72 Smith, above n 19, 48–49.

73 This is partly due to the fact that, unlike parents, children do not owe a fiduciary duty to one another. It is also because we do not expect as much from children as we do from adults.

74 This is, in one sense, an appeal to the child's developing sense of moral responsibility towards those close to him/her.

75 Crouch and Elliott, above n 33, 284.

76 Schoeman, above n 23, 57.

77 Schoeman, above n 23.

78 Donchin, above n 6, 243.

79 Nelson and Nelson, above n 5, 70.

80 Nelson and Nelson, above n 5, 70.

81 See, for example, Marilyn Friedman 'Feminism and Modern Friendship: Dislocating the Community' (1989) 99 *Ethics* 275; Adrienne Asch and Gail Geller, 'Feminism, Bioethics and Genetics' in Susan M Wolf (ed), *Feminism & Bioethics: Beyond Reproduction* (Oxford University Press, 1996), 318, 341.

82 Samantha Brennan, 'Recent Work in Feminist Ethics' (1999) 109 *Ethics* 858, 869.

83 Nelson and Nelson, above n 5, 70. Vulnerable family members not only include women and children, but also those who are chronically ill, frail and elderly or dependent on family members with 'greater prestige, mobility and resources'.

84 Donchin, above n 6, 241.

85 Nelson and Nelson, above n 5, 70.

86 Nelson and Nelson, above n 5, 70.

87 Donchin, above n 6, 243.

88 Donchin, above n 6, 242.

89 Carol Gilligan, *In a Different Voice: Psychological Theory and Women's Development* (Harvard University Press, 1982, 1993 edn). More recently, see Held, above n 20.

90 Meyers, above n 64, 16. Meyers notes that 'people's relationships with others are often unchosen yet constitutive of their identity'.

91 Meyers, above n 64, 16.

92 Meyers, above n 64, 16.

93 Anne Donchin, 'Reworking Autonomy: Toward a Feminist Perspective' (1995) 4 *Cambridge Quarterly of Healthcare Ethics* 44, 51. Brennan argues that '[a]s long as the interests of individuals and the interests of the group can diverge, there is a role for moral rights to play': above n 82, 870.

94 G Pennings, R Schots and I Liebaers, 'Ethical Considerations on Preimplantation Genetic Diagnosis for HLA Typing to Match a Future Child as a Donor of Haematopoietic Stem Cells to a Sibling' (2002) 17 *Human Reproduction* 534, 537. See also Nancy S Jecker, 'Conceiving a Child to Save a Child: Reproductive and Filial Ethics' (1990) 1 *The Journal of Clinical Ethics* 99, 102. Ross makes a similar argument: Ross, above n 52, 43–44.

95 Jecker, ibid, 102.

96 See, for example John Rawls, *A Theory of Justice* (Oxford University Press, 1972), 114–17, esp 114.

97 Jecker argues that even though parents are required to do far more for offspring than offspring are required to do for siblings, offspring still owe far more to siblings than to strangers because of the presence of a 'close relationship': Jecker, above n 94, 103.

98 Smith, above n 19, 41.

99 Smith, above n 19, 51.

100 Smith, above n 19, 51.

101 Virginia A Sharpe, 'To What Extent Should We Think of Our Intimates as "Persons"? Commentary on "Conceiving a Child"' (1990) 1 *The Journal of Clinical Ethics* 103, 106.

102 I am referring to traditional liberal theory, including the works of Kant and Mill, which still largely dominate Western bioethics. In more recent years, feminist philosophers have introduced a relational element into liberal theory. See, for example, a detailed discussion of 'relational autonomy' in Catriona Mackenzie and Natalie Stoljar (eds), *Relational Autonomy: Feminist Perspectives on Autonomy, Agency, and the Social Self* (Oxford University Press, 2000).

103 In particular, bioethical debate has been dominated by Beauchamp and Childress' ethical framework known as 'principlism', which includes autonomy, nonmaleficence, beneficence and justice. In response to feminist criticisms that their notion of autonomy under-estimated the importance of intimate relationships, Beauchamp and Childress offered what has been described as a form of 'weak relational autonomy', which suggests that individuals can always choose their social relations: Donchin, above n 6, 238.

104 Meyers, above n 64, 14.

105 Schoeman, above n 23, 56.

106 Attributed to Jeremy Bentham in John Stuart Mill, *Utilitarianism* (Project Gutenberg EBook reprinted from Fraser's Magazine, 7th edn, Longmans, Green, and Co, 1879), <http://www.gutenberg.org/ebooks/11224> (accessed 24 April 2013).
    For a discussion of favouritism within families, see Nelson and Nelson, above n 5, 64; Smith, above n 19, 49.

107 Bernard Williams, 'Persons, Character and Morality', in *Moral Luck: Philosophical Papers, 1973–1980* (Cambridge University Press, 1981), 18.

108 Nelson and Nelson, above n 5, 65.

109 Meyers, above n 64, 15.

110 Williams, above n 107, 18.

111 Schoeman, above n 23, 48.

112 Schoeman, above n 23, 48.

113 Sharpe, above n 101, 104.

114 Sharpe, above n 101, 105. This is consistent with the Aristotelian idea that where there is friendship there is little need for justice (*Nicomachean Ethics* 1155a27): see Sherman, above n 29, 295.

115 Sharpe, above n 101, 106. Not all theorists believe that impartialist ethical theories are incompatible with intimate relationships. See, for example, Nancy S Jecker, 'Impartiality and Special Relations' in Diana Tietjens Meyers, Kenneth Kipnis and Cornelius F Murphy (eds), *Kindred Matters: Rethinking the Philosophy of the Family* (Cornell University Press, 1993), 74. Jecker attempts to reconcile 'moderately impartial' principles with the mor-ality of intimate relations. Jecker is one of four authors who present different theoretical approaches to family morality in Part I of *Kindred Matters*. Despite their different theore-tical approaches, however, all authors agree that family members have special obligations to one another: Meyers, above n 64, 19.

116 Sharpe, above n 101, 106.

117 Smith, above n 19, 50.

5 A relational model for selective reproduction

5.1 Introduction

The relational approach to the welfare of the child proposed in Chapter 4 encompasses both individual and collective interests. The individual interests of a child and the collective interests the child shares with his/her family may not, however, always coincide. A relational decision-making model must therefore acknowledge and accommodate individual and collective interests within a family. This chapter proposes a relational model for selective reproduction that requires the interests of the child to be born to be considered in connection with the interests of other family members. I draw from relational approaches proposed in the context of general medical decision-making to devise a collaborative decision-making process that attempts to reconcile family interests where possible.

As discussed in Chapter 4, a relational approach to the welfare of the child may at times require some of the individual interests of the child to be born to be compromised in favour of other family interests. Compromising the interests of a child does not sit easily with the traditional concept of 'best interests' that is frequently employed in relation to decision-making involving children.[1] A relational approach more accurately reflects, however, the way in which 'everyday' decisions are generally made within families. A relational decision-making model should, nevertheless, ensure that the basic needs of the child to be born are not sacrificed. It is therefore important to determine the point at which acceptable compromise becomes unacceptable sacrifice to prevent the child to be born from being exploited, abused or neglected. There is increasing support for relational medical decision-making models in Western medicine, although not specifically in the context of assisted reproduction. Rather than detracting from the welfare of the child to be born, I argue that a relational model promotes a broader conception of the welfare of the child by acknowledging the relational nature of the interests of the child within the context of his/her family and the importance of intimacy to human flourishing.

I begin this chapter by examining, in section 5.2, the nature of general decision-making within families. In particular, I analyse the scope of parental duties and discretion and the impact of familial character on family decision-making.

In section 5.3, I propose a test for determining when necessary compromise becomes unacceptable sacrifice in order to protect the child to be born from exploitation, abuse and neglect. In section 5.4, I examine the role of families in general medical decision-making and explore some relational models developed in this context. In particular, I investigate a 'process model' of informed consent, whereby the values and preferences of the patient take shape through a shared process of decision-making with his/her family. The idea of a relational medical decision-making model is not novel. It has gained some momentum in recent times by ethicists who are sceptical of the bias in Western bioethics towards the individual patient.[2] To date, however, a relational decision-making model has not been adopted in the context of assisted reproduction. In section 5.5, I draw from the relational approaches discussed in section 5.4 to develop a relational decision-making model for selective reproduction based on a modified collaborative decision-making process.

5.2 General family decision-making

The 'best interests' of the child is rarely the sole or predominant principle in family decision-making. Parents often make decisions for their children that are not necessarily based on their individual or best interests. Everyday decisions that have a life-shaping impact on children, such as place of residence, type of education and division of leisure and work within a family are not (and cannot be) made solely on the basis of the individual interests of one particular child. These decisions are instead made based on a myriad of factors, including the needs and interests of individual family members, the capacity of other family members to satisfy those needs and interests, the nature of the relationships within a family, and the character of a particular family. In Chapter 4, I argued that compromise is an essential part of intimate family life, particularly in families where there is more than one child. In this section, I explore the basis on which parents make everyday decisions about their children. In particular, I consider the duties parents have to their children, the nature of parental discretion, and the impact of familial character on family decision-making.

5.2.1 *Parental duty and discretion*

Parents have a duty to ensure that the basic needs of their children are met but, beyond this, parental decision-making is largely discretionary. Significantly, parents do not generally make decisions based on the best interests of one particular child. Instead, parents can and should take account of the interests of other family members, including themselves, when making family decisions. The following is an outline of some basic parental duties and discretions.

Parents have a general duty to care for and nurture their children by virtue of their fiduciary relationship with them.[3]

Children require nourishment, shelter, education, care, protection, respect, intimacy and love in order to develop physically, intellectually and emotionally. Many of these 'primary goods' are enshrined as rights under international Convention.[4] Parents must attend to the basic needs of their children by providing them with a threshold level of each of these 'primary goods'.[5] If parents fail to satisfy their child's basic needs, they 'waive their right to be their child's surrogate voice'.[6]

Provided parents satisfy the basic needs of their children, parental decision-making is discretionary.[7]

Parents can choose how they will attend to their children's basic needs. For example, some parents may decide to enrol their children in an exclusive private school, whereas others may prefer 'home schooling' for their children. Furthermore, while parents must satisfy the basic needs of each child, they 'need not maximize the procurement of primary goods for their children'.[8] The level of each primary good provided by parents will depend to a large extent on their priorities and preferences. As Lainie Friedman Ross points out, '[p]arents will place different emphases on different primary goods'.[9] She argues that in a 'liberal pluralistic society in which there is no agreed conception of the good', parents should have flexibility in 'procuring primary goods for their children'.[10] Parents must ensure that their children's basic needs are met, by providing, ' ... a threshold level of each primary good for their child, but beyond that, parents can consider not only the child's self-interests but also the interests of the child as a member of a particular family and community'.[11] So, for example, parents are not required to give their children the best education they can afford, provided they give them an adequate level of education to enable them to develop normally.[12] Similarly, while parents must satisfy their children's basic nutritional needs, they need not provide their children with the highest quality diet available to them.

Parents are also responsible for the welfare of their family as a whole and should take into consideration the interests of all family members who are likely to be affected by a decision.

Many decisions parents make in respect of one child will impact not just on the individual child but on the whole family. This is particularly pertinent where there is more than one child. In ordinary life, it is common for children within the same family to have conflicting interests. Parents with more than one child regularly make decisions that require compromise by one child for the welfare of another sibling or the family as a whole. For example, if one child has special needs and requires special education, the parents may decide to uproot the family and move closer to a special educational facility. The decision to accommodate the special needs of one child is likely to compromise the interests of other children in the family who may be forced to leave their friends and familiar environment.[13] Similarly, families may devote more family resources to a child with an exceptional talent to enable that child to pursue that talent. For example, if one child is a gifted pianist, the parents may devote considerable time and effort into helping that child achieve his/ her full potential as a concert pianist. This may impinge on some of the activities of the other siblings, who may not get an equivalent share of the family's resources. Obviously, it would not be satisfactory for parents to neglect or abuse one family member to benefit another. However, the collective nature of family sometimes requires a family to give 'a preferential share of what it has to a particular member, because of her particular vulnerabilities or talents'.[14] Ultimately, the parents must judge whether the compromises required from the other children are justified by the gains to the needy or gifted child.

In addition to the interests of their children, parents have their own interests that will legitimately impact on their decision-making.

Most significantly, 'parents have an interest in *parenting* – that is, in sharing a life with, and directing the development of, their child'.[15] Thus, although parents have parental duties in relation to a child, parents should not be viewed purely as 'agent(s) of the child's welfare'.[16] Thomas Murray proposes a more apposite model for the parent–child relationship based on 'mutualism', which focuses on 'the central importance of the *relationship*, without losing sight of the individuality of the parties'.[17] Mutualism recognises that the interests of the parents and child are interconnected and that parents have an interest in promoting the child's flourishing. According to Archard, 'the shared life of a parent and child involves an adult's purposes and aims at the deepest level'.[18] It is therefore important to respect a parent's parenting choices, provided they meet the child's basic needs, as these go to the heart of parental identity. Outside parenting, parents also have their own self-regarding interests, which may not directly relate to their child's flourishing. These interests include building a career, having an independent identity (beyond that of a mother or father), and leading a satisfying life. It would be unreasonable to expect parents to give up all interests outside their children when they become parents. These interests should also be recognised in family decision-making.

It is important for parents to openly acknowledge the various interests that impact on family decision-making.

By openly acknowledging broader family interests, parents are better placed to address potential conflicts between the interests of the child and those of the family, honestly and fairly. This, in turn, enables parents to genuinely promote the interests of all their children. Parents sometimes feel compelled to rationalise their decisions on the basis that they are in the best interests of their children, when this is neither true nor necessary. Such rationalisations can be dangerous and may ultimately erode the genuine interests of children. Parents regularly make decisions about childcare, education, where their family lives, what type of car they drive, how much time they spend with their children, even how much television their children watch, based on their own interests as well as their children's needs. Parents need to acknowledge their own and other family interests when making decisions that impact on individual family members if they are to make responsible and fair decisions. Parents may feel uncomfortable justifying decisions that impact on their children on a basis other than the best interests of the child. No parent wants to believe that they are not looking out for their child's best interests. However, we need to openly recognise that, while parents have certain duties in respect of children, there are other interests beyond those of children that influence family decision-making.

For example, the decision to put an infant or child into formal childcare[19] is not a decision based solely on the interests of the child. Rather, it is a decision generally motivated by the interests of other family members, particularly parents. There are many reasons why parents choose childcare, including: affordability; it enables parents to pursue careers and financially support the whole family, particularly women who are freed from traditional gendered roles; and it gives parents, particularly single parents, a break from the constant demands of parenting. While childcare may provide some benefits to a child, there is ongoing debate about whether childcare facilities provide optimal care, particularly for infants and children aged under 2.[20] In this sense the debate becomes unrealistic as there are many care arrangements, both in and outside the home, that are unlikely to be optimal for children.[21] If we accept that the decision to use childcare, as with many other familial decisions, is based on the interests of the family as a whole, the debate can move from arguments about what is in the child's best interests to one focused on ensuring that childcare facilities satisfy the basic needs of children. In reformulating the debate, it is important to bear in mind that a child's basic needs extend beyond the physical needs for care, food and shelter, and include the child's need for love, intimacy and affection.

5.2.2 Impact of familial character on family decision-making

Compromise within families is not limited to accommodating the varying needs and interests of children and parents, but is also related more broadly to familial character or identity. Familial character imbues family members with a sense of collective identity and meaning. As with any other collective, 'a family can affirm certain values and repudiate others *en famille*, so that the small details of the daily routine form a mosaic of shared meaning'.[22] In other words, families are viewed 'as institutions with independent ideals and as invested with meanings of their own'.[23] According to Hilde and James Lindemann Nelson, contributing to the family mosaic 'can promote a feeling of solidarity among family members which is in itself a deep source of personal satisfaction'.[24] Families need a certain degree of freedom to pursue their own projects, which in turn provide their individual members with meaning and identity.

Familial character is influenced by the particularities within a family, including 'the personalities and life situations of specific family members, as well as common practices or traditions to which families may have allegiance'.[25] At least in the early years, familial character is shaped significantly by parental preferences and values. For example, parents who value sport or the arts may take a child to weekly football matches or ballet performances in the hope of instilling in the child a passion for that particular form of recreation. Or perhaps the parents hold no such illusions, but simply want to take the family along in any event simply because they enjoy watching football or ballet. The parents' actions may have little to do with the child's welfare, as they are unlikely to be able to demonstrate the specific value of attending football or ballet performances. Rather, 'parents intervene in their children's lives on the basis of undemonstrable views that there are things that matter apart from a child's own interest'.[26] Parents also, on occasion, expose their children to small risks of serious harm in pursuing these interests. For example, by driving to the football on a rainy winter's night, parents subject their child to a small risk of being involved in a car accident.

Familial character does not justify a *carte blanche* on parental authority. As discussed in Chapter 4, parents can and should represent the interests of the family as a whole as well as their own interests. Furthermore, as children grow and develop their own identities, they will have more influence about familial character and decision-making. Familial character is influenced by the individual preferences and needs of all family members, which are continually evolving, and by the family history, religion, culture and values that its members inherit. At times, the interests of the family as a whole may take precedence over the interests of particular family members. However, provided parents attend to the basic needs of their children, they should be free to distribute benefits and burdens according to the priorities within their family. James Lindemann Nelson argues that it is important to allow families the freedom to pursue family projects, which provide meaning, definition and character, even though the pursuit of such projects may deviate from impartial theories of justice:

> The way in which families choose their projects, distribute their energies, and assign their burdens and benefits may serve goals other than those picked out by general theories of justice ... They express what might be regarded as familial character, as those reasons for which people have the deep and abiding interest they do in forming and maintaining families.[27]

It is integral to a meaningful life that families are able to pursue their own interests and distribute benefits and burdens in a way that reflects the family's particular character even though this may, at times, involve compromise by individual family members. According to Bernard Williams, 'deep attachments to other persons will express themselves in the world in ways which cannot at the same time embody the impartial view'.[28] Ferdinand

Schoeman similarly argues that, in relation to family decisions concerning a child:

> factors other than the parents' responsibility for promoting the child's interests may be taken into account legitimately. These other factors can roughly be characterised as concerns emerging from the desire to promote the family's welfare or character. Such a perspective does not entitle parents to sacrifice their children's lives or welfare, although it does permit parents to compromise the child's interests for ends related to family welfare.[29]

It is important to recognise the value of familial character in order to understand the intricate basis on which decisions are made within families and the individual compromise that this sometimes entails. Families have their own identities, which will influence the way in which decisions are made and vary according to the particularities of each family. If parents are required to focus on the individual interests of one particular member, much of the familial character that creates meaning and fosters identity would be eroded.

5.3 Necessary compromise and unacceptable sacrifice

The power imbalance that exists among family members demands that children be afforded some independent protection 'lest they be treated, Cinderella-like, as mere conveniences to advance others' ends'.[30] For example, conceiving a saviour sibling through PGD to be a 'tissue farm' is clearly unacceptable. All children should be protected from abuse, neglect and exploitation.[31] Children who are not yet born are in a particularly vulnerable position as they have no opportunity to influence the decisions made by the rest of the family prior to their birth. The child to be born as a result of PGD clearly requires some protection. The more difficult issue is how far the state should intrude into decisions about selective reproduction in order to protect the welfare of the child.

5.3.1 Limiting state involvement in family decision-making

There are strong reasons for limiting state involvement in family decision-making. Given the inherent and instrumental value of intimate families discussed in Chapter 4, state interference with parental discretion should be minimised. According to Schoeman, 'state scrutiny of, and intervention into, family affairs is highly disruptive of familial relationships' and should therefore be kept to a minimum.[32] Sarah Elliston points out that state oversight of parental decision-making would not only undermine parents' ability to care for their children and family but 'would in any event be impossible for the state to effectively monitor and police'.[33] Furthermore, in families with more than one child, parents have obligations to all their children. Allen Buchanan and Dan Brock argue that failure on the part of parents to maximise the individual interests of any particular child is not an adequate reason for state intervention, '[P]arents' obligations toward their other children as well as their own legitimate self-interests can conflict with doing what *maximises* the child's well-being, and sometimes may take precedence over it'.[34] According to Buchanan and Brock, state intervention should be limited to cases in which parents fail to promote the basic needs of the child.[35] Ross similarly argues for a minimal state intervention into parental discretion:

> Parents need the moral and legal space within which to make decisions that will facilitate their child's long-term autonomy, not only her present-day autonomy. Moreover, third party intrusion, by physicians or the state, should be resisted unless negligent and abusive decisions are in the making.[36]

State intervention is justified to protect children from abuse, neglect and exploitation. However, what constitutes abuse, neglect or exploitation will vary according to the circumstances and the particular relationship in question.[37] Different types of relationships carry different moral obligations. As previously discussed, parents have a fiduciary duty to attend to the basic needs of their children. Failure to do so will constitute abuse, neglect and/or exploitation on behalf of the parents and justify state intervention.

A relational model for selective reproduction can and should provide a threshold level of protection to the child to be born to ensure that his/her basic needs are met. While there is no evidence to suggest that families seeking PGD are more likely to deny the basic needs of a child than any other family, concerns about commodification and harm pose a potential threat to the 'primary goods' of respect and protection from harm. A minimum threshold for these two primary goods, below which state interference is justified, is necessary in order to protect the child to be born from exploitation, abuse or neglect. Saviour sibling selection provides a useful case study for exploring how the primary goods of respect and protection from harm might be preserved in selective reproduction generally.

5.3.2 Respecting the child as an individual

The first concern raised in relation to saviour sibling selection is the possibility that parents may commodify the child to be born by creating him/her for the sole purpose of saving their existing ill child. Although a remote possibility, society would be derelict in its duty to children to not only allow, but assist, parents to conceive children solely as commodities. In Chapter 3, I argued that parental motivation is a relevant consideration in saviour sibling selection. The reasons people have for wanting a child are, however, complex and often multi-factorial. I therefore contended that the state should only intervene in decisions to select a saviour sibling (on the basis of parental motivation) in extreme cases where parents clearly have no interest in the child to be born beyond his/her role as a stem cell donor. I concluded that counselling is an important process for exploring parental motivation for saviour sibling selection, not only to protect the child to be born from commodification but also to assist parents in making genuinely informed decisions prior to conception and into the future.

The difficulty lies in ascertaining when parents intend to conceive a child solely as a commodity as opposed to wanting a child for his/her own sake. Commodification of a child is not something to which parents would readily admit. Furthermore, as discussed in Chapter 3, it is likely to be difficult to separate parents' reasons for conceiving a child because of a genuine desire for a child from those linked to an attempt to save another child. Although parental motives for seeking a saviour sibling are likely to be mixed and complex, at least some attempt should be made to identify parents who do not genuinely desire a child for his/her own sake through counselling. In relation to other types of selection, it may be easier to ascertain parental motivation. For example, individuals who desire a male child to satisfy cultural expectations may have a clearer sense of why they are seeking PGD. As discussed below, counselling is seen as beneficial to patients in making informed decisions. In Australia, attempts have been made in the past to ascertain parental motivation for saviour sibling selection through counselling[38] and parental motives remain a relevant consideration under the NHMRC ART Guidelines.[39]

The process of counselling in assisted reproduction aims to assist patients to explore and understand their own motives in seeking treatment, thereby enhancing their capacity to make fully informed decisions.[40] Counsellors help patients reflect on the long- and short-term implications of the proposed treatment for themselves, their family and the child to be born. They also encourage patients to develop realistic expectations about treatment outcomes and explore appropriate coping strategies.[41] Counsellors aim to create a supportive environment, which is conducive to honest exploration of parental motives, by developing rapport, establishing a relationship of trust, using empathy and breaking down barriers.[42] The counselling process does, however, have some limitations. According to Adrienne Asch and Gail Geller, counsellors can 'display subtle biases' through the questions they ask and the information they provide or omit,[43] which may impact on the value of the information obtained. Careful attention should therefore be directed towards minimising the impact of bias in the counselling process.

Using PGD to select a child with specific genetic traits is morally complex. Parental motivation is particularly important when selection is sought for reasons unrelated to any therapeutic benefit for the child to be born. Commodification becomes a genuine concern when patients seek a particular 'type' of child or a child for a specific reason that does not enhance the health outcomes for the prospective child. Apart from saviour sibling selection, this may occur when patients seek a child of a particular sex for social reasons or when they seek a deaf child for reasons associated with 'cultural identity'. If PGD becomes more widely available, clinics should provide families seeking PGD with sufficient information, appropriate counselling and ethical guidance to explore and develop their values and preferences in relation to complex ethical reproductive decisions. A clinical ethicist could assist clinicians and counsellors in creating an 'open moral space' within which parents can explore and reflect upon their motivations for selective reproduction.[44]

Decisions to allow PGD for ethically controversial purposes that are unrelated to any therapeutic benefit for the child to be born, such as saviour sibling selection, should also be subject to independent review to ensure that the prospective parents do not intend to exploit the child to be born by treating him/her solely as a means to an end. The complex nature of parental motivation highlights the importance of process in cases where patients are seeking PGD to select a particular 'type' of child. Counselling and ethical guidance form an integral part of the process by creating a supportive environment in which patients can explore their own motivations for seeking particular genetic traits in a child. This exploration of parental motivation also acts as a safeguard for the interests of the child to be born by revealing potentially harmful motives for selecting a particular type of child.

5.3.3 Protecting the child from harm

The second concern about saviour sibling selection is that the child to be born will be harmed, either physically or psychosocially. As with all applications of PGD, there are potential risks of physical harm to the child born as a saviour sibling associated with embryo biopsy and ART. There is also a future risk of physical harm to saviour siblings if future donations are required. Lastly, there is a theoretical risk of psychosocial harm associated with being conceived as a donor. An assessment of what constitutes acceptable risk of harm is necessary in order to ensure that the child to be born as a result of PGD receives a threshold level of protection from harm. One way of determining an acceptable risk of harm is by requiring that the child experience a balance of benefit over harm or a net benefit overall. In Chapter 3, I argued that the claim by some commentators that saviour siblings experience an individual net benefit is unconvincing.[45] In any event, as already discussed, parents frequently expose their children to small risks of harm for which there is not necessarily an overriding individual benefit.[46] An individual net benefit approach is therefore inconsistent with general decision-making within families as it 'ignores the benefits to the family as a group'.[47] A more holistic approach is needed to determine when state intervention is necessary to prevent unacceptable risk of harm to the child to be born as a result of PGD.

Several slightly different approaches to determining unacceptable risk of harm in medical decision-making involving families have been developed in the context of intra-familial donations. All of these approaches differ from an individual net benefit approach in that they allow for the child to be exposed to some risk of harm without necessarily requiring any overriding individual benefit to that child. In this respect, the approaches more accurately reflect general decision-making within families, where the welfare of the family as a whole is a relevant consideration. Applying each of these approaches to saviour sibling selection, I conclude that, on the current evidence available, using PGD to select a saviour sibling does not generally pose an unacceptable risk of harm to the child to be born. I then propose a threshold level of protection from harm for the child to be born as a result of PGD.

5.3.3.1 'Constrained parental autonomy'

Ross adopts an approach to medical decision-making involving children, which she describes as 'constrained parental autonomy'.[48] This approach states that parents can expose their children to procedures involving 'minimal risk' and 'minor increase over minimal risk' of harm. For any greater risk, a competent child's consent is necessary and an incompetent child's participation is impermissible.[49] Ross' categories are based on 'the likelihood and degree of risk and harm'.[50] Ross defines 'minimal risk' as, 'No more risk than that which a child typically experiences, or ... no more risk than that which is encountered in many activities to which parents typically expose their children for educational purposes'.[51] In the context of intrafamilial donations, Ross classifies blood donation as carrying the *minimal risk* of a small bruise and slight fatigue.[52] By way of contrast, she claims that the main risks and harms of bone marrow donation, namely anaesthesia and temporary pain, involve a *minor increase over minimal risk* but 'are within the realm of risks to which parents often subject their children'.[53] On the other hand, kidney donations, which involve anaesthesia, major surgery, potential major complications and a long recuperation period, are classified by Ross as involving *more than a minor increase over minimal risk*.[54]

5.3.3.2 Significant risk of serious harm that is unreasonable

Elliston suggests a slightly different test to Ross, based on 'whether the parents' decision poses a significant risk of serious harm to the child and whether it is unreasonable'.[55] According to the first limb of Elliston's test, judicial scrutiny is justified where there is a significant risk of serious harm to the child. However, the second limb of Elliston's test provides that a parental decision involving significant risk of serious harm to a child may be acceptable if it is considered by a court to be reasonable.[56] In the context of parents consenting to bone marrow donations by their incompetent children, Elliston argues that 'it is reasonable for parents to make decisions that take account of the needs of all their children, rather than because they are in the donor child's best interests'.[57] Elliston's standard of significant risk of serious harm appears to roughly correlate with Ross' standard of 'more than a minor increase over minimal risk'. Elliston cautions, however, that:

... given the uncertainty about potential risks and benefits, and the possibility for parents and those concerned with the care of the sick child to underestimate harm to the proposed donor, [sibling donation] is a situation where I consider that some independent scrutiny is justified.[58]

Elliston suggests that, in most cases, judicial scrutiny would not be necessary and independent review by a statutory authority 'would provide an appropriate level of oversight'.[59] She concludes that parents who consent to bone marrow donation between siblings would not generally be deemed to be acting unreasonably. However, some cases of bone marrow donation may pose a significant risk of serious harm to the child which is unreasonable. For example, Elliston argues that the degree of distress for a child who is a reluctant donor may increase the level of risk of harm to the child 'beyond acceptable limits'.[60]

5.3.3.3 Role of relationship in determining acceptable risk of harm

The final two tests I discuss differ from the tests already examined in that they expressly highlight the direct bearing that relationship has on determining an acceptable risk of harm.[61] Analysing the approach by US courts to sibling donations, James Dwyer and Elizabeth Vig offer a general formula for determining what constitutes acceptable risk of harm as an alternative to the 'best interests' test applied by the courts. They state that there must be a 'moral match between the relationship and the risks to the donor relative to the benefits to the recipient'.[62] According to Dwyer and Vig, '[d]ifferent relationships justify different risks relative to various benefits'.[63]

Lynn Jansen offers a slightly different approach based on 'intimate attachment' between persons, which recognises that a child's well-being can be bound up with the well-being of another.[64] According to Jansen, when an intimate attachment exists between a donor and recipient, 'the interests of the child donor will be furthered by the donation'.[65] Jansen concludes that intimate attachments usually exist between members of a family but are not limited to family relationships.[66] She further contends that parents should be considered the 'presumptive authorities' in determining when an intimate attachment exists between their child and another person.[67] Lastly, Jansen provides a similar limitation on parental decision-making to Ross and Elliston by stating that where the donation involves a significant increase over minor risk to the donor there should be routine judicial review of parental decisions.[68]

5.3.3.4 Does saviour sibling selection cause unacceptable harm?

On any of the above formulations of threshold risk, saviour sibling selection is not likely to cause unacceptable harm to the child to be born. Arguably, the most significant risk is the future risk of physical harm associated with a bone marrow donation in the event that the initial cord blood transplant proves unsuccessful. This risk seems acceptable according to any of the above approaches, provided the relationships within the existing family are sufficiently close. On current evidence, the general risks posed by the PGD process appear to be less significant than the risks posed by a bone marrow transplant. There is therefore a strong likelihood that a child selected using PGD to be a saviour sibling will have a sufficiently intimate relationship with the existing sibling to justify the level of risk involved.

Nevertheless, PGD regulation should clearly outline a threshold level of protection from harm for the child to be born and establish mechanisms for ongoing review and guidance in relation to the risk of harm posed by saviour sibling selection and other controversial applications of PGD. In the context of saviour sibling selection, for example, it is possible that further empirical evidence may reveal a higher risk of physical or psychosocial harm to saviour siblings than that which is currently understood from studies on the embryo biopsy process, ART and sibling bone marrow donors. It is also possible that the individual circumstances of a particular case may pose a greater risk than usual to the child to be born. For example, counselling may reveal that parents seeking a saviour sibling are not sufficiently psychologically stable to support the child to be born in the event that the cord blood donation proves unsuccessful.

As with sibling donations generally, parents and treating physicians may not, on their own, be able to objectively assess the risk of harm to a saviour sibling. Family members may also disagree, either between themselves or with the treating physician, about the level of harm posed to the unborn child. Given the ethical complexities surrounding intra-familial donations, parents would arguably benefit from clinical ethics consultation during the decision-making process. For instance, a clinical ethicist could work in conjunction with parents, the treating physician and the counsellor to assess the risk of harm to the child to be born in each case and could mediate any disputes that arise.

5.3.3.5 A threshold level of protection from harm

Given the vulnerable position of the child to be born as a result of PGD, the child should receive a threshold level of protection from harm. All of the approaches already outlined provide that independent scrutiny of decisions is required when the risk of harm to a child becomes significant. Although the approaches differ on how they define significant risk of harm, they roughly equate to the same standard. For simplicity, I shall adopt the language used by Elliston of 'significant risk of serious harm' as the threshold for state intervention in relation to assisted reproductive treatments. Elliston acknowledges that the terms 'significant' and 'serious' may be criticised as indeterminate. However, 'there will always be an interpretive element in judging whether a parental decision crosses the threshold for state intervention'.[69]

It would be helpful to include a definition of 'significant risk of serious harm' in ART legislation to provide some clarity. For example, the phrase might be defined as 'more than a minor increase over the harm than that which a healthy child normally experiences', based on Ross' formulation for constrained parental autonomy discussed above. The health care team should guide patients in determining what constitutes a significant risk of harm in cases involving PGD.

As discussed in Chapter 2, PGD is currently allowed in the UK and Australia to detect serious genetic conditions and improve ART outcomes. The risk of harm to the child to be born in these cases is minimal as current evidence suggests that the risks associated with ART and embryo biopsy are low. Using PGD to select a child for non-therapeutic reasons carries additional risks of harm for the child to be born, depending on the reason for selection. Saviour sibling selection, while allowed in the UK and Australia, is more tightly regulated to protect the welfare of the child to be born and applications are approved on a case-by-case basis. Other controversial types of selection, such as social sex selection and selecting for disability, are currently prohibited in the UK and Australia. Selective reproductive choices that raise genuine concerns about harm to the child to be born should be independently reviewed on a case-by-case basis to ensure that the welfare of the child to be born is adequately protected. In some cases, the risk of harm may be deemed acceptable where the relationship between family members and specific family circumstances suggest that the welfare of the child will be enhanced overall.

A relational approach is relatively novel in the context of assisted reproduction. There has, however, been growing recognition of the importance of broader family interests in relation to general medical decision-making. Although the child to be born is in a different position to a patient facing medical treatment, similar issues arise in both scenarios.

5.4 Role of families in medical decision-making

Given the traditional emphasis in Western bioethical debate on individual patient autonomy, the role of the family in medical decision-making may seem, at best, marginal. There are good reasons for protecting patient autonomy, given that patients are in an especially vulnerable position by virtue of their illness and will be directly and often profoundly affected by the consequences of treatment decisions. However, there are several bioethical writers who have 'begun to shift the balance in bioethics so that family interests are weighed in concert with – not against – patient autonomy'.[70] Nelson argues that 'standard accounts of medical ethics obscure what is particularly morally significant about families'.[71] Some bioethicists argue for a greater role for the family in medical decision-making, even when the patient is a competent adult.[72] Rather than rejecting patient autonomy, these bioethicists are essentially proposing different conceptions of relational autonomy in the field of bioethics.[73]

Relational autonomy is based on a premise that persons are 'socially embedded'.[74] In contrast to the traditional approach to individual patient autonomy, a relational perception of patient autonomy 'requires active concern for others'.[75] According to Roy Gilbar and Ora Gilbar, ' ... autonomy can be developed only in the context of social relationships with others who cultivate this capacity, and ... personal autonomy can be implemented through reference to shared social norms and values'.[76] Given that persons are, at least in part, 'defined by their relationships and their interconnectedness with others',[77] it makes sense to take into account the interests of intimate family members who will be affected by a medical decision alongside those of the patient. Although relatively new in the context of Western bioethics, a family-focused approach to medical decision-making is common in other cultures.[78] My focus in this section is to argue that greater family involvement in medical decision-making is not inconsistent with Western bioethical principles and can in fact enhance patient outcomes.

5.4.1 *Position of the child to be born is analogous to that of a patient*

It may seem misplaced to discuss the notion of autonomy in relation to a child who is not yet born in the context of selective reproduction. The child to be born as a result of selective reproduction does not have any decision-making capacity because he/she is not yet in existence. However, the position of the child is analogous to that of a patient requiring general medical treatment in two significant respects. First, both the prospective child and the patient will be directly affected by the relevant treatment decision. Decisions about general medical treatment and decisions to select a child using PGD are likely to impact directly on the bodily integrity of the patient and the child to be born, respectively. In the case of the child to be born as a saviour sibling, the decision will not only impact on the child's very existence but also the use of that child's tissue at the time of birth and possibly into the future. As discussed in Chapter 3, the fact that a child is not yet in existence does not mean that policymakers should ignore the future interests of the child to be born as a result of PGD, which may conflict with the interests of the family as a whole. For example, the prospective child has future interests in being treated with respect and protected from harm – some of which may be compromised by particular types of selection using PGD. Like a patient facing a treatment decision, the child to be born as a result of PGD has interests, albeit future ones, that will be affected by the relevant decision.

Second, both the child to be born and the patient are vulnerable and in need of some protection in the decision-making process. A competent patient's decision-making capacity may be significantly compromised or diminished due to illness and the patient may not be able to defend his/her interests. In relation to patients facing treatment, Nelson points out that 'considerations about vulnerability and personal privacy and integrity must be acknowledged'.[79] The plight of the child to be born is even more precarious because the child is not in existence at the time a decision is made and therefore has no capacity to influence the decision or defend his/her future interests. The prospective child has no input into the decision, which will ultimately determine not only that child's very existence but his/her role within the family in a profound way. As a consequence of their vulnerable positions, both the patient and the child to be born rely, to varying degrees, on others to represent and defend their interests in the decision-making process.

The following discussion reveals the impact that family relationships can have on medical decision-making and explores different relational models for dealing with potentially conflicting individual and collective interests within families. I draw on various aspects of these models to propose a relational model for selective reproduction in section 5.5.

5.4.2 Medical decision-making involving families

Mark Kuczewski describes the increased focus on the role of family in medical decision-making in recent years as 'the natural progression and development of medical ethics'.[80] 'Having focused on the rights of the patient for so long, it follows that ethicists now wish to map the relationships surrounding the individual that may affect medical decision-making'.[81] Kuczewski's 'process model' for medical decision-making provides a new lens through which to view family relationships in relation to medical decisions. According to Kuczewski, a patient's family members have a critical role to play in the *process* of informed consent to medical treatment. Instead of perceiving the patient's interests as separate to, and in potential conflict with, those of his/her family, Kuczewski views informed consent as a process of genuinely shared decision-making in which the patient's decision is influenced by discussions with his/her physician and family. Before I discuss Kuczewski's process model to family decision-making and its potential application to PGD, I shall briefly outline and critique three different relational approaches to medical decision-making that have influenced Kuczewski and bioethical debate on the role of family in medical decision-making generally.

5.4.2.1 Three relational approaches to medical decision-making

John Hardwig instigated the debate about the role of families in medical decision-making in 1990 when he argued that the focus should shift from the individual patient towards a broader consideration of the patient's family.[82] Hardwig proposes a radical approach to relational autonomy in medical decision-making by advocating that the traditional patient-centred medical ethic be replaced with a presumption that the interests of the patient and family members that are of the same magnitude should be given equal weighting. However, he argues that this presumption will generally be overridden by the patient's interests in optimal health and longer life.[83]

Because a patient's medical decisions often dramatically affect the interests of members of that patient's family, Hardwig argues that medical decisions should be made by taking into account the medical and nonmedical interests of both the patient and other family members, 'To be part of a family is to be morally required to make decisions on the basis of thinking about what is best for all concerned, not simply what is best for yourself'.[84] For example, certain treatment options may be more costly than others and may have a significant financial impact on the patient's family. There may also be significant burdens placed on family members who provide ongoing care and support for the patient. Hardwig proposes that the family, rather than just the patient alone, should make medical treatment decisions. To this end, he argues that 'family conferences' should be required when a treatment decision is likely to impact on the lives of family members.[85] Such family conferences would not be limited to an advisory or supportive function but would operate as decision-making forums.

Nelson builds on Hardwig's view of family relationships as involving overlapping and mutually affecting interests by claiming that they also provide contexts of intimacy. Nelson argues that the intimacy and mutual commitment on which families are based create a sense of moral responsibility between family members, giving further weight to the claim that family interests ought to be included in medical decision-making.[86] According to Nelson, the intimate nature of family relationships creates not only a potential clash of individual interests but also a clash between the interests of individuals and the collective interests they share as members of a family. It is therefore important to protect the character of the family as an intimate collective in the decision-making process.

When a dispute emerges between a patient and family members, Nelson recommends that 'conflicts [be] met with efforts to mediate, to facilitate consensus, or to forge acceptable compromise'.[87] He suggests that an independent advocate should represent the interests of incompetent patients in mediation.[88] In contrast to Hardwig, Nelson suggests that we should begin with the presumption that a competent patient has decision-making authority, but acknowledge that this presumption is rebuttable and a family should have an option to challenge patient authorisation on the basis of family interests.[89] Nelson's model represents a view of medical decision-making involving families that is sensitive to both the values protected by patient-centredness in current medical practice and the inherent value of intimate relationships.

Jeffrey Blustein's approach to relational patient autonomy is slightly different as he separates out the decision from the process of making the decision. Blustein argues that 'the locus of decisional authority should remain with the individual patient' but that, ' ... family members, by virtue of their closeness to and intimate knowledge of the patient are often uniquely qualified to shore up the patient's vulnerable autonomy and assist him or her in the exercise of autonomous decisionmaking'.[90] According to Blustein, families are 'an important resource for patients' in helping them make fully informed treatment decisions.[91] Short of giving family members any share of decisional authority, Blustein suggests that procedures need to be devised 'that acknowledge the moral weight of their legitimate interests'.[92] It is the role of the physician to enhance the patient's autonomy by facilitating discussion between patients and those with whom they are intimate to give patients 'opportunities for serious reflection on their choices'.[93] However, although patients should be encouraged to include the interests of family members in medical decision-making, Blustein stresses that the choice itself belongs to the patient. Blustein argues that it is necessary to protect individual decision-making rights because, even in harmonious families, the interests of individual members will at times conflict with those of the rest of the family. According to Blustein, '[i]ndividual rights are needed because a significant degree of diversity may exist even in a group united by a common conception of the good'.[94]

5.4.2.2 Critique of the three approaches to medical decision-making

While the medical decision-making models for families discussed above reflect slightly differing conceptions of relational autonomy, they fall short of a truly collaborative decision-making model. Kuczewski claims that Hardwig, Nelson and Blustein ultimately 'remain trapped by the individualism implicit in the doctrine' of informed consent, which dominates medical ethics.[95] All three approaches recognise that the patient is generally in a vulnerable position and requires 'advocacy and protection'.[96] They all entail a presumption in favour of the decisional authority of the patient but recognise that family interests should be taken into account to some degree in the decision-making process. Lastly, and significantly, the debate is ultimately framed in terms of a conflict between the interests of the patient and those of the family. The debate focuses on the question of whose interests should take precedence when those of the patient and family conflict. With some exceptions, most conflicts are settled in favour of the patient. Kuczewski acknowledges that framing the issue in terms of conflicting interests 'has an initial attraction because of its clarity and practicality'.[97] However, simply providing an answer fails to explain 'the more general phenomenon of the family's place in medical decisionmaking'.[98]

Kuczewski rejects the way in which the problem of conflicting interests within families is framed as one which must be answered in either/or terms and should generally be resolved in favour of the patient.[99] The problem, according to Kuczewski, is that medical ethics has developed in the shadow of a legalistic doctrine of informed consent, which is in turn based on an 'individual profile rather than a family portrait'.[100] As a result, the family is usually conceived of as comprising competing interests, which leads to ethicists arguing about the relative merits of these rival interests. This confuses the role of the family in medical decision-making as '[t]he profundity of the links and bonds between family members is hidden from view in these legalistic discussions of interests and rights'.[101] Kuczewski describes this legalistic approach as an 'event model of informed consent'[102] because the focus is on the event of receiving consent from the patient, who is assumed to have a defined set of values. According to this approach, the role of the family is generally confined to vouching for the patient's competence.[103] Kuczewski contrasts this approach with a 'process model' of informed consent, in which consent is viewed as a process of shared decision-making whereby the values and preferences of the patient take shape through discussions with his/her physician and family.[104]

5.4.2.3 A 'process model' for medical decision-making

An alternative approach to the role of family in medical decision-making focuses on process and the respective roles of the patient, family and physician. Instead of asking whose interests should take precedence when those of the patient and family conflict, Kuczewski says we should be asking what are the respective roles of the patient, family members and physician in the medical decision-making process. In this sense, Kuczewski goes further than Blustein, who separates out the decision from the process, by making the process the main focus of his decision-making model.[105] According to Kuczewski, the discussions through which the patient's values and preferences take shape are 'not prior to the event of giving consent, but, in a sense, [are] the process of informed consent'.[106] Kuczewski's process model of decision-making sees family members not as representing a separate group of interests to be weighed against the interests of the patient, but as performing an integral role in the decision-making process. By engaging in the decision-making process, family members assist the patient by taking part 'in the patient's narrative self-discovery that helps her to reconnect with her values and give them meaning as expressed in choices'.[107] In cases where the patient's values have not yet been developed, family plays an important role in discovering and shaping those values. Kuczewski argues that '[b]ecause we discover our values in dialogue with those closest to us, the family is naturally an integral part of this process'.[108] Family members can, however, sometimes exert undue influence on patients, which does not assist them in forming their views but amounts to coercion. In such cases, Kuczewski acknowledges that a physician may need to seek recourse through 'formal institutional mechanisms' to protect a vulnerable party.[109]

Of all the relational models discussed in this section, Kuczewski's model comes closest to a genuinely collaborative medical decision-making model. For Kuczewski, the process model of informed consent is a collaborative form of decision-making that involves 'active roles for physicians and families in the medical decisionmaking process'.[110] As these roles will vary according to the circumstances of each case, clear guidance is needed to define and circumscribe the various roles in the relevant context. In section 5.5, I explore a relational decision-making model for selective reproduction based on Kuczewski's process model and outline the various roles played by health professionals and prospective parents in this context.

5.5 A relational model for selective reproduction

A relational decision-making model for selective reproduction reflects the importance of intimate family to the welfare of the child to be born. Although it is impossible to have a fully collaborative decision-making model when the prospective child cannot participate in the decision-making process, a modified version of Kuczewski's process model can be applied to selective reproduction. The relational model I propose involves a shift in focus from the interests of the child to be born to those of the family as a whole and establishes a modified collaborative decision-making process for dealing with the various interests within a family. The interests of the child to be born remain important within this framework but must be considered in connection with the interests of other family members. At the end of this section, I outline some general features of a relational model for selective reproduction.

5.5.1 *Shift in focus from child to be born to family as a whole*

As discussed in section 5.4, family members often play an important role in medical decision-making. The interests of a patient's family should be considered in relation to many medical decisions – not just because the family is likely to be affected by the treatment decision, but also because the intimacy and mutual commitment on which intimate families are based creates a sense of moral responsibility between family members. Furthermore, families play an integral part in the personal narrative on which a patient's values and preferences are formed and transformed. Despite the recent bioethical debate about the importance of family input into medical decision-making, the role of the family in medical decisions involving children has been impeded by a strong focus on the 'best interests' of the child in paediatric and reproductive medicine.[111] Just as some bioethicists have argued for a shift from a patient-centred to a relational medical decision-making model, there are strong reasons to move from a decision-making model for selective reproduction that centres on the child to be born to one in which the interests of the family are also taken into consideration.

Notwithstanding the direct impact on and vulnerability of the child to be born as a result of PGD, the underlying justifications for a relational medical decision-making model also apply to selective reproduction. Existing family members are likely to be affected by a decision to select a child using PGD. The introduction of a new child into a family under ordinary circumstances will, at a minimum, alter the family dynamic and reduce the share of parental resources available for existing members. Selecting a child for a particular reason adds an additional element of complexity and different family members may be affected in various ways. Selecting a saviour sibling, for example, will clearly have a profound impact on the life of the existing ill child who needs a stem cell transplant. It will also impact heavily on the parents and other siblings who have close bonds with the ill child.

The additional justification for a relational model for medical decision-making highlighted by Nelson, based on the intimate nature of family relationships, also applies to selective reproduction. I argued in Chapter 4 that children, in particular, depend on intimate families for love, protection, nurturing, socialisation and identity. Furthermore, the future interests of the child to be born will be influenced by his/her family in the same way that a patient's values and preferences are influenced by family. The decision to use PGD should not, therefore, be based solely on the individual interests of the child to be born but should also openly and honestly reckon with the interests of existing family members. Even in cases where the welfare of the child to be born requires independent review, the child's interests should be represented as 'not necessarily estranged from those of her family'.[112] As far as possible, a collaborative decision-making process should be employed to explore the various interests within a family seeking selective reproduction.

5.5.2 Modified collaborative decision-making process

In Chapter 4, I highlighted the relational nature of the welfare of the child to be born by arguing that the child has both individual and collective interests that are shared with his/her family. A relational model for selective reproduction should provide an effective process for dealing with the various individual and collective interests that exist within a family. In this section, I draw from Kuczewski's process model to argue that instead of focusing on the potential conflict between the interests of the child to be born and those of his/her family, attention should be redirected to collaborative decision-making.

While much of Kuczewski's discussion (which relates to competent patients) is not directly relevant to selective reproduction, we can draw from his model by not approaching questions about the various family interests involved in selective reproduction in 'either/or' terms. Instead, we should view the welfare of the child to be born within the context of the family into which the child will be born, as the child's future values and preferences are likely to be influenced by his/her family's values and beliefs. For example, you would not apply Catholic doctrine to a Jewish family wishing to use PGD, as the child to be born would not be raised according to Catholic values. The prospective child will ultimately emerge from the initial role or purpose for which he/she has been conceived to become an individual with his/her own values and preferences. However, those values and preferences will necessarily be shaped by the values and belief systems of his/her family. Furthermore, as the child's future welfare depends not only on satisfaction of his/her individual interests but also on the child's relationships with other family members, any conflict of interests cannot be solved by simply balancing the child's individual interests against other family interests.

Clearly Kuczewski's process model, which involves a genuine collaboration between the patient, his/her family and the physician, cannot be fully replicated for selective reproduction. First and foremost, the child to be born as a result of PGD cannot have any input into the decision-making process that will determine the child's very existence. Another significant point of difference is that the treating physician is not primarily representing the interests of the child to be born, but is in fact treating the patients seeking PGD. The relational model I propose for selective reproduction is therefore based on a modified collaborative decision-making process. Importantly, my model requires that the interests of the child be viewed within the social context of the family into which the child will be born rather than as essentially separate to, and to be balanced against, the interests of his/her family.

5.5.3 *General features of a relational model for selective reproduction*

In this section, I sketch out the general features of my relational model for selective reproduction. Given the importance of context in shaping relational models, I return to my saviour sibling selection case study at various points to flesh out the details of how my model might work in practice. The relational model I propose could, however, be adapted to apply to other forms of selective reproduction. I draw from the general features of a relational decision-making model to develop a revised regulatory framework for saviour sibling selection in Chapter 6.

5.5.3.1 *A relational model requires consideration of the interests of all family members, not just those of the child to be born*

Not only will existing family members be affected by selective reproductive decisions, but the child to be born will share collective interests with his/her family. It is therefore important to clearly identify and evaluate the various interests at stake in the decision-making process, some of which are individual and others which are shared. In the context of saviour sibling selection, these include the future interests of the child to be born, the interests of the existing ill child in receiving a stem cell transplant,[113] the interests of the parents in saving the life of their existing child, the interests of the parents in having another child, the interests of any other siblings who will be affected by the decision, and the shared interests of the family as an intimate collective.

5.5.3.2 *A 'process model' is preferable to a conflict-based model for managing individual and collective interests within a family*

A balance must be struck between protecting the individual interests of the child to be born and promoting the interests of the family in the decision-making process. Instead of asking whose interests should take precedence when the interests of the child to be born appear to conflict with the interests of his/her family, regulation should focus on the decision-making process and the respective roles of the family and their healthcare team. It is important that individual and collective family interests be explored, as far as possible, in a supportive environment that promotes the intimate nature of family. By creating an 'open moral space' within which to explore the various interests of family members, decisions can be made that promote the welfare of the child to be born as well as the valuable intimate relationships that exist within a family.[114] In some cases, entrenched conflict between family members may require more formal mediation. I clarify the roles of family and the healthcare team in the decision-making process in more detail below.

5.5.3.3 The decision-making process should openly and respectfully explore the family's values, beliefs and preferences as these are relevant to the welfare of the child to be born

Ascertaining the values, beliefs and preferences of a family seeking selective reproduction is an important part of the decision-making process because the future values, beliefs and preferences of the child to be born will be influenced by those of his/her family. If the family is 'the soil out of which the [child's] values and preference grow',[115] a realistic assessment of the welfare of the child to be born requires an understanding of the values, beliefs and preferences of the family into which that child will be born. Given that existing family members may not have made decisions about selective reproduction before, they are unlikely to have fully developed the value system necessary to support their decision. The decision-making process is therefore an important collaborative project of 'mutual self-discovery'[116] for the whole family, whose values and preferences are likely to be in transformation. The ethical complexities raised by selective reproduction create a need for some form of clinical ethics consultation over and above what may be provided by ART physicians and counsellors. Clinical ethicists can play a key role in keeping open the moral space necessary to explore the values, beliefs and preferences of all family members.

5.5.3.4 The roles of prospective parents and members of the healthcare team (physician, counsellor and clinical ethicist) should be clearly outlined

Given the active roles I propose for families and members of the healthcare team in the decision-making process, the various roles should be clearly defined and differentiated to avoid confusion.

(a) Role of prospective parents in determining the welfare of the child to be born

Parents generally play an important role in determining the welfare of their children.[117] Prospective parents seeking PGD should therefore actively contribute to determinations about the welfare of the child to be born. Because the welfare of a child is intertwined with the welfare of his/her family, it is reasonable for prospective parents to make decisions that take account of the needs of all family members, not just those of the child to be born. However, because the child to be born is noticeably absent from the decision-making process, he/she requires some additional protection to ensure that his/her interests are not subordinated to the interests of existing family members. This does not, however, mean that the child's future interests should be removed from the social context into which the child will be born. As already discussed, the child's values, beliefs and preferences will inevitably be influenced by those of his/her family.

Although I propose that the prospective parents should be the primary decision-makers, existing children within the family should also be actively involved in the decision-making process where appropriate. All family members should be given information, counselling and ethical guidance during the decision-making process. General guidance on the welfare of the child to be born should be provided through legislation or policy guidelines and reinforced by the treating clinic. Case specific information and support in relation to PGD should be provided by a multi-disciplinary team of healthcare professionals within the treating clinic. I discuss the various roles of the treating healthcare professionals in more detail below.

(b) Role of healthcare professionals in treating the family as an intimate collective and protecting the welfare of the child to be born

Given the medical, psychological and ethical complexities surrounding PGD, clinics should provide families with relevant information, counselling and ethical guidance to enable them to make fully informed and ethically sound decisions.

The role of the treating healthcare team should be clearly defined to ensure that they are not solely representing the interests of the patients seeking PGD any more than they are acting solely as advocate for the child to be born. Rather, the team should aim to treat the family as an intimate collective. The focus should be on a collaborative, inclusive and supportive decision-making process that promotes the welfare of the family as a whole, without sacrificing the interests of the child to be born. To this end the healthcare team's role is to assist family members in determining and promoting their individual and collective interests in an open collaborative decision-making process. Within the team, different healthcare professionals can provide different forms of assistance.

A physician's primary role is to relieve a patient's pain and suffering and restore his/her health. In the context of PGD, the ART physician's role is to assist patients to conceive a healthy baby with particular genetic traits. For example, in the case of saviour sibling selection, the parents desire a baby who will be a direct tissue match for an existing ill sibling. The ART physician must also promote the welfare of the child to be born. To help families make informed decisions about PGD, the ART physician should provide family members with all relevant information. For saviour sibling selection this will include: all other treatment options for the existing sibling; the likely success rates for conceiving a direct tissue match; and the risks associated with PGD for all family members. In alerting patients to the risks for the child to be born, the ART physician assists in promoting the welfare of the child to be born.

Counselling plays an integral role in the decision-making process.[118] Counsellors should support patients and relevant family members in their consideration of the welfare of the child to be born and how the interests of family members interlace with those of the prospective child. As part of this process, counsellors should help patients explore their motivation in seeking to have another child, in particular whether they desire a child in his/her own right. For instance, in the context of saviour sibling selection, it is important to help parents look beyond their immediate desire to save their existing ill child and appreciate that a new child will be created with his/her own interests and needs. Counselling should also address the implications for the whole family in the event that the donation of cord blood stem cells by a saviour sibling is unsuccessful. Lastly, family members may require counselling to explore and further develop their own value system in the context of selective reproduction. Counselling should at least attempt to be value-neutral and non-directive in the sense that families are encouraged to explore their own value systems independently of the values and beliefs of individual counsellors. There is, however, significant debate about what non-directive counselling involves and whether or not it is entirely achievable or entirely appropriate in all contexts.[119]

Given the complex ethical questions raised by selective reproduction, a clinical ethicist should also actively participate in the decision-making process. The role of the clinical ethicist should not be that of an expert moral authority who ultimately determines the 'right' outcome in any particular case. Rather, a clinical ethicist should facilitate moral deliberation that can lead to consensus using a 'discourse ethics' approach.[120] Where consensus is more difficult to achieve, the clinical ethicist should attempt to resolve conflict through mediation.[121] Margaret Urban Walker explains that 'ethicists are architects of moral space within the health care setting, as well as mediators in the conversations taking place within that space'.[122] As already discussed, patients and other family members should be given sufficient moral space within which to explore the various family interests affected by selective reproduction. By openly acknowledging the various interests at stake, decisions can be made that promote the welfare of the child to be born as well as the welfare of the family into which he/she will be born. I discuss clinical ethics consultation and the role of the clinical ethicist in more detail in Chapter 6.

5.5.3.5 Guidance should be given as to how the welfare of the child to be born is likely to be adversely affected by selective reproduction

The two major concerns for the welfare of the child to be born as a result of PGD are commodification and harm. The risks of harm associated with ART and the embryo biopsy process appear to be low, although further empirical evidence is needed to examine any long-term impacts on the child to be born. Different types of selection carry varying risks of commodification and harm. In this chapter, I have focused on the risks associated with saviour sibling selection. I outlined a threshold level of respect and protection from harm to protect the child to be born as a result of PGD from exploitation, abuse or neglect.

Concerns about commodification and harm are not limited to saviour sibling selection and arise in relation to other non-therapeutic applications of PGD, including social sex selection or selecting a child with a disability. Controversial types of selection that raise genuine concerns about commodification or harm to the child to be born should be subject to independent review. Regulation should clarify when the risk of commodification or harm is likely to be unacceptable, for example, when counselling reveals that the prospective parents do not genuinely desire a child for his/her own sake or there is a significant risk of serious harm to the child to be born. In line with a relational approach, any potential harm to the child to be born should be considered within the context of the family into which that child will be born. In the context of saviour sibling selection, for example, a higher risk of physical harm to the child to be born might be allowed in families with an exceptionally stable and supportive network that could mitigate any negative effects on the donor child.

5.5.3.6 Complex decisions should be subject to independent review to ensure that the welfare of the child to be born has been given due consideration

Decisions to use PGD in cases where commodification and harm are genuine concerns, such as saviour sibling selection, should be independently reviewed to protect the child to be born from exploitation, abuse or neglect. While this could be done by a court or administrative tribunal, a separately constituted clinical ethics committee is arguably more appropriate as it is less formal, quicker and closer to the clinical setting. Clinical ethics committees are a relatively new phenomenon in the UK and Australia and are not without their critics.[123] In Chapter 6, I examine the nature and role of clinical ethics committees and address some of the criticisms that have been levelled against them. In the context of selective reproduction, a clinical ethics committee should apply a relational conception of the welfare of the child by considering not only the interests of the child to be born, but also the interests of his/her parents and siblings, the collective interests of the family and the nature of existing relationships within the family.

5.5.3.7 Decisions about selective reproduction should be recorded and clinics should attempt to monitor the long-term effects on children born as a result

Given the importance of the decision-making process in the relational model I propose, transparency in decision-making is essential. Clinics should record decisions to allow PGD and the purposes for which it is sought. In complex cases where review by a clinical ethics committee is required, such as saviour sibling selection, accurate recording will assist clinical ethics committees in assessing whether the welfare of the child to be born has been effectively safeguarded in the decision-making process. In particular, physicians, counsellors and ethics counsellors should independently report on their consultations with families seeking saviour sibling selection.

As discussed in Chapter 2, the full extent of the impact of the PGD and its various applications on the welfare of the child to be born is, as yet, unknown. Clinics should make efforts to monitor the long-term physical and psychosocial effects on children born as a result of PGD to improve welfare assessments in the future. In addition to recording requirements, regulation should therefore also encourage ongoing monitoring of children born as a result of PGD.

5.6 Conclusion

Compromise is an integral part of family life. While parents generally seek to promote the welfare of their children, family decisions are rarely based solely on the individual interests of one particular child. Instead, decisions are made according to the needs of family members, the capacity of other family members to meet those needs, the nature of relationships within a family, and the character and preferences of a particular family. In the context of general medical treatment decisions, there is increasing support for a relational approach to decisions that impact on family members. A relational decision-making model for selective reproduction reflects the complex basis on which decisions are generally made within families by acknowledging that some of the individual interests of the child to be born may need to be compromised in favour of the welfare of the family.

A relational model for selective reproduction should not, however, sacrifice a child's basic needs in favour of the welfare of the family as a whole. In order to protect the welfare of the child to be born, PGD regulation should provide the child to be born with a threshold level of respect and protection from harm. Regulation should clarify when the risk of commodification or harm is likely to be unacceptable, for example, when counselling reveals that prospective parents do not genuinely desire a child for his/her own sake or there is a significant risk of serious harm to the child to be born. Physicians, counsellors, clinical ethicists and prospective parents all play key roles in creating an open moral space within which to explore the welfare of the child in the context of the family into which he/she will be born. A separately constituted clinical ethics committee should review decisions to proceed with particular applications of PGD where there is a genuine risk to the child to be born, such as saviour sibling selection, to ensure that the child is not at risk of exploitation, abuse or neglect. The ethics committee should make an assessment of the welfare of the child based on considerations of risk, benefit and relationship.

In Chapter 6, I propose a detailed regulatory framework for saviour sibling selection based on the relational decision-making model outlined in this chapter. I do not propose a simple formula for promoting the welfare of the child in this context. This is because 'the notion of an intimate attachment and the corresponding notion of a child's well-being being bound up with another are not precise ideas'.[124] As Nelson points out, 'Recognising that the concerns of intimacy can have a legitimate call upon the way a person lives makes of morality a messier thing, but if that mess were cleaned up, much of significant human value would be lost'.[125]

Notes

1 The 'best interests' of the child is a fundamental principle in international law: Convention on the Rights of the Child, opened for signature 20 November 1989, [1991] ATS 4 (entered into force 2 September 1990). The Convention requires the best interests of the child to be the primary concern of parents and public bodies in all actions concerning children: Arts 3(1), 18(1). The 'best interests' test is also applied by UK and Australian courts exercising inherent *parens patriae* jurisdiction to make orders in respect of children and pursuant to legislation concerning children. See, for example, Children Act 1989 (UK), s 1(1) and Family Law Act 1975 (Cth), s 60A.

2 See, for example, John Hardwig, 'What about the Family?' (1990) 20 *The Hastings Center Report* 5; James Lindemann Nelson, 'Taking Families Seriously' (1992) 22 *The Hastings Center Report* 6; Jeffrey Blustein, 'The Family in Medical Decisionmaking' (1993) 23 *Hastings Center Report* 6. Mark G Kuczewski, 'Reconceiving the Family: The Process of Consent in Medical Decisionmaking' (1996) 26 *The Hastings Center Report* 30. By way of contrast, family-centred medical decision-making models are common in East Asia: see below n 78.

3 For a discussion of the ethical basis of parental duties, see David William Archard, *Children, Family and the State* (Ashgate, 2003), 94.

4 Convention on the Rights of the Child, above n 1. The Convention only comes into effect, however, once a child is born; Ruth McNair, *Outcomes for Children Born of ART in a Diverse Range of Families* (Victorian Law Reform Commission, 2004). The term 'primary goods' is used by Rawls in *A Theory of Justice*, to describe 'things that every rational (person) is presumed to want': John Rawls, *A Theory of Justice* (Oxford University Press, 1971), 62.

5 Lainie Friedman Ross, 'Health Care Decisionmaking by Children: Is it in Their Best Interest?' (1997) 27 *The Hastings Center Report* 41, 49–50.

6 Lainie Friedman Ross, *Children, Families, and Health Care Decision Making* (Clarendon Press, 1998), 49. Ross cites the judgment of Justice White in the US case, *Wisconsin v Yoder*, 406 US 205 (1972), 48–49. The Supreme Court held in this case that Amish parents could remove their children from high school on religious grounds. However, Justice White stressed that a blanket exemption from all schooling would breach parental duties to their children.

7 Archard, above n 3, 96.

8 Ross, above n 6, 43.

9 Ross, above n 6, 49.

10 Ross, above n 6, 49, 50.

11 Ross, above n 6, 50.

12 This was the approach taken by the US Supreme Court in *Yoder* 406 US 205 (1972), above n 6. The Supreme Court was influenced in that case by the fact that Amish parents allow their children to acquire a basic education.

13 Example adapted from G Pennings, R Schots and I Liebaers, 'Ethical Considerations on Preimplantation Genetic Diagnosis for HLA Typing to Match a Future Child as a Donor of Haematopoietic Stem Cells to a Sibling' (2002) 17 *Human Reproduction* 534, 537. For a series of examples in family life where a child might be expected to compromise his/her interests for the sake of a sibling, see James Dwyer and Elizabeth Vig, 'Rethinking Transplantation between Siblings' (1995) 25 *Hastings Center Report* 7, 10.

14 Hilde and James Lindemann Nelson use the phrase 'morality of intimacy': Hilde Lindemann Nelson and James Lindemann Nelson, *The Patient in the Family: An Ethics of Medicine and Families* (Routledge, 1995), 64.

15 Archard, above n 3, 97.

16 Archard, above n 3, 96. Archard describes this as a 'stewardship' account of parenting, as opposed to a proprietarian account of parenting where the child is viewed as the property or extension of the parent: 96–97.

17 Thomas H Murray, *The Worth of a Child* (University of California Press, 1996), 61.

18 Archard, above n 3, 96.

19 I am referring here to a childcare centre, crèche, or daycare nursery.

20 The literature on the childcare debate is vast and beyond the scope of this book. Purported benefits of childcare include stimulation, socialisation, and immunity-building. Purported disadvantages of childcare include an increase in childhood illness, lack of privacy and inflexibility in daily routine. Historically, the main concerns about childcare have arisen out of attachment theory and the work of John Bowlby. See, for example, Steve Biddulph, *Raising Babies: Should Under 3's go to Nursery?* (Harper Thorsons, 2006). However, other studies suggest that good quality childcare is not harmful to child development: Osnat Erel, Yael Oberman and Nurit Yirmiya, 'Maternal versus non-maternal care and seven domains of children's development' (2000) 126 *Psychological Bulletin* 727.

21 Children cared for in the home by parents or extended family may not always be better cared for than children in formal childcare. For example, a parent who is constantly stressed and unable to cope with the demands of a small child or a grandparent, and who puts the child in front of the television for extended hours is not providing optimal care for the child.

22 Nelson and Nelson, above n 14, 68.

23 Ferdinand Schoeman, 'Parental Discretion and Children's Rights: Background and Implications for Medical Decision-Making' (1985) 10 *The Journal of Medicine and Philosophy* 45, 56.

24 Nelson and Nelson, above n 14, 68.

25 Nelson and Nelson, above n 14, 68.

26 Nelson, above n 2, 8.

27 Nelson, above n 2. Nelson argues that families make choices that may not reflect distributive justice or utilitarian principles.

28 Bernard Williams, *Moral Luck: philosophical papers, 1973–1980* (Cambridge University Press, 1981), 18.

29 Schoeman, above n 23, 57.

30 Anne Donchin, 'Autonomy and Interdependence: Quandaries in Genetic Decision Making' in Catriona Mackenzie and Natalie Stoljar (eds), *Relational Autonomy: Feminist Perspectives of Autonomy, Agency, and the Social Self* (Oxford University Press, 2000) 236, 243.

31 These terms are overlapping to some extent. For example, a child conceived solely as a source of body parts is not only exploited and physically abused, but also neglected in the sense that his/her basic need for respect is ignored.

32 Schoeman, above n 23, 58.

33 Sarah Elliston, *The Best Interests of the Child in Healthcare* (Routledge-Cavendish, 2007), 30.

34 Allen E Buchanan and Dan Brock, *Deciding for Others: The Ethics of Surrogate Decision Making* (Cambridge University Press, 1989), 236.

35 Buchanan and Brock, ibid, 235.

36 Ross, above n 6, 41.

37 For a detailed discussion of how the nature of a relationship impacts on whether a child is abused or neglected, see Ross, above n 6, 47–48.

38 See previous Victorian policy on saviour sibling selection: Infertility Treatment Authority (ITA), *Tissue Typing in Conjunction with Preimplantation Genetic Diagnosis* (adopted February 2003, updated January 2004), [2.3].

39 National Health and Medical Research Council (NHMRC), *Ethical Guidelines on the Use of Assisted Reproductive Technology in Clinical Practice and Research 2004 (as revised in 2007 to take into account the changes in legislation)* (June 2007) (NHMRC ART Guidelines), [12.3].

40 See, for example, Australian and New Zealand Infertility Counsellors Association, *Guidelines for Professional Standards of Practice Infertility Counselling* (October 2003) (ANZICA Guidelines), [1.2.2].

41 ANZICA Guidelines, ibid, [1.2.1].

42 Telephone conversation between the author and Rita Alesi (Manager of Counselling Services, Monash IVF) on 17 July 2009.

43 Adrienne Asch and Gail Geller, 'Feminism, Bioethics and Genetics' in Susan M Wolf (ed), *Feminism & Bioethics: Beyond Reproduction* (Oxford University Press, 1996) 318, 341.

44 For a discussion of the importance of ethics consulting in keeping moral space open in health care settings, see Margaret Urban Walker, 'Keeping Moral Space Open: New Images of Ethics Consulting' (1993) 23 *Hastings Center Report* 33.

45 See Chapter 3, section 3.5.3.

46 See discussion at section 5.2.2.

47 Ross, above n 6, 43.

48 Ross, above n 6, Chapter 3, esp 50–52.

49 Ross, above n 6, 119.

50 Ross, above n 6, 112.

51 Ross, above n 6, 83–85. Ross prefers the latter variation as children may face some risks in their everyday lives, with which they may not cope well and to which parents would not intentionally expose them. For example, a child may be bullied at school or a child with cancer may be exposed to regular lumbar punctures. These possibilities would not justify exposing a child to risk of harm commensurate with bullying or a lumbar puncture for non-therapeutic purposes.

52 Ross, above n 6, 113.

53 Ross, above n 6, 29, see also 43, 113.

54 Ross, above n 6, 113.

55 Elliston, above n 33, 257, see also 37–40. Schoeman proposes a similar standard to Elliston by arguing that state intervention be limited to preventing 'imminent and serious harm': Schoeman, above n 23, 60.

56 Elliston, above n 33, 37.

57 Elliston, above n 33, 258.

58 Elliston, above n 33, 260.

59 Elliston, above n 33, 261.

60 Elliston, above n 33, 261.

61 The importance of relationship is implicit in the other tests. For example, Ross argues that parents should be able to consent to a child's participation in intrafamilial donations that entail minimal to a minor increase over minimal risk. Ross contends that such

transplants promote the well-being of the sick child and the well-being of the family as a whole, on which the donor child's well-being depends: Ross, above n 6, 115. Similarly, the second tier of Elliston's test, based on reasonableness, is an attempt to view the assessment of risk within the social context of the family.

62 Dwyer and Vig, above n 13, 11.

63 Dwyer and Vig, above n 13, 11.

64 Lynn A Jansen, 'Child Organ Donation, Family Autonomy, and Intimate Attachments' (2004) 13 *Cambridge Quarterly of Healthcare Ethics* 133, 139.

65 Jansen, ibid, 141.

66 Given that intimate relationships can exist between friends as well as siblings, Jansen argues that 'to restrict child organ donations to siblings would be arbitrary': Jansen, above n 64, 139.

67 Jansen, above n 64, 140.

68 Jansen, above n 64, 134, 140.

69 Elliston, above n 33, 36.

70 Carol Levine, 'Family Caregiving' in *From Birth to Death and Bench to Clinic: The Hastings Bioethics Center Briefing Book for Journalists, Policymakers, and Campaigns* (2008) 63, 65.

71 Nelson, above n 2, 6.

72 Nelson, above n 2, 6. See also Hardwig, above n 2.

73 Roy Gilbar and Ora Gilbar, 'The Medical Decision-Making Process and the Family: The Case of Breast Cancer Patients and their Husbands' (2009) 23 *Bioethics* 183, 185. For a detailed discussion of relational autonomy, see Catriona Mackenzie and Natalie Stoljar (eds), *Relational Autonomy: Feminist Perspectives of Autonomy, Agency, and the Social Self* (Oxford University Press, 2000).

74 Mackenzie and Stoljar, ibid, 4.

75 Gilbar and Gilbar, above n 73, 185.

76 Gilbar and Gilbar, above n 73.

77 Paul Lauritzen, *et al*, 'The Gift of Life and the Common Good: The Need for a Communal Approach to Organ Procurement' (2001) 31 *The Hastings Center Report* 29, 32.

78 For example, a family-centred medical decision-making model is generally preferred by East-Asians and Mexican-Americans: Daniel Fu-Chang Tsai, 'How Should Doctors Approach Patients? A Confucian Reflection on Personhood' (2001) 27 *Journal of Medical Ethics* 44; Leslie J Blackhall, *et al*, 'Ethnicity and Attitudes toward Patient Autonomy' (1995) 274 *Journal of American Medical Association* 820. There are, however, problems associated with family-centred decision-making models in some cultures, particularly patriarchal ones: Edwin Hui, 'Parental Refusal of Life-Saving Treatments for Adolescents: Chinese Familism in Medical Decision-Making Re-Visited' (2008) 22 *Bioethics* 286. The complex relationship between cultural norms and medical decision-making models is beyond the scope of this book.

79 Nelson, above n 2, 10.

80 Kuczewski, above n 2, 30.

81 Kuczewski, above n 2, 30.

82 Hardwig, above n 2.

83 Hardwig argues that 'life, health and freedom from pain and handicapping conditions are extremely important goods for virtually everyone' and are therefore highly significant considerations in all treatment decisions: above n 2, 7.

84 Hardwig, above n 2, 6.

85 Hardwig notes that a third party such as the treating physician need not always convene such conferences: above n 2, 9.

86 Nelson, above n 2, 10.

87 Nelson, above n 2, 11. It is questionable whether a physician can realistically discharge his/her fiduciary duties to the patient, while attempting to objectively mediate family disputes about treatment. Hardwig foreshadowed this dilemma when he stated,

'[p]hysicians are trained to be especially responsive to medical interests and we may well want them to remain that way'. See Hardwig, above n 2, 8.

88 Nelson, above n 2, 11. Nelson stresses that the advocate should represent the patient 'as a person, not simply as a self-interest maximizer'.

89 Nelson, above n 2, 11. Kuczewski argues that the practical outcome of this right of rebuttal means that Nelson's position is virtually identical with Hardwig: Kuczewski, above n 2, 31.

90 Blustein, above n 2, 6. Blustein draws on the work of Jay Katz, who distinguishes between 'choices' and 'thinking about choices': at 12. See Jay Katz, *The Silent World of Doctor and Patient* (Free Press, 1984), 111.

91 Blustein, above n 2, 6.

92 Blustein, above n 2, 11.

93 Blustein, above n 2, 12

94 Blustein, above n 2, 10.

95 Kuczewski, above n 2, 31.

96 Kuczewski, above n 2, 31.

97 Kuczewski, above n 2, 31.

98 Kuczewski, above n 2, 31.

99 Kuczewski, above n 2, 31, 36. This criticism is perhaps less apt for J L Nelson's approach, which recognises the inherent value of intimate families and the attempts to preserve intimate relationships through mediation.

100 Kuczewski, above n 2, 30.

101 Kuczewski, above n 2, 31.

102 Kuczewski, above n 2, 32.

103 Kuczewski, above n 2, 33.

104 Kuczewski, above n 2, 32–33. Kuczewski makes a further distinction between two types of process model. He uses the term 'interpretive model' to describe a situation where the patient already has well-developed values and the physician and family assist the patient in interpreting those values and translating them into preferences and treatment decisions. He uses the term 'deliberative model' to describe the situation where the patient does not have the necessary values relevant to a given case and the physician and family assist the patient in developing new values.

105 Kuczewski acknowledges that there will be cases of unresolvable conflict between a patient (who has developed and stable views) and his/her family, for which a legalistic event-based model is appropriate. However, he argues that this 'either/or' way of thinking has wrongly dominated the debate about the role of family in medical decision-making: above n 2, 36.

106 Kuczewski, above n 2, 34.

107 Kuczewski, above n 2, 34.

108 Kuczewski, above n 2, 34.

109 Kuczewski, above n 2, 36.

110 Kuczewski, above n 2, 35.

111 For a discussion of the 'best interests' approach in the UK and Australia, respectively, see Sarah Elliston, above n 33; and Alastair Nicholson, 'Children's Rights in the Context of Infertility Treatment' (Speech delivered at the Infertility Treatment Authority One Day Symposium, Melbourne, 2 November 2006); Victorian Law Reform Commission (VLRC), *Assisted Reproductive Technology & Adoption*, Final Report (2007) (VLRC Report), 46.

112 Nelson, above n 2, 11.

113 I have assumed, for the purposes of this book, that the existing ill child is agreeable to, and desirous of, a bone marrow transplantation following the birth of a saviour sibling.

114 For a discussion of the importance of open moral space within healthcare institutions generally, see Walker, above n 44. Walker specifically envisages a role for clinical ethicists in guiding this process.

115 Nelson and Nelson, above n 14, 36.

116 Kuczewski, above n 2, 35.

117 For a detailed analysis of why parents are generally well-placed to make treatment decisions of behalf of their children, see Buchanan and Brock, above n 34, 233–34. Buchanan and Brock provide four reasons to support their position: (a) parents care deeply about their children; (b) parents bear the consequences of treatment choices; (c) parents have a right, within limits, to raise their children according to their own standards and values; and (d) family is a valuable social institution, particularly in its role in fostering intimacy, and family members must have significant authority to carry out their roles as carers.

118 A current UK study suggests that ART counsellors have concerns about the nature of their role in 'welfare of the child' assessments: Ellie Lee, Jan Macvarish and Sally Sheldon, 'Assessing Child Welfare under the Human Fertilisation and Embryology Act: The New Law: Summary of Findings' (University of Kent, September 2012) <http://blogs.kent.ac.uk/parentingculturestudies/files/2012/06/Summary_Assessing-Child-Welfare-final.pdf> (accessed 24 April 2013). This reinforces the need to clearly articulate the purpose and role of counselling in the decision-making process through regulation.

119 The complex debate about non-directive counselling is beyond the scope of this book. For a detailed discussion of the nature of non-directive genetic counselling and the problems it raises, see Jon Weil, *et al*, 'The Relationship of Nondirectiveness to Genetic Counselling: Report of a Workshop at the 2003 NSGC Annual Education Conference' (2006) 15 *Journal of Genetic Counseling* 85; Clare Williams, Priscilla Alderson and Bobbie Farsides, 'Is Nondirectiveness Possible within the Context of Antenatal Screening and Testing?' (2002) 54 *Social Sciences & Medicine* 339; Glyn Elwyn, Jonathon Gray and Angus Clarke, 'Shared Decision Making and Non-Directiveness in Genetic Counselling' (2000) 37 *Journal of Medical Genetics* 135.

120 For a detailed discussion of the role of 'discourse ethics' in medical decision-making, see Janet Farrell Smith, 'Communicative Ethics in Medicine: The Physician-Patient Relationship' in Susan M Wolf (ed), *Feminism & Bioethics: Beyond Reproduction* (Oxford University Press, 1996), 184. See also David J Casarett, Frona Daskal and John Lantos, 'The Authority of the Clinical Ethicist' (1998) 28 *Hastings Center Report* 6. These commentators draw on Habermas' theory of 'discourse ethics' to formulate a model of clinical ethics consultation that focuses on consensus: Jürgen Habermas, *Moral Consciousness and Communicative Action* (MIT Press, 1990).

121 Walker, above n 44, 39–40. See also Casarett, Daskal and Lantos, ibid, 8–9.

122 Walker, above n 44, 33.

123 For a discussion of some of the problems associated with clinical ethics committees, see Shiela McLean, 'Clinical Ethics Committees, Due Process and the Right to a Fair Hearing' (2008) 15 *Journal of Law and Medicine* 520; Daniel Sokol, 'The Unpalatable Truth about Ethics Committees' (2009) 339 *British Medical Journal* 891.

124 Jansen, above n 64, 139.

125 Nelson, above n 2, 9.

6   Regulating saviour sibling selection

6.1 Introduction

A key feature of the relational model for selective reproduction I proposed in Chapter 5 is that the interests of family members are taken into account in connection with the interests of the child to be born. This chapter explores how regulation might support this relational model. I focus specifically on saviour sibling selection in order to 'map out' a relational framework for regulation in this area. While other controversial forms of selective reproduction are currently prohibited in the UK and Australia, saviour sibling selection is regulated in both countries by legislation and/or policy guidelines. I discuss how a relational framework for regulating saviour sibling selection differs from the existing 'harm-based' and 'best interest' models that exist in the UK and Australia, respectively, and could lead to different decisions to those made under current UK and Australian regulation.

I begin in section 6.2 by addressing a preliminary question about whether selective reproduction should be regulated at all. I argue that the state plays an important role in regulating selective reproduction under a relational model. Regulation can improve the decision-making process and protect the child to be born from exploitation, abuse and neglect. I briefly explore different regulatory models in section 6.3 before outlining some key general features of a relational framework for saviour sibling selection. Lastly, in section 6.4, I highlight the similarities and differences between my proposed relational framework and the existing frameworks in the UK and Australia for saviour sibling selection. In particular, my relational framework aims to provide a less restrictive and more nuanced approach to decision-making in the complex area of selective reproduction.

6.2 Should we regulate selective reproduction?

In Chapter 5, I argued that a relational model for selective reproduction could assist prospective parents in deciding whether or not to use PGD to select a child with specific genetic traits. I also proposed a threshold level of protection from commodification and harm for the child to be born. In this section,

I build on these findings to argue that selective reproduction should be regulated. First, regulation can *support* patients by ensuring they receive adequate information, counselling and ethical guidance in the decision-making process. Second, retaining the welfare of the child provision (in a modified form) can *protect* the child to be born from exploitation, abuse and neglect. I begin by exploring the purpose of regulating assisted reproduction generally, before concentrating on the regulation of selective reproduction.

6.2.1 Regulating assisted reproduction

The term 'regulation' has a 'bewildering variety of meanings'[1] and can denote a vast array of different controls. According to the public interest theory of regulation, regulatory intervention is justified where there is likely to be market failure in achieving public interest goals.[2] In the area of medicine and healthcare, the vulnerability of patients and information asymmetries justify regulation in some form. Medical practitioners in the UK and Australia are regulated by a combination of legislation, professional guidelines and common law principles.[3] Fertility specialists in the UK and Australia are regulated over and above the legal and ethical restraints on medical practitioners generally. Brazier has observed, with some scepticism, that '(r)eproductive medicine is singled out as special, as a part of medicine of such particular social concern and significance that the state should have a direct stake in its evolution'.[4] In this section, I explore whether the 'special' nature of assisted reproduction justifies regulation beyond that which already applies to the medical profession.

Advancements in assisted reproductive technology have raised a plethora of ethical and legal questions, which cannot easily be ignored. According to Brownsword, there is 'little virtue in leaving genetics to the play of subjective preference and the market'.[5] Regulation in the UK and Australia has, however, focused on a limited sector of reproductive medicine involving IVF and related technologies. According to Brazier, '(r)egulation of reproductive medicine remains partial and selective'.[6] Skene similarly points out that in Australia there are many areas of reproductive medicine that are not specifically regulated.[7] For example, a woman can take contraception to prevent the birth of a child, undergo surgical sterilisation, have a sterilisation reversed, repair her fallopian tubes to assist conception and inseminate herself with donor sperm, all free of legislative interference.[8]

The selective or random nature of regulation within reproductive medicine is arguably unjustified. In some areas of reproductive medicine there may be stronger reasons for regulation than there are for IVF, based on the prevention of harm. For example, Brazier has observed that self-insemination using fresh sperm carries risk to the woman of HIV or other sexually transmitted disease that is not present for IVF.[9] Inconsistencies within the regulatory landscape for reproductive medicine do not, however, undermine legitimate reasons for regulating assisted reproduction. In fact, the justifications for regulating assisted reproduction may well support a broader regulatory net over reproductive medicine.[10] There is significant support for state involvement in assisted reproduction. According to Szoke, the state plays an important role in resolving any conflicts which may exist over reproductive technologies and 'formalising an expression of the public interest'.[11] Cannold and Gillam similarly argue for the legitimacy of state involvement in regulating assisted reproductive treatments:

> ... the state has an obligation to protect the interests of its citizens and regulation is a legitimate method of achieving this. It is possible that ART can be practised in ways that threaten the interests of at least some citizens and so, in principle, it is ethically permissible for the state to regulate in such situations.[12]

Various justifications have been given for regulating assisted reproduction, reflecting concern for patients, doctors, the embryo, the child to be born, the expenditure of public funds and general standards of morality.[13] Johnson suggests a narrower role for regulation. He argues that, as a broad principle, 'regulation should be restricted to the *support* of those who should be capable of making an informed decision and to the *protection* of those incapable of protecting themselves'.[14] In the context of assisted reproduction, regulation should therefore support patients seeking treatment and protect those who may be born as a result. Savulescu takes a similar approach to ART regulation when he states that 'we should consider the vulnerable and consider the children by balancing the risks and benefits'.[15] I propose three broad justifications for regulating assisted reproduction: (a) quality control; (b) respect for the embryo; and (c) protection of the child to be born. These justifications are consistent with the regulatory parameters for ART proposed by Johnson and Savulescu.

The first reason for regulating assisted reproduction is to support patients seeking treatment by controlling the quality of ART services. Quality control is integral to public confidence in ART services. An independent report in New Zealand on preimplantation genetic diagnosis stated that:

> [e]nsuring that the health and safety of both the persons accessing fertility services and the embryos produced as a result of assisted reproductive procedures are protected to the highest standard possible is a major factor in gaining public confidence in any regulatory framework.[16]

Regulation can ensure high standards of treatment within clinics through inspection and quality assurance requirements.[17] A regulatory framework that imposes standards and accreditation requirements can protect patients from some of the health risks associated with ART and prevent their exploitation by 'maverick doctors' or their abuse by 'rank amateurs'.[18] Quality control can, and should, extend beyond ensuring high technical standards within clinics to establishing a supported decision-making process, with adequate information, counselling and ethical guidance.

The second justification for regulating ART, respect for the embryo, lies at the heart of the regulation of assisted reproduction in the UK.[19] In 1984, the Warnock Committee determined that the embryo had a special status, entitling it to 'some protection in law'.[20] The Warnock Committee adopted a gradualist approach to the developing moral status of the embryo in order to reconcile reproductive liberty with some level of protection for the embryo.[21] The gradualist approach allows specific infertility treatment to be carried out, subject to careful evaluation of the reasons for the creation and use of embryos in respect of the treatment. The STC in the UK reaffirmed the gradualist approach in its 2005 Report, concluding that ART remains a legitimate interest of the state.[22]

Protecting the welfare of the child to be born is the third justification for regulating assisted reproduction. As discussed in Chapter 3, the welfare of the child to be born is a key feature in UK and Australian regulation. According to a liberal theory of law, regulation that restricts individual activity is justified to prevent harm to others. This can be traced back to John Stuart Mill who stated that 'the only purpose for which power can be rightfully exercised over any member of a civilised community, against his will, is to prevent harm to others'.[23] In a liberal democracy, the state is therefore justified in placing limits on reproductive liberty in order to prevent harm to the child to be born, particularly given that the child is incapable of protecting him/herself. However, as Gavaghan points out, 'the concept of "harm" is not as straightforward as Mill ... perhaps assumed, and it is especially problematic in relation to "genesis" questions, that is, decisions about who should be born'.[24] Furthermore, it is possible that the child to be born may be 'wronged' even though he/she is not strictly 'harmed'. In response to Kantian concerns about commodification, state intervention may be justified to ensure that any child to be born as a result of ART is not treated 'simply as a means', whether or not the child can be said to be harmed.[25] The dilemma of how far the state should regulate assisted reproduction to protect the welfare of the child to be born can be approached on the basis that 'any intervention into reproductive choice must have a sound ethical basis and also take into account evidence of harm to children or to society'.[26]

6.2.2 Regulating selective reproduction

The justifications for regulating assisted reproduction apply to selective reproductive treatments involving PGD. There are, however, two key reasons for specifically regulating selective reproduction, which arise out of the discussion in Chapter 5.

First, regulation can improve the decision-making process, not only for patients contemplating selective reproduction, but also for members of the healthcare team assisting them. This reason falls within the first justification for assisted reproduction – quality control. In Chapter 5, I highlighted the importance of the decision-making process in dealing with the individual and collective interests that exist within a family. I argued that the various interests within a family seeking PGD should be considered within an 'open moral space'. Clinicians, counsellors and ethicists play key roles in promoting a supporting collaborative and constructive environment in which ethically complex and emotionally charged decisions about selective reproduction can be made. Regulation should outline the various roles of treating healthcare professionals involved in PGD to ensure that patients receive adequate information, counselling and ethical guidance when making treatment decisions. By promoting transparent processes through clear protocols, regulation provides a basis for effective and efficient decision-making. It also enables practice to develop in accordance with clearly established principles, which ensures greater consistency in decisions and builds a common foundation for future cases.

Second, regulation can protect the child to be born from exploitation, abuse and neglect. This reason falls within the third justification for assisted reproduction – protecting the welfare of the child to be born. As discussed in Chapter 2, there are potential risks of physical harm associated with the embryo biopsy process and ART generally. There are also additional risks of harm associated with particular types of selection. For example, there is a potential risk of psychosocial harm to saviour siblings associated with being selected as a donor for an existing child. Saviour sibling selection also involves a future risk of physical harm to the donor child if peripheral blood or bone marrow donations are required at a later date. There is currently insufficient evidence to suggest that either the physical or psychosocial harm that may be caused by saviour sibling selection is of a level that constitutes exploitation, abuse or neglect. Further empirical evidence may, however, reveal otherwise. Significantly, there are no longitudinal studies of the long-term physical and psychosocial impacts on saviour siblings. Regulation should safeguard the welfare of the child to be born in order to protect the child from any risk that may be revealed in future studies. Given the lack of empirical evidence in this area, regulation should therefore facilitate further longitudinal research into the long-term risks to the child born as a result of PGD. This could be achieved through a nationally coordinated system for monitoring the effects on children born using PGD.

There is also the risk, which I discussed in Chapter 2, that certain types of selection may commodify the child to be born. The concern about commodification is frequently raised in the debate about saviour siblings, who might potentially be brought into existence solely as a means to saving the life of an existing child. The state should protect the child to be born against the unlikely but possible scenario where parents want another child to act, in effect, as a 'tissue farm' for an existing sibling. There are already common law and legislative protections in relation to ongoing tissue donation in the UK and Australia, which I outlined in Chapter 3.[27] These protections should minimise any harm to saviour siblings associated with future tissue donations. However, as mentioned in Chapter 2, it is possible that a child may still be commodified even if he/she is not ultimately harmed.[28] The fact that the parents intend to have another child purely as a source of tissue is sufficient to warrant state involvement to prevent the child being treated by his/her parents as a commodity. Parents should not be assisted in conceiving a child solely as a commodity if, for example, counselling reveals that the parents have no genuine desire to care for their new child and intend to treat the child as a 'tissue farm' (whether or not they are likely to be successful in this pursuit).

6.2.3 *Welfare of the child principle*

As discussed in Chapter 3, the welfare of the child principle is entrenched in Australian and UK ART legislation through the welfare of the child provision.[29] However, some commentators are cynical about the role of the welfare principle in assisted reproduction. According to Brazier, the welfare provision in UK legislation has essentially been used to protect the child to be born by restricting access to ART.[30] Walker similarly argues that the welfare provision in Victorian legislation is vague and its application has led, in the past, to discrimination.[31] Other commentators contend that the welfare of the child principle should not be relied on as a justification for interfering with an individual's reproductive liberty.[32]

In this book, I argue that the welfare of the child provision should be retained in ART legislation but the focus of regulation should shift from 'gate-keeping' to one that genuinely assists families as a whole. The relational approach I propose in Chapter 4 reconceptualises the welfare of the child to clearly embrace the collective interests a child shares with his/her family as well as the child's individual interests. The relational model for selective reproduction I propose in Chapter 5 places a strong emphasis on information, counselling and ethical guidance to enable patients seeking PGD to reach an informed decision for their family, including the child to be born. According to my relational model, it is the clinic rather than Parliament or the offices of a statutory body through which individual decisions about the welfare of a child within a family should be made. Such decisions ought to be made on a case-by-case basis, within a commonly accepted framework of parameters set down in legislation and more detailed policy guidelines. A case-by-case approach means that guidelines can evolve as new information and evidence surfaces and not remain static, as legislation tends to be.

A relational model for selective reproduction achieves two distinct regulatory goals. First, it enhances quality control in a broad sense. It not only assists prospective parents in deciding whether or not to use PGD, but also assists healthcare practitioners to support the parents in making their decision. Second, it promotes the welfare of the child to be born by protecting the child from exploitation, abuse and neglect. In response to the critique by some liberal justice theorists that reproduction is private and no business of the state,[33] a relational model for selective reproduction can be seen as enhancing parental choice by supporting prospective parents throughout the decision-making process. In section 6.3, I map out a relational framework for regulating saviour sibling selection that aims to navigate parents through the ethical minefield of saviour sibling selection whilst protecting the child to be born from exploitation, abuse and neglect.

6.3 A relational framework for regulating saviour sibling selection

Selective reproduction affects the interests of not only the child to be born but also the child's parents and any existing children within the family. Saviour sibling selection is a good example of how the various interests within a family may both align and conflict. The relational framework outlined here focuses on saviour sibling selection but could be adapted to apply to other forms of selective reproduction as they become available. Of the different regulatory models that might be used to implement a relational framework for regulating selective reproduction, I have chosen a permissive regulatory model.

6.3.1 *Different regulatory models*

Currently, a range of models on the regulatory spectrum operate in the area of assisted reproduction in the UK and Australia, some of which are more prescriptive than others. The licensing model in the UK confers considerable discretion on the HFEA within a relatively permissive legislative framework. By way of contrast, legislation in the State of Victoria is more prescriptive,[34] with criminal sanctions imposed on medical practitioners who fail to comply with their statutory obligations. There is also considerable variation between Australian states and territories. For example, the 'criminal model' in Victoria can be contrasted against the 'professional model' operating in NSW.[35] Legislation in the State of NSW has been described as 'light touch'[36] as it aims to complement the national system of professional regulation. ART physicians in Australia must follow the national guidelines on ART established by the NHMRC (NHMRC ART Guidelines), which leave 'a large amount of discretion' to clinics.[37] ART services in the UK and the various jurisdictions within Australia are regulated by legislation, policy guidelines or a combination of both.

Different regulatory models have their own advantages and disadvantages. Permissive regulatory frameworks may offer greater flexibility than prescriptive models but can lack predictability and consistency, leading to regulatory uncertainty.[38] In some jurisdictions, the regulatory model may also be influenced by constitutional factors. For example, Australia is a federation of states and territories, and constitutional limitations on the legislative power of the Commonwealth Parliament make national legislation in the area of assisted reproduction difficult to achieve.[39] Some commentators have suggested that national guidelines are more appropriate for regulating ART services in Australia than legislation, which varies from state to state.[40] A national approach arguably reduces regulatory duplication, ensures common ethical standards, prevents 'reproductive tourism' between states[41] and improves national data collection for longitudinal studies on the welfare of the child who is born. It is possible for Australian states and territories to cede responsibility for ART regulation to the Commonwealth.[42] However, as current debate in Australia involving national healthcare, hospitals and education reveals, this is a solution fraught with difficulty, not least because political allegiances at state and federal levels seldom align.[43]

The complex regulatory analysis required to evaluate the 'continuum of regulatory options'[44] that exist for ART treatments is beyond the scope of this book. The focus here is to establish a relational framework for regulating saviour sibling selection that could be implemented through legislation and/or policy guidelines in various countries. For present purposes, I base my relational framework on a permissive regulatory model that includes both legislation and policy guidelines. Brownsword contrasts 'hard law' legislation with 'soft law' guidelines or codes of practice and argues that, paradoxically, compliance may be improved by soft, as opposed to hard, law.[45] However, because 'soft law' regimes lack formal monitoring mechanisms, soft law works best when it operates 'in the shadow of a ... harder law regime'.[46] A balance must be struck between clarity and flexibility in regulating selective reproduction. Legislation, which is subject to the rigours of parliamentary debate, can establish broad guiding principles and determine boundaries to protect the public interest in relation to issues 'of major community concern'.[47] Policy guidelines can then operate at a lower level to provide more detailed guidance on specific forms of selective reproduction, such as saviour sibling selection. A major benefit of guidelines is that they can be detailed, practical, flexible and responsive to technological developments and changing community concerns.[48] In other words, guidelines can evolve more easily as practice develops. Guidelines can also be formulated and amended by informed specialists outside the orbit of parliament and political agendas.

It is important that policy guidelines are made in a transparent manner, by a body with sufficient expertise, and with an opportunity for input from key stakeholders. As discussed in Chapter 2, the HFEA, a UK statutory authority, was criticised for its lack of transparency and consistency in developing policy on saviour sibling selection and the welfare of the child. Concerns were also raised about the HFEA's expertise and ability to make ethical decisions, given its lay membership.[49] Lastly, the HFEA's dual roles as regulator and policymaker have been described by some as incompatible and leading to ad hoc decision-making.[50] The purpose and role of the HFEA recently came under scrutiny, as part of the UK Government's review of arm's length bodies in the health area, although the government opted to retain the HFEA.[51] Another option is to confer policy-making on a specialist advisory committee. Specialist advisory committees are sometimes criticised for being 'talking shops', expensive bureaucracies or extremely politicised.[52] However, these concerns can be addressed by clearly defining the role of the committee, embedding their policies within the regulatory scheme, and removing political control over appointments.[53] An example of an effective national advisory committee is the Australian Health Ethics Committee (AHEC), a Principal Committee of the NHMRC, with expertise in philosophy, clinical medical practice and nursing, disability, law, religion and health consumer issues.[54] The AHEC formulated the NMHRC ART Guidelines in Australia, which regulate ART in all Australian states and territories except to the extent they are inconsistent with state legislation.

A regulatory regime that aims to influence behaviour has three core elements: standards; processes for monitoring compliance with those standards; and mechanisms for enforcing the standards.[55] The relational framework proposed in this chapter focuses on standards to improve the decision-making process for selective reproduction and protect the welfare of the child to be born. It is important, however, to mention briefly how these standards might be monitored and enforced. To ensure compliance with the regulatory scheme, legislation should impose auditing, reporting and monitoring requirements on ART clinics with appropriate sanctions for non-compliance. One way in which the threshold level of protection for the child to be born could be enforced is by creating an offence for clinicians to engage in any form of ART where the child to be born is at risk of abuse, neglect or exploitation. Another is to suspend the operation of the contravening ART clinic. In addition to these measures, clinicians could be required to undergo additional training and education on the welfare of the child. Independent annual auditing by a professional body such as the Royal College of Obstetricians and Gynaecologists or British Fertility Society in the UK or the Fertility Society of Australia, would further enhance compliance and transparency. Compliance with the standards imposed in legislation and policy guidelines should be linked to accreditation, in a similar way to the NHMRC ART Guidelines in Australia.[56]

An additional element of ethical oversight can be provided through clinical ethics consultation. I propose two separate stages of ethical oversight in my relational model for selective reproduction. First, a clinical ethicist should provide ethics counselling to assist patients in the decision-making process. Second, a separately constituted CEC should independently review complex cases, such as saviour sibling selection, to ensure that they comply with the ethical criteria set out in legislation and policy guidelines. In Australia, clinics must currently seek advice from a CEC (or relevant state or territory regulatory authority) when requested to provide PGD for saviour sibling selection, although the role of the CEC is not authoritative.[57] Clinical ethics consultation is an integral part of my proposed regulatory framework for selective reproduction and requires some further clarification.

6.3.2 *Clinical ethics consultation*

The two stages of ethical oversight in my relational model represent different forms of clinical ethics consultation – one advisory (ethics counselling) and the other more authoritative (ethics review). One of the key problems raised in relation to clinical ethics consultation services is the lack of clarity about their precise role and function.[58] It is therefore necessary to clarify the different roles I envisage for clinical ethics consultation services in the decision-making process for selective reproduction.

At the first stage of ethical oversight, a clinical ethicist working within the healthcare team should provide *ethics counselling* to assist patients in deciding whether to select a particular embryo using PGD. Clinical ethics consultation is becoming more common in the area of healthcare, particularly in the US[59] and, more recently, the UK.[60] Some hospitals in Australia offer clinical ethics consultation services, although these services are currently more *ad hoc* than their US and UK counterparts.[61] In the UK and Australia, clinical ethics consultations more commonly occur with clinicians than patients or family members.[62] This is understandable given that clinical ethics consultation services have generally developed in response to the need of clinicians involved in ethically complex cases.[63] Ethics counselling for patients seeking selective reproductive treatments and their families is, however, an essential element of the relational model outlined in Chapter 5.

I propose that a clinical ethics consultant[64] work alongside the ART physician and counsellor to help patients and direct family members navigate their way through the complex ethical questions that arise in relation to selective reproduction. The clinical ethicist should facilitate moral deliberation and consensus using 'discourse ethics' rather than act as an expert moral authority or arbiter in cases of discord. Where consensus is not achievable, the clinical ethics consultant should assist by mediating any disputes that arise and helping patients, any existing children, and members of the healthcare team to engage meaningfully in the decision-making process. The ethics consultant should also ensure that the interests of the child to be born are given adequate consideration.[65] The ethics consultant should not make a decision for patients, but help to inform and guide patients to make a decision within the framework of policy guidelines discussed earlier.

Once patients have made a decision to proceed with PGD, a second stage of *ethics review* of the decision should be promptly carried out in ethically complex cases, such as saviour sibling selection, by a separately constituted CEC.[66] In contrast to ethics counselling, the CEC would have a decision-making role at the ethics review stage and would focus more on the welfare of the child to be born than the interests of the patients seeking treatment. An authoritative role for CECs in assisted reproduction is consistent with the recommendation by the VLRC in Australia that CECs should be more than an advisory body in complex ART cases and should have a decision-making capacity.[67] The CEC's objective would be to ensure that the welfare of the child is given due consideration in accordance with relevant ART regulation by routinely reviewing decisions to proceed with saviour sibling selection. Upon review, a CEC should refuse treatment if it is of the view that the child to be born is at risk of abuse, neglect or exploitation based on criteria set out in policy guidelines and in accordance with guiding principles in relevant ART legislation. A CEC should also refer decisions to proceed with treatment back to the clinic for further consideration in cases where, in the opinion of the CEC, the process has been so flawed that the patients cannot have made a fully informed decision.

Currently, in the UK and Australia, CECs have what has been described as an 'advisory or informal' rather than a 'decision-making' role.[68] In the context of assisted reproduction, the Australian NHMRC ART Guidelines specifically require clinics considering applications for saviour sibling selection to seek *advice* from a CEC but the decision to proceed ultimately rests with individual clinics.[69] By way of contrast, in the US there has been increased judicial support for conferring a decision-making role on CECs to enable them to resolve 'complex and sensitive issues in health care'.[70] A more authoritative role for CECs would directly impact on patient's rights to access assisted reproductive treatment. It is therefore important to ensure that safeguards are in place to ensure that the decision-making process is transparent, consistent and accords procedural fairness to patients. McLean emphasises the importance of appropriate skills mix on CECs and due process in the way they conduct their proceedings.[71]

In terms of skills, a properly constituted CEC should have the appropriate expertise to assess the welfare of the child in the context of assisted reproduction.[72] This would require members from a variety of disciplines, including assisted reproductive medicine, law, ethics and child psychology and/or psychiatry. Members should be provided with ongoing training and support to ensure they fully understand and operate within the regulatory framework for ART and competently engage with clinical ethical issues. Currently, there is a lack of guidance and support for CECs in the UK and Australia in contrast to human research ethics committees (HRECs). Unlike HRECs, CECs are a hospital-driven phenomenon and are not subject to the same level of regulation. A national framework for CECs should therefore be established, setting out their membership, procedures and reporting requirements, to ensure fair and consistent decision-making by CECs at a national level.

To ensure due process and transparency in decision-making, CECs should provide a statement of reasons in support of their decision upon request. There should also be some form of independent evaluation of the decision-making processes of CECs for quality control purposes. Lastly, decisions by a CEC to refuse treatment should be subject to review by an independent decision-making body within the traditional legal framework, such as a specialist review panel, tribunal or court of law.[73] Review by a CEC of ethically complex decisions about selective reproduction is more appropriate at first instance than external review by a panel, court or tribunal, which is likely to be more formal, time-consuming, and removed from the clinical setting. Ideally, all clinics offering selective reproduction should have recourse to a regional CEC. A local CEC has benefits over a national ethics committee[74] because it is closer to the clinical setting and able to make decisions that reflect the circumstances of individual cases.[75] The value in localised CECs lies in their ability to 'provide support that is responsive and relevant to local circumstances'.[76] CECs should rely on information provided by all participants involved in the treatment decision, including patients. The healthcare team should provide a detailed report to the regional CEC, providing the background to and reasons for treatment decisions. Where any member of the healthcare team is concerned that the child to be born is at risk of exploitation, abuse or neglect, he/she should provide details of the concerns in the team's report to the CEC. Patients should be given an opportunity to respond to concerns raised to 'ensure that the patient's voice is heard, that she can participate fully in treatment decisions, exercise her decisional authority, and challenge those who oppose her'.[77]

Given the relative infancy of CECs in the UK and Australia, significant structural and procedural reforms are needed if CECs are to engage in ethics review of selective reproductive decisions. These reforms are warranted as clinical decision-making becomes increasingly ethically complex, particularly in cases involving beginning and end of life decisions. The potential lack of independence by ART clinicians who feel sympathetic to their patients provides a strong argument for the involvement of CECs in the decision-making process. As some commentators point out, 'there is a residual unease amongst doctors' in assessing the welfare of the child in the context of ART.[78] This concern has been echoed by the STC in the UK and the VLRC in Australia. For instance, the medical director of a UK infertility clinic submitted to the STC that '[i]t is possible for us clinicians in particular to become so "wrapped up" in what we perceive to be best for the couple that we do not see the wider picture'.[79] A recent empirical study of UK ART clinics confirms that staff continue to struggle with the small number of 'difficult cases' they experience.[80] Similarly, in Australia, the VLRC consultation process revealed that clinics encounter cases where they are unsure about a particular risk to a child to be born.[81] In addition to ethics review, CECs can also play an educative role by disseminating policy guidelines in a manner that can be easily digested and applied by individual clinics. As Doyal has pointed out, 'CECs can play a valuable role in disseminating national guidance, which has been presented in long documents and may not be readily assimilated by busy clinicians'.[82]

6.3.3 Outline of regulatory framework

In Chapter 5, I proposed some general features of a relational model for selective reproduction. In order to support this relational model, regulation should perform three main functions. First, *clear guidance* is needed on the availability of controversial treatments, such as saviour sibling selection, and the various individual and shared interests within a family that may be affected. Second, regulation should establish a *collaborative decision-making process* to manage individual and shared interests within families, which may not necessarily coincide. Third, regulation should provide a *threshold level of protection for the child to be born*. For ease of reference, I refer to the general features of my relational model from Chapter 5 that correlate with each of these three main functions. My relational framework includes a combination of hard law (legislation) and soft law (policy guidelines) initiatives to achieve these goals in the context of saviour sibling selection. Although my proposed framework focuses on saviour sibling selection, many of the elements could be adapted for other controversial types of selection in the future.

6.3.3.1 Guidance on saviour sibling selection and the interests at stake

'A relational model requires consideration of the interests of all family members, not just those of the child to be born'

Past experience in the UK provides a good example of the problems that can arise when a parliament fails to engage fully with the ethical debate about new reproductive technologies. The Hashmi and Whitaker cases discussed in Chapter 2 highlighted a need for the UK Parliament to legislate specifically on saviour sibling selection to avoid inconsistent decision-making by the HFEA and legal challenge. There are compelling reasons for the availability of new and controversial reproductive technologies to be addressed by parliaments through democratic debate rather than by the courts. Brownsword argues that judicial determinations on new assisted reproductive technologies raise problems of incrementalism in the regulation of ART, lack of institutional accountability and regulatory uncertainty.[83] ART legislation should therefore clearly sanction controversial applications of PGD that are to be allowed, such as saviour sibling selection, as is now the case in the UK.

A relational model for selective reproduction should also be endorsed in ART legislation through guiding principles that clearly articulate the various interests at stake. In particular, guiding principles should require treatment decisions to involve consideration of the individual interests of the child to be born, the prospective parents and any existing siblings as well as the collective interests of the family as a whole.

More detailed guidance on the specific nature of the various family interests that may be relevant to specific types of selection should be contained in policy guidelines, which can be developed as new applications of PGD arise. Policy guidelines on saviour sibling selection should include the following relevant interests:

(a) The future interests of the child to be born in being treated with respect and protected from harm.
(b) The interests of the parents in saving the life of their existing child and in having another child.
(c) The interests of the ill child in receiving a bone marrow transplant and having a sibling.
(d) The interests of any other siblings who will be affected by the decision.
(e) The collective interests of the family as a whole in the life and health of each of its members.

6.3.3.2 A collaborative decision-making process

'A "process model" is preferable to a conflict-based model for managing individual and collective interests within a family'

'The decision-making process should openly and respectfully explore the family's values, beliefs and preferences as these are relevant to the welfare of the child to be born'

'The roles of prospective parents and members of the healthcare team (physician, counsellor and clinical ethicist) should be clearly outlined'

The relational model proposed in Chapter 5 reflects a modified collaborative decision-making process for dealing with the various interests within a family. It devolves treatment decisions to patients in consultation with their health-care team, subject to approval by a CEC in ethically complex cases. In cases where there are no concerns by the healthcare team about the welfare of the child to be born, treatment decisions should be made by the prospective parents in consultation with their healthcare team in accordance with guiding principles in ART legislation and relevant policy guidelines. In ethically complex cases, such as saviour sibling selection, legislation should require clinics to refer treatment decisions to a CEC for review.

This decision-making model enhances and supports reproductive choice, allows decisions to be made on a case-by-case basis according to individual circumstances, and ensures that the welfare of the child to be born is adequately protected. Legislation should endorse a relational model for selective reproduction through its guiding principles by specifying that the interests of the child to be born must be considered in connection with, rather than in opposition to, the interests of his/her family. More detailed guidance on the decision-making process should be contained in policy guidelines, the focus of which should be to improve decision-making so that prospective parents can make informed and ethically reasoned decisions.

To enable parents to make genuinely informed and reasoned decisions about saviour sibling selection within a supported environment, policy guidelines should outline the following features of the decision-making process:

(a) Treatment decisions should be made by parents in consultation with their healthcare team, which should consist of an ART physician, counsellor and clinical ethicist.
(b) Where appropriate, all existing children should be given an opportunity to contribute to the discussion about selective reproduction.
(c) It is reasonable for parents to make decisions that take account of the needs of all their children.
(d) Individual and collective family interests should be explored in a supportive environment that promotes the intimate nature of family.
(e) The values, beliefs and preferences of all family members should be discussed in a non-judgemental manner, within an 'open moral space'.
(f) The healthcare team should provide and discuss information with sensitivity to cultural diversity and religious beliefs.
(g) Where there is a difference of opinion between family members about treatment, a 'discourse ethics' approach should be taken to resolve potential conflicts wherever possible.
(h) Where there is entrenched conflict between family members, an attempt should be made to settle the conflict through mediation, although the parents should ultimately make the treatment decision.

Policy guidelines should also clearly outline the respective roles of the prospective parents and members of the healthcare team (ART physician, counsellor and clinical ethicist) in the decision-making process. The following roles are tailored to saviour sibling selection:

(i) *Parents* seeking saviour sibling selection should actively contribute to a determination about the welfare of the child to be born.
(j) The *healthcare team* should assist parents in determining whether or not to proceed with saviour sibling selection by providing relevant information, counselling and ethical guidance to parents and, where appropriate, existing children within the family.
(k) Where any member of the healthcare team is of the opinion that the child to be born is at risk of exploitation, abuse or neglect, the member should outline his/her concerns in detail to the regional CEC.
(l) The *ART physician* should provide parents and any existing children involved in the decision-making process with relevant information on saviour sibling selection, including:[84]

- information about the tissue typing tests required;
- the latest evidence about any risk associated with ART and embryo biopsy;
- the likely success rates for conceiving a direct tissue match;
- the likely success rates for achieving a successful outcome for the existing child;
- the likely impact of saviour sibling selection on all family members; and
- all other treatment options for the existing sibling.

(m) The *counsellor* should support parents and any children involved in the decision-making process by:[85]

- exploring the motivation of parents seeking a saviour sibling;
- addressing the implications of undergoing treatment for parents, their existing children and any child born as a result;
- providing personal and emotional support to parents and any existing child who is likely to be affected by a decision to select a saviour sibling;
- encouraging parents and existing children to develop realistic expectations about treatment outcomes;
- promoting discussion about appropriate coping strategies in the event that the saviour sibling is ultimately unsuccessful in curing the existing ill child; and
- advising parents about additional services and support networks that are available.

(n) The *clinical ethicist* should provide ethics counselling throughout the decision-making process by:

- assisting all family members to explore their own preferences, values and beliefs in the context of saviour sibling selection;
- facilitating moral deliberation and consensus through 'discourse ethics'; and
- where consensus is not achieved, mediating any disputes that arise.

6.3.3.3 A threshold level of protection for the child to be born

'Guidance should be given as to how the welfare of the child to be born is likely to be adversely affected by selective reproduction'

'Complex decisions should be subject to independent review to ensure that the welfare of the child to be born has been given due consideration'

'Decisions about selective reproduction should be recorded and clinics should attempt to monitor the long-term effects on children born as a result'

Lastly, ART regulation should establish a clear threshold level of protection to the child to be born, who is incapable of asserting him/her own interests. Instead of containing a vague reference to the welfare of the child, legislation should specify clear limits on assisted reproductive treatments to protect the welfare of the child to be born. A 'minimum welfare' approach should be adopted, similar to current HFEA policy, which creates a presumption in favour of treatment unless the child to be born is at risk of exploitation, abuse or neglect.

Legislation should expressly prohibit PGD in cases where there is a risk of exploitation, abuse or neglect and establish broad criteria for determining when such a risk exists. Based on the threshold level of protection proposed in Chapter 5, a child is at risk of exploitation, abuse or neglect when either: (a) the parents do not want another child for his/her own sake (commodification); or (b) there is a significant risk of serious harm to the child to be born (harm). Legislation should broadly define the phrase 'significant risk of serious harm' but otherwise leave these determinations to clinicians and CECs. As discussed in Chapter 5, 'significant risk of serious harm' might be defined as 'more than a minor increase over the level of harm that a healthy child normally experiences'.[86]

More detailed guidance on specific risks associated with particular applications of PGD should be included in policy guidelines. Such guidelines can be reviewed from time to time, as more evidence becomes available, and are more easily amended than legislation. The following guidance is tailored to saviour sibling selection:

Specific guidance on *commodification*:

(a) Parental motivation for having a child is complex and multifaceted and rarely entirely altruistic.
(b) How the parents are likely to treat the child once s/he is born is more important than parental motivation for having the child.

Specific guidance on *harm*:

(c) Harm includes physical, psychological and social harm, in particular:
  - possible physical harm associated with ART and embryo biopsy;
  - any likely long-term psychological and social implications associated with selection; and
  - any intrusive surgery to which the child to be born may be exposed in the future.
(d) Parents regularly expose their children to some risk of harm.
(e) The intimate nature of family relationships sometimes justifies imposing a greater risk of harm on family members than would otherwise be justified in relation to strangers.
(f) The nature and intimacy of existing relationships within the family should be taken into account.
(g) A significant risk of serious harm falls outside the realm of risks to which parents often subject their children.
(h) A saviour sibling may donate bone marrow in the future but should not donate any non-regenerative or whole organs.

General guidance should also be given about balancing risk and benefit in the context of specific relationships. Relevant factors for saviour sibling selection include:

(i) The circumstances of the family seeking treatment, including:[87]
  - the nature of relationships within the existing family;[88]

- the demands of ART treatment on the parents while caring for the existing child; and
- the extent of social support available within the extended family.

(j) The severity of the condition of the existing child, including:[89]

- the degree of suffering associated with their condition;
- the speed of degeneration in progressive disorders;
- the prognosis, including all treatment options;
- the availability of other sources of tissue; and
- the availability of other effective therapy/alternative treatment options.

(k) The likelihood of a successful outcome.
(l) The consequences of an unsuccessful outcome.

Policy guidelines should direct clinics and families to consider the risk of commodification and harm in relation to all applications for PGD. Given the concerns about the welfare of saviour siblings, decisions about saviour sibling selection should be referred to a regional CEC for independent review in accordance with the guiding principles set out in ART legislation. Policy guidelines should outline the role of the CEC in saviour sibling cases as follows:

(m) A CEC should review all decisions to proceed with saviour sibling selection and determine that treatment should not be provided where:

- the child to be born is at risk of exploitation, abuse or neglect; or
- the decision-making process has been so flawed that the parents cannot have made a fully informed decision.

Provided the threshold level of protection is satisfied, parents should not be denied treatment on the basis of the 'welfare of the child'.

Lastly, good record-keeping is important for transparency and consistency in decision-making. Policy guidelines should require clinics to keep accurate records to ensure that the decision-making process has complied with ART legislation and policy guidelines. CECs must be satisfied on the basis of the report of the healthcare team that the welfare of the child has been satisfactorily safeguarded in accordance with the relevant regulatory scheme. In addition to record-keeping, policy guidelines should also encourage ongoing monitoring of children born as a result of PGD and improved data collection. As discussed earlier in the chapter, ongoing longitudinal research is needed to improve welfare assessments about children selected using PGD to be saviour siblings. Policy guidelines should require clinics to make arrangements for inviting and encouraging patients and their families to take part in long-term follow-up studies of physical and psychosocial effects on saviour siblings and their families.[90] The information obtained by clinics should be reported and recorded on a national registry to assist further research in this area.

6.4 Differences from UK and Australian regulation

The relational framework for saviour sibling selection outlined above differs from the current regulatory frameworks in the UK and Australia in several ways and may ultimately lead to different outcomes in some cases.

The first difference is that my relational framework expressly articulates a *broader range of interests* to be considered in the decision-making process than current UK and Australian ART regulation. ART legislation in the UK and Australia focuses on the welfare of the child to be born but gives little attention to other relevant interests within families or how those other interests interact with those of the child to be born. For example, legislation in the Australian States of Victoria and SA requires the welfare and interests of the child to be born to be treated as paramount but does not mention the interests of existing children or the parents in seeking treatment.[91] As Chapter 3 revealed, it is difficult to comprehend how saviour sibling selection could ever be justified on the interests of the existing child alone. Legislation in the UK and the State of WA refers to some interests beyond those of the child to be born. In the UK, for example, legislation requires consideration to be given to the welfare of both the child to be born and 'any other child that may be affected by the birth',[92] whereas legislation in WA specifically requires consideration of the welfare and interests of both participants and the child to be born.[93] In neither jurisdiction, however, are the collective interests of family expressly articulated.

Saviour sibling selection provides an excellent example of how the interests of parents and existing children are relevant to decisions about selective reproduction. The decision to select a saviour sibling is primarily motivated by the interests of the parents and the existing ill child. It makes sense, therefore, to openly acknowledge these other interests in the decision-making process so that they can be managed alongside the interests of the child to be born. Acknowledging other family interests also avoids the need to rationalise saviour sibling selection on the basis that it is in the interests of the child to be born, as has been done in the past. The interests of other family members are, to some extent, addressed by current HFEA policy on saviour sibling selection, which reinforces the statutory obligation on clinics to consider the condition of the ill child, including the degree of suffering and prognosis.[94] The policy also requires clinics to consider the family circumstances of parents seeking treatment, although it does not directly mention the interests of the parents seeking a saviour sibling.[95] Lastly, HFEA policy on the welfare of the child states that clinics are expected to consider the wishes of all involved without discrimination.[96] There is no guidance, however, as to how the various interests within a family should be managed.

The second difference between my relational framework for saviour sibling selection and regulatory frameworks in the UK and Australia relates to *who makes treatment decisions and how they are made*. My framework devolves decisions about saviour sibling selection to parents in consultation with their healthcare team, subject to approval by a CEC in complex cases. In the UK, the HFEA licenses clinics to provide PGD for saviour sibling selection on a case-by-case basis. The STC in the UK recommended that decisions about assisted reproductive treatment be devolved to patients and clinicians rather than a statutory authority, to ensure minimal state intrusion into reproductive decision-making.[97] The UK Government opted instead to maintain the HFEA's role in licensing PGD on the basis that it improves consistency and accountability.[98] The HFEA reviewed its case-by-case approach to licensing saviour sibling selection in late 2009 and, in January 2010, determined to continue this approach for the time-being.[99] A key factor in favour of adopting a case-by-case approach is the fact that 'there are still-unresolved ethical and social concerns' regarding saviour siblings and very little information on the benefits and risks of the treatment.[100]

In Australia, the NHMRC ART Guidelines devolve decisions about PGD to clinics in accordance with certain requirements.[101] In particular, clinics must seek advice from a CEC in relation to decisions involving saviour sibling selection.[102] As already discussed, the NHMRC ART Guidelines apply to all states and territories, except to the extent they are inconsistent with state legislation. In the State of Victoria, for example, doctors must determine patient eligibility for treatment in accordance with statutory criteria and treatment decisions may be reviewed by an independent review panel. Victorian legislation authorises treating clinics to provide assisted reproductive treatment to patients who, in the view of a doctor, are infertile or at risk of passing on a heritable disease or disorder.[103] If a patient does not meet the eligibility criteria in Victorian legislation, the Patient Review Panel may authorise treatment (including PGD) that is for a therapeutic goal and consistent with the best interests of the child to be born.[104]

There are clear advantages in allowing prospective parents to be directly involved in essentially private reproductive decisions. In a liberal democratic society, any intervention by the state into the reproductive choices of individuals should be based on sound ethical principles and take into account evidence of harm to children or society. According to the STC, 'there are no compelling reasons for a statutory authority to make judgements on whether or not a family can [select a saviour sibling], provided they fall within parameters set by Parliament'.[105] Generally speaking, parents are better placed than statutory authorities, clinics or specialist panels to make decisions about the welfare of their own children. A 'lighter touch' approach to regulation is also consistent with public opinion in the UK, which suggests that decisions about PGD should be made by affected families in consultation with clinicians.[106] As the STC noted, there is no evidence that parents would use PGD for 'trivial' reasons to a degree that would harm the child to be born as a result of the procedures.[107] The focus of PGD regulation should therefore be to assist prospective parents in the ethically complex decision-making process.

A collaborative decision-making process with some independent ethical oversight is important for controversial applications of PGD, such as saviour sibling selection, as the individual interests of the child to be born may not always coincide with those of his/her family. Instead of focusing on the potential conflict between the interests of family members, collaborative decision-making enables parents to explore the various interests with guidance from their healthcare team within an 'open moral space'. Existing children should also be given an opportunity to contribute to the discussion, where appropriate. My relational framework promotes a collaborative decision-making process by outlining the ways in which healthcare professionals can support prospective parents in making decisions about selective reproduction. As some commentators have pointed out, the current roles of clinicians and statutory bodies as gatekeepers of assisted reproductive treatment is problematic.[108] The welfare of the child is better protected through independent ethical oversight by a CEC, which ensures a threshold level of protection to the child to be born. My framework also has a strong focus on ethics counselling, which does not currently exist in the UK and Australian decision-making models. Providing prospective parents with the ethical support needed to make ethically informed and defensible decisions should provide an additional layer of protection for the child to be born.

My relational framework shares the case-by-case approach to saviour sibling selection that has been adopted in the UK and Australia. There is merit to a case-by-case approach to controversial applications of PGD as the circumstances of each case will vary significantly. As King points out, although an in-principle decision has been taken by the UK Parliament in relation to saviour sibling selection, the ethical issues surrounding treatment 'are still alive in the details and variability between individual cases'.[109] A case-by-case approach can also accommodate new information and technological developments as they arise. For example, as discussed in Chapter 3, further longitudinal studies are needed on the impacts of selection on saviour siblings. As this information arises, it can be fed into the decision-making process in individual cases. Technological advancements may also impact on the level of harm caused to the embryo during the biopsy process, which may be relevant to the welfare of the child to be born.

The third difference between my relational framework and UK and Australian regulation relates to the *level of protection afforded the child to be born*. My framework provides for a threshold level of protection that is similar to the 'harm-based' approach to the welfare of the child articulated in UK HFEA policy. HFEA policy contains a presumption of treatment unless information suggests there is a 'risk of significant harm or neglect'.[110] My threshold level of protection also expressly protects the child to be born from exploitation. This extends the harm-based approach to include Kantian concerns about commodification that may not result in any harm to the child. By creating a presumption in favour of treatment, subject to a threshold level of protection, my framework provides clear parameters for clinics to work within that should minimise unfair discrimination based on subjective considerations. This 'minimum welfare' approach is preferable to the 'best interests' approach that applies in at least some Australian jurisdictions. In Victoria and SA, for example, the welfare and interests of the child to be born are to be treated as paramount. As previously discussed, a 'best interests' approach has the potential to discriminate against the infertile and erode reproductive choice, particularly when there is a lack of clear guidance on the nature of the interests of the child to be born.

Lastly, my relational framework does not include *two restrictions* on saviour sibling selection that have been applied in the UK and Australia and which appear to have no clear justification. First, the distinction that currently applies in the Australian States of Victoria, SA and WA, by virtue of the eligibility requirements for assisted reproductive treatment, between PGD for tissue typing in conjunction with detection of a heritable condition and PGD for tissue typing alone is unjustified and should be removed.[111] The fact that parents who are not infertile or at risk of passing on a genetic disease are not eligible for treatment means that parents whose existing child suffers from a non-heritable condition cannot use PGD for tissue typing alone in order to select a saviour sibling. The risk/benefit analysis for the child to be born is, however, the same, whether or not tissue typing is carried out alone or in conjunction with PGD to detect a heritable condition. As discussed in Chapter 2, the HFEA removed the restriction on PGD for tissue typing alone from its policy on saviour sibling selection in 2004, following widespread public criticism and debate in the UK about its inconsistent decisions in the Hashmi and Whitaker cases. My relational framework permits PGD, whether or not the existing sibling suffers from a heritable condition.

Second, both the UK and Australia limit PGD for tissue typing to donation between siblings.[112] My relational framework does not limit the use of PGD to selecting a child with compatible tissue for a sibling if the family is sufficiently close to justify a donation by the child to be born to another family member, such as a parent. My approach to assisted reproduction is more consistent with existing regimes for tissue donation by minors. For example, Victorian legislation permits regenerative tissue to be removed from a child for transplantation to either a sibling or a parent in certain circumstances.[113] The Family Court of Australia has also allowed a child to donate bone marrow under its 'welfare jurisdiction' in two separate cases to an aunt and, more recently, a cousin.[114] In the UK, the STC criticised the HFEA for restricting the use of tissue typing to donations between siblings.[115] According to the STC, a distinction between siblings and other members of the family would need to be based on evidence that suggests that 'the psychological impact on the child, and the nature of the family's relationship, would be different if the recipient of the stem cells were not a sibling'.[116]

6.5 Conclusion

There are strong reasons for regulating ART and, specifically, selective reproduction. Regulation is not only important in protecting the child to be born from exploitation, abuse and neglect, but it can also improve the decision-making process. Instead of unduly restricting reproductive liberty, a permissive regulatory approach can enhance parental choice by supporting prospective parents in making ethically complex and emotionally charged decisions. The relational framework proposed in this chapter aims to achieve this goal.

Within legislatively determined parameters and in accordance with more detailed policy guidelines, essentially private decisions about selective reproduction should be made by patients in consultation with their healthcare team rather than by a statutory body or clinic. As the STC noted, '(d)ecisions made at a local level have the advantages of speed and proximity to the clinical setting'.[117] It is, however, worth paying heed to Jayson Whitaker's comment (based on his personal experience as the father of a saviour sibling) that, while clinical decisions should be left to the patient and doctor, 'there does need to be some voice of reason in there'.[118]

Legislation should establish clear parameters for selective reproduction, within which more detailed policy can be developed. Carefully formulated policy guidelines on particular forms of selective reproduction can support parents facing difficult treatment decisions by clarifying the roles of the prospective parents and members of their healthcare team in the decision-making process. Ethically complex treatments, such as saviour sibling selection, should be independently reviewed by regional CECs, which can provide another layer of ethical oversight. My relational regulatory framework aims to provide parents with the 'voice of reason' needed to make well-informed decisions about selective reproduction whilst also protecting the welfare of the child to be born.

Notes

1 Anthony Ogus, *Regulation: Legal Form and Economic Theory* (Clarendon Press, 1994), 1.
2 Ogus, ibid, 2–3.
3 In the UK, see Medical Act 1983 (UK); General Medical Council, *Good Medical Practice* (13 November 2006), <http://www.gmc-uk.org/static/documents/content/GMP_0910. pdf> (accessed 4 December 2012). In Australia, see Health Practitioner Regulation National Law Act, as in force in each state and territory; Australian Medical Association, *Code of Ethics of the Australian Medical Association* (2004, revised 2006), <https://ama.com. au/codeofethics> (accessed 24 April 2013).
4 Margaret Brazier, 'Regulating the Reproduction Business?' (1999) 7 *Medical Law Review* 166.
5 Roger Brownsword, 'Regulating Human Genetics: New Dilemmas for a New Millennium' (2004) 12 *Medical Law Review* 14, 15.
6 Brazier, above n 4, 169.
7 Skene notes, however, that 'whilst these areas are not specifically regulated by legislation, there are laws that regulate them incidentally': Loane Skene, 'Why Legislate on Assisted Reproduction?' in Ian Freckelton and Kerry Petersen (eds), *Controversies in Health Law* (Federation Press, 1999), 266, 267.
8 Skene, ibid. In relation to the UK, see Brazier, above n 4, 170.
9 Brazier, above n 4, 170.

10　For example, Brazier suggests that the licensing of fertility specialists in the UK, which promotes high standards of medical practice, could be extended to all emerging specialties: above n 4, 167.

11　Helen Szoke, 'The Nanny State or Responsible Government?' (2002) 9 *Journal of Law and Medicine* 470, 481. Szoke recognises that resolution by the state will not satisfy all parties in a pluralist society.

12　Leslie Cannold and Lynn Gillam, 'Regulation, Consultation and Divergent Community Views: The Case of Access to ART by Lesbian and Single Women' (2002) 9 *Journal of Law and Medicine* 498, 501–2.

13　See, for example, House of Commons Science and Technology Committee Fifth Report of Session 2004–5, *Human Reproductive Technologies and the Law*, HC7–1 (24 March 2005) (STC Report), [33]; Victorian Law Reform Commission (VLRC), *Assisted Reproductive Technology & Adoption*, Final Report (2007) (VLRC Report), 45; Don Chalmers, 'Professional Self-regulation and Guidelines in Assisted Reproduction' (2002) 9 *Journal of Law and Medicine* 414, 425–26.

14　Martin H Johnson, 'The Art of Regulation and the Regulation of ART: The Impact of Regulation on Research and Clinical Practice' (2002) 9 *Journal of Law and Medicine* 399, 405. Johnson envisages that the first category would include patients and possibly doctors. He suggests that the second category would include children (desired and existing), the embryo, and gamete donors.

15　Submission by Julian Savulescu to the House of Commons Science and Technology Committee: STC Report, above n 13, [36].

16　Human Genome Research Project, *Choosing Genes for Future Children: The Regulatory Implications of Preimplantation Genetic Diagnosis* (Human Genome Research Project, 2006), 328.

17　STC Report, above n 13, [317]–[319]. See also Committee of Inquiry into Human Fertilisation and Embryology, *Report of the Committee of Inquiry into Human Fertilisation and Embryology*, Cmnd 9314 (July 1984) (Warnock Report), [13.3].

18　Brazier, above n 4, 167. See also, Progress Educational Trust (PET), 'Parents or Parliament: Embryo Testing, Who Decides?', Public Debate (London, 16 July 2007).

19　Brazier states that the case for ART regulation made by the Warnock Committee was based on a pre-eminent concern for embryos and a focus on regulating standards: Brazier, above n 4, 172. In Australia, the status of the embryo has been the focus of detailed discussion in relation to the regulation of embryo research and cloning: Senate Community Affairs Legislation Committee, *Report on the Provisions of the Research Involving Embryos and Prohibition of Human Cloning Bill 2002*, October 2002, 2–8, <http://www.aph.gov.au/Parliamentary_Business/Committees/Senate_Committees?url=clac_ctte/completed_inquiries/2002–4/emb_cloning/report/index.htm > (accessed 24 April 2013).

20　Warnock Report, above n 17, [11.17].

21　Warnock Report, above n 17, [11.17].

22　STC Report, above n 13, [46].

23　John Stuart Mill, 'On Liberty' in Mary Warnock (ed), *Utilitarianism and On Liberty* (Blackwell Publishing, 2nd edn, 2003), 88, 94.

24　Colin Gavaghan, *Defending the Genetic Supermarket: Law and Ethics of Selecting the Next Generation* (Routledge-Cavendish, 2007), 37–38.

25　Gavaghan, ibid, 41, 51–54.

26　STC Report, above n 13, [390].

27　See discussion in Chapter 3, section 3.5.1.

28　See discussion in Chapter 2, section 2.3.

29　In the UK, see Human Fertilisation and Embryology Act 1990 (UK) (HFE Act (UK)), c 37, s 13(5). In Australia, see Assisted Reproductive Treatment Act 2008 (Vic), s 5(a) (ART Act (Vic)); Assisted Reproductive Treatment Act 1988 (SA), s 4A; and Human Reproductive Technology Act 1991 (WA), s 23 (1)(e) (HRT Act (WA)).

30　Brazier, above n 4, 174.

31 Kristen Walker, 'Should There Be Limits On Who May Access Assisted Reproductive Services? A Legal Perspective' in Jennifer Gunning and Helen Szoke (eds), *The Regulation of Assisted Reproductive Technology* (Ashgate, 2003), 123, 131–33.

32 See, for example, Emily Jackson, 'Conception and the Irrelevance of the Welfare Principle' (2002) 65 *Modern Law Review* 176; Amel Alghrani and John Harris, 'Reproductive Liberty: Should the Foundation of Families Be Regulated?' (2006) 18 *Child and Family Law Quarterly* 191.

33 For example, John Harris builds on Dworkin's work on individual rights by arguing that individuals have a right to procreative autonomy: John Harris, 'Rights and Reproductive Choice' in John Harris and Soren Holm, *The Future of Human Reproduction* (Oxford University Press, 1998), 5. See also John Robertson, Helen Bequaert Holmes and Cynthia B Cohen, *Children of Choice: Freedom and the New Reproductive Technologies* (Princeton University Press, 1994).

34 The current ART Act (Vic) is, however, less prescriptive than its predecessors, the Infertility (Medical Procedures) Act 1984 (Vic) and the Infertility Treatment Act 1995 (Vic).

35 Kerry Petersen, 'Regulating Preimplantation Genetic Diagnosis: A Criminal Model Versus a Professional Model' (2009) 17 *Journal of Law and Medicine* 452, 456–60.

36 Malcolm Smith, 'Reviewing Regulation of Assisted Reproductive Technology in New South Wales: The Assisted Reproductive Technology Act 2007 (NSW)' (2008) 16 *Journal of Law and Medicine* 120, 120.

37 Smith, ibid, 130. The NHMRC ART Guidelines do, however, prohibit PGD to detect non-serious genetic conditions, for social sex selection and for selecting in favour of a genetic defect or disability: NHMRC, *Ethical Guidelines on the Use of Assisted Reproductive Technology in Clinical Practice and Research 2004 (as revised in 2007 to take into account the changes in legislation)* (June 2007) (NHMRC ART Guidelines), {12.2].

38 Brownsword, above n 5, 31.

39 The Commonwealth Parliament does not have express power to legislate in relation to the provision of ART services or health and medicine generally: Australian Constitution 1900, s 51.

40 Skene, above n 7, 267.

41 The VLRC reported that the absence of uniform ART legislation has led to 'reproductive tourism' within Australia, whereby people who are ineligible for treatment in one state travel to unregulated states to undergo treatment: VLRC Report, above n 13, 44, 55.

42 In 2002, the Commonwealth Parliament enacted national legislation on human embryo research and cloning technologies through a co-operative federal agreement by the Council of Australian Governments (COAG): Prohibition of Human Cloning Act 2002 (Cth) and the Research Involving Human Embryos Act 2002 (Cth). Although these schemes have a long history in Australia, they are not without their problems. The decision of the High Court in *R v Hughes* (2000) 202 CLR 535 casts some doubt on the constitutional validity of Commonwealth-State co-operative schemes. National frameworks are also undermined where states fail to pass corresponding legislation. For example, in December 2006, the national ban on therapeutic cloning was lifted by the Australian Parliament. Although COAG leaders agreed in April 2007 to use their best efforts to introduce corresponding legislation in their respective jurisdictions by 12 June 2008, the State of WA maintains an absolute prohibition on therapeutic cloning: Human Reproductive Technology Act 1991 (WA), s 53C.

43 In the absence of a specific referral of power or agreement by the states and territories, the Commonwealth Parliament could potentially use one or more of its powers under the Constitution, such as its financial assistance power, to indirectly legislate on ART. For a discussion of other potential Commonwealth powers that might support national ART legislation in Australia, see Sharon Scully, 'Does the Commonwealth Have Constitutional Power to Take Over the Administration of Public Hospitals?' (Research Paper No 36, Parliamentary Library, Parliament of Australia, 2009).

44 Szoke, above n 11, 35.

45 Brownsword, above n 5, 18.

46 Brownsword, above n 5, 18.

47 Helen Szoke, 'Australia – A Federated Structure of Statutory Regulation of ART' in Jennifer Gunning and Helen Szoke (eds), *The Regulation of Assisted Reproductive Technology* (Ashgate, 2003), 75, 78.

48 Szoke, ibid, 81.

49 STC Report, above n 13, [196]–[98].

50 See STC Report, above n 13, [363]; Joint Committee on the Human Tissue and Embryos (Draft) Bill Session 2006–7, *Human Tissues and Embryos (Draft) Bill*, HL 169/HC 630-I and II (August 2007) (Joint Committee Report), [36]; Iain McDonald, Rachel Anne Fenton and Fiona Dabell, 'Treatment Provisions: Proposals for Reform of the Human Fertilisation and Embryology Act 1990' (2007) 29 *Journal of Social Welfare and Family Law* 293, 294.

51 Department of Health (UK), *Consultation on Proposals to Transfer Functions from the Human Fertilisation and Embryology Authority and the Human Tissue Authority*, Consultation Paper (June 2012); Department of Health (UK), *Government Response to the Consultation on Proposals to Transfer Functions from the Human Fertilisation and Embryology Authority and the Human Tissue Authority* (January 2013) (Government Response). The UK Government will, however, conduct an independent review of how the HFEA carries out its functions in 2013: Government Response, [69].

52 STC Report, above n 13, [348]–[352].

53 STC Report, above n 13, [350]–[51].

54 NHMRC, *Australian Health Ethics Committee (AHEC)* (2012), <http://www.nhmrc.gov.au/about/committees/ahec/index.htm> (accessed 24 April 2013). See also National Health and Medical Research Council Act 1992 (Cth), s 36(1).

55 Christine Parker, *et al* (eds), *Regulating Law* (Oxford University Press, 2004), 1.

56 As discussed in Chapter 2, all clinics offering ART services in Australia must comply with the NHMRC ART Guidelines for accreditation by the Reproductive Technology Accreditation Committee.

57 NHMRC ART Guidelines, above n 37, [12.3].

58 Sheila McLean, 'Clinical Ethics Committees, Due Process and the Right to a Fair Hearing' (2008) 15 *Journal of Law and Medicine* 520, 521.

59 CECs have provided ethics consultation services in the US since the early 1970s: F Rosner, 'Hospital Medical Ethics Committees: A Review of their Development' (1985) 253 *Journal of American Medical Association* 2693. A 2007 survey of US hospitals revealed that 81% of hospitals have an ethics consultation service: E Fox, S Myers and R Pearlman, 'Ethics Consultation in United States Hospitals: A National Survey' (2007) 7 *American Journal of Bioethics* 13.

60 Although CECs have been in existence in the UK since the mid-1990s, they initially focused on guideline and policy development: E M Meslin, *et al*, 'Hospital Ethics Committees in the United Kingdom' (1996) 8 *HEC Forum* 301; Anne Slowther, *et al*, 'Clinical Ethics Support Services in the UK: An Investigation of the Current Provision of Ethics Support to Health Professionals in the UK' (2001) 27 (Suppl 1) *Journal of Medical Ethics* i2. A 2011 survey of UK CECs revealed that the CECs have become increasingly involved in case consultations in recent years: Anne Slowther, Leah McClimans and Charlotte Price, 'Development of Clinical Ethics Services in the UK: A National Survey' (2012) 38 *Journal of Medical Ethics* 210.

61 In Victoria, for example, the Royal Women's Hospital Clinical Ethics Advisory Group and the Royal Children's Hospital Clinical Bioethics Committee provide clinical consultation services. While there are no national figures on the number of clinical ethics committees operating in Australian hospitals, the numbers are probably quite low. Lynn Gillam estimated in 2009 that 10%–20% of hospitals in Australia had clinical ethics committees: Lynne Gillam, 'Human Research Ethics Committees' (Paper presented at the Centre for Human Bioethics Intensive Bioethics Course, Alexandra, Victoria, 3 December 2009).

62 For example, the Clinical Ethics Response Group (CERG) at the Royal Children's Hospital in Victoria, Australia, provides ethical advice to clinicians at their request. While the role of the CERG is still evolving, parents are not generally involved in ethics consultations: information provided by Associate Professor Lynn Gillam, Academic Director, Children's Bioethics Centre, Royal Children's Hospital to author on 28 April 2010. In recent years, clinical ethical services in the UK are increasingly accepting consultation requests from patients and family members. For example, a 2011 study by Slowther revealed that consultation requests were accepted from patients and family members by 49% of services, although several services reported that, in practice, most consultation requests come from clinicians: Slowther, McClimans and Price, above n 60, 212.

63 Slowther, McClimans and Price, above n 60, 213.

64 For a discussion of the challenges in credentialing clinical ethics consultants, see Fox, Myers and Pearlman, above n 59.

65 According to Fiester, an ethics consultant who acts as mediator is 'responsible for protecting everyone's interests and is obligated and accountable for ensuring that no one is marginalized or voiceless': Autumn Fiester, 'Mediation and Advocacy' (2012) 12 *American Journal of Bioethics* 10, 10.

66 To avoid undue delay, CECs should be required to review cases within one to two weeks. In the State of Victoria, for instance, the Royal Women's Hospital Clinical Ethics Advisory Group (CEAG) and The Royal Childrens' Hospital Clinical Bioethics Committee (CBC) generally convene within a week's notice: email from Margaret Coady (Committee Member, CEAG) to Michelle Taylor-Sands, 25 March 2010; The Royal Children's Hospital Melbourne, Children's Bioethics Centre, *Clinical Ethics Service*, <http://www.rch.org.au/bioethics/clinical.cfm?doc_id=12222> (accessed 24 April 2013).

67 VLRC Report, above n 13, 62–63.

68 See McLean, above n 58, 522; VLRC Report, above n 13, 63.

69 NHMRC ART Guidelines, above n 37, [12.3]. ART legislation in the State of WA also expressly acknowledges the role of clinical ethics committees: HRT Act (WA), s 21.

70 McLean, above n 58, 523. See, for example, *Re Quinlan* (1976) 355 A 2d 647, 671; *Re AC* (1990) 573 A 2d 1235, 1237.

71 McLean, above n 58, 525–28.

72 The VLRC recommended that CECs should generally include a child development expert, a psychologist or psychiatrist with expertise in the prediction of risk of harm to children, and a doctor with experience in ART: VLRC Report, above n 13, 63. Given the ethical and legal aspects of the role I am proposing for CECs, I would add an ethicist and a lawyer to the list.

73 In Australia, for example, the Patient Review Panel in the State of Victoria has the power to determine whether treatment should be provided where patients are denied treatment: ART Act (Vic), s 85.

74 One example of a national ethics committee is the New Zealand National Ethics Committee on Assisted Reproductive Technology (ECART). ECART, a national statutory body, approves ART procedures in New Zealand in accordance with the national guidelines issued by the New Zealand Advisory Committee on Assisted Reproductive Technology (ACART): Human Genome Research Project, above n 16, 232, 314.

75 STC Report, above n 13, [353]. Ideally, each clinic would have its own CEC. However, it would be appropriate for smaller clinics to have recourse to a CEC at a larger clinic operating within the same region.

76 Slowther, *et al*, above n 60, i2.

77 S M Wolf, 'Ethics Committees and Due Process: Nesting Rights in a Community of Caring' (1991) 50 *Maryland Law Review* 798, 858.

78 S E Mumford, E Corrigan, E and M G R Hull, 'Access to Assisted Conception: A Framework of Regulation' (1998) 13 *Human Reproduction* 2349, 2353.

79 STC Report, above n 13, [374].

80 Ellie Lee, Jan Macvarish and Sally Sheldon, 'Assessing Child Welfare under the Human Fertilisation and Embryology Act: The New Law: Summary of Findings' (University of Kent, September 2012), 5

81 VLRC Report, above n 13, 62. See also 2001 UK study by Slowther, which provides the following statistics on the perceived need for CECs: 89% in favour; of these, 62% for a CEC, 26% for an individual clinical ethicist and 12% for some other model of clinical ethics service: Slowther, *et al*, above n 60, i4.

82 Submission by Len Doyal to the STC: STC Report, above n 13, [342]. See also Len Doyal, 'Clinical Ethics Committees and the Formulation of Health Care Policy' (2001) 27 (Suppl 1) *Journal of Medical Ethics* i44, i47.

83 Roger Brownsword, 'Reproductive Opportunities and Regulatory Challenges' (2004) 67 *The Modern Law Review* 304, 319–20.

84 Some of these are contained in existing UK and Australian ART policy documents: HFEA, *Code of Practice* (8th edn, first published 2009, revised October 2011) (HFEA, *Code of Practice*), Guidance Note 10, [10.26]; NHMRC ART Guidelines, above n 37, [12.5].

85 Some of these are based on the Australian and New Zealand Infertility Counsellors Association (ANZICA), *Guidelines on Professional Standards of Practice Infertility Counselling* (October 2003) (ANZICA Guidelines).

86 This test is based on Ross' definition of *minor increase over minimal risk of harm*, discussed in Chapter 5, section 5.3.3.1.

87 Some of these are based on HFEA, *Code of Practice*, above n 84, Guidance Note 10, [10.25].

88 While it can be difficult to judge the nature of relationships within families, this is effectively what US courts have done in the context of cases involving organ donations by siblings. See discussion by Dwyer and Vig in relation to *Hart v Brown* and *Strunk v Strunk*: James Dwyer and Elizabeth Vig, 'Rethinking Transplantation Between Siblings' (1995) 25 *Hastings Center Report* 7.

89 Some of these are based on HFEA, *Code of Practice*, above n 84, Guidance Note 10, [10.23].

90 HFEA, *Code of Practice*, above n 84, Guidance Note 10, [10.28].

91 The guiding principles in the ART Act (Vic) refer to the health and well-being of women undergoing treatment and the right of those seeking treatment to protection from discrimination: s 5(d), (e). However there is no express recognition of parents' general interests in seeking treatment.

92 HFE Act (UK), s 13(5)

93 HRT Act (WA), s 23(1)(e).

94 HFEA, *Code of Practice*, above n 84, Guidance Note 10, [10.23].

95 HFEA, *Code of Practice*, above n 84, Guidance Note 10, [10.25].

96 HFEA, *Code of Practice*, above n 84, Guidance Note 10, [8.7].

97 STC Report, above n 13, [390].

98 Department of Health, *Review of the Human Fertilisation and Embryology Act: Proposals for Revised Legislation (Including Establishment of the Regulatory Authority for Tissue and Embryos)*, Cm 6989 (2006) (White Paper), [2.44].

99 HFEA, *Minutes of Authority Meeting* (20 January 2010) (HFEA Minutes), [10.13].

100 David King, 'The Case for Case-by-Case Regulation of PGD' (2010) 541 *BioNews*, <http://www.bionews.org.uk/page_53438.asp> (accessed 24 April 2013).

101 Clinics are required to use open and consistent decision-making and patients are entitled to understand and participate in decisions about their care: NHMRC ART Guidelines, above n 37, [5.3]. Clinics offering PGD must be provided with relevant information and counselling, including genetic counselling: at [12.4], [12.5].

102 NHMRC ART Guidelines, above n 37, [12.3].

103 ART Act (Vic), s 10(2).

104 ART Act (Vic), s 15(3).

105 STC Report, above n 13, [129].

106 PET, above n 18.
107 STC Report, above n 13, [251].
108 Brazier, above n 4, 178. Walker, above n 31, 131–34. For a detailed discussion of the different ways in which clinicians may act as gatekeepers for ART, see John H Pearn, 'Gatekeeping and Assisted Reproductive Technology: The Ethical Rights and Responsibilities of Doctors' (1997) 167 *Medical Journal of Australia* 318.
109 King, above n 100.
110 HFEA, *Code of Practice*, above n 84, Guidance Note 8, [8.15].
111 See discussion in Chapter 2, section 2.5.2.2.
112 HFE Act (UK), Schedule 2, s 1ZA(1)(d); NHMRC ART Guidelines, above n 37, [12.3]. In the State of Victoria, however, the Patient Review Panel may potentially allow parents to use PGD to select a tissue-matched embryo for the benefit of other relatives: *JS and LS v Patient Review Panel (Health and Privacy)* [2011] VCAT 856 (8 April 2011) [38]–[39].
113 Human Tissue Act 1982 (Vic), s 15.
114 *In the Marriage of GWW and CMW* (1997) 136 FLR 421; *Re Inaya (special medical procedure)* (2007) 213 FLR 278.
115 STC Report, above n 13, [129].
116 STC Report, above n 13, [129]. For a detailed discussion about the inconsistencies surrounding the 'parental exception' to the use of PGD for tissue typing, see Gavaghan, above n 24, 160–62. See also, Stephen Wilkinson, *Choosing Tomorrow's Children: The Ethics of Selective Reproduction* (Oxford University Press, 2010), 124–27.
117 STC Report, above n 13, [353].
118 STC Report, above n 13, [373].

7 Conclusion

Advancements in assisted reproductive technologies during the last 20 years have increased the potential for parents to select the genetic traits of their children. Some types of selection are more controversial than others and raise questions about how much choice parents should have over the characteristics of their children. Using PGD to screen out serious genetic diseases, for example, is generally considered to be more acceptable than using this technology to select a particular 'type' of child, such as a saviour sibling or a child of a particular sex or physical appearance. The latter forms of selective reproduction raise ethical concerns about the welfare of the child to be born and the nature of the parent/child relationship. These ethical concerns pose new regulatory challenges, which have not always been adequately addressed in the past. As revealed in Chapter 2, early attempts to regulate saviour sibling selection in the UK were met with widespread criticism and legal challenge. A significant obstacle faced by the HFEA in developing its early policy on saviour sibling selection was the fact that there was no clearly articulated ethical approach underlying the welfare of the child provision in UK ART legislation.

At the heart of the problem of regulating selective reproduction is the fact that, although reproductive decision-making is generally thought of as a private matter, enabling parents to select the genetic traits of their children has potential adverse implications for society as a whole and, more specifically, the child to be born. The primary goal of this book has been to explore the concerns associated with the welfare of the child in selective reproduction and to propose a regulatory solution that adequately protects the child to be born without unduly curtailing reproductive choice. As discussed in Chapter 3, concerns about commodification and harm have dominated the debate about selective reproduction and led to an individualistic approach to the welfare of the child to be born that is reflected in UK and Australian regulation. While the individual interests of the child are important, the welfare of the child is inextricably connected with the welfare of his/her family. The relational approach to the welfare of the child to be born proposed in Chapter 4 provides a more comprehensive account of the child's individual and collective family interests.

The welfare of a child is not, however, necessarily synonymous with the welfare of his/her family. There must be limitations on how far parents can compromise the welfare of an individual child in order to promote the welfare of the family as a whole. In Chapter 4, I explored the limits on what parents can expect from their children by analysing the nature of families and their concomitant obligations. I contended that individual compromise by family members (including children) is an essential element of the intimacy that exists within families and is justified on the basis of familial duty. The compromise entailed by familial duty need not be voluntary or based on constructive consent because membership alone provides the foundation for moral responsibility to family. Furthermore, the duty owed by family members to one another is greater than the duty owed to strangers because intimate relationships involve a higher level of mutual obligation and reliance than non-intimate relationships. Put simply, we do more and expect more from family members because of the intimate nature of family relationships. A different range of principles applies to obligations of family membership than the impartial moral principles grounded in modern liberal theory. This does not mean that general moral constraints should not operate within families, raising related questions about when and how the state should intervene to protect children from their families.

There comes a point at which necessary compromise by an individual family member becomes unacceptable sacrifice. Clearly it is unacceptable, for example, to allow parents to conceive a saviour sibling as a 'tissue farm' for an existing child. The child to be born as a result of selective reproduction is in a particularly vulnerable position as he/she does not have a 'voice' in the decision-making process. Although there are good reasons to limit state interference in family decision-making, the state should intervene to prevent abuses of parental discretion and to ensure that the interests of the child to be born are not overlooked altogether in decisions about selective reproduction. In Chapter 5, I argued that state interference is justified to protect children from exploitation, abuse and neglect. In such cases, the nucleus of well-being and well-acting that is essential to intimate relationships within families has broken down and a disconnection occurs between the welfare of the child and the welfare of his/her family. Drawing on the concerns about commodification and harm discussed in Chapter 2, I recommended that regulation confer a threshold level of respect and protection from harm to the child to be born as a result of selective reproduction. This 'minimum threshold' approach is similar to current HFEA policy on saviour sibling selection, which creates a presumption in favour of treatment unless the child is at risk of serious harm or neglect.

The relational model for selective reproduction outlined in Chapter 5 attempts to reconcile individual and collective interests within families as far as possible. In contrast to the predominantly 'harm-based' and 'best-interests' models for selective reproduction in the UK and Australia, respectively, my relational model requires the interests of the child to be born to be considered in connection with the interests of other family members. This more accurately reflects the way decisions are frequently made within families and is gaining increasing support in the context of medical decision-making generally. Central to the relational model proposed is a collaborative decision-making process, with active roles for families and members of their healthcare team. I proposed a new role for a clinical ethicist to assist families in navigating the ethical minefield of selective reproduction by facilitating moral deliberation and consensus through ethics counselling and mediating any disputes that arise. The role of the clinical ethicist is to create an 'open moral space' for prospective parents and other relevant family members to explore and attempt to reconcile the various interests at stake in accordance with their individual values, beliefs and preferences. I also recommended that a separately constituted CEC review complex decisions about selective reproduction, such as saviour sibling selection, to ensure that the welfare of the child to be born is given proper consideration.

The relational framework for regulating saviour sibling selection mapped out in Chapter 6 provides an example of how a relational model might be implemented through a combination of legislation and policy guidelines. The framework proposed is not intended to be definitive but is offered as a start-ing point, to trigger debate about how regulation might better reflect the relational nature of the welfare of the child in assisted reproduction. I opted for a flexible permissive regulatory framework that supports parents in the decision-making process and protects the child to be born from exploitation, abuse and neglect, without unnecessarily restricting reproductive choice. My proposed regulatory framework essentially performs three main functions.

First, it provides general guidance on the various individual and shared interests within a family seeking selective reproduction through guiding principles in legislation. The guiding principles proposed specify that treat-ment decisions should involve consideration of the interests of the child to be born, the interests of his/her parents, the interests of any existing siblings and the collective interests of the family as a whole. More detailed guidance on the specific nature of these interests within the context of saviour sibling selection is contained in policy guidelines.

Second, my proposed regulatory framework establishes a robust decision-making process to manage individual and shared interests within families (which will not necessarily coincide). I recommended that legislation endorse a relational approach by requiring the interests of the child to be born to be considered in connection with the interests of his/her family. My proposed policy guidelines implement a relational decision-making model by outlining the roles of parents and members of their healthcare team in the context of saviour sibling selection. This requires ART physicians, counsellors and clin-ical ethicists to assist parents by providing relevant information, counselling and ethical guidance, respectively.

Third, my proposed framework confers a threshold level of protection on the child to be born through legislation, which expressly prohibits PGD where there is a risk of exploitation, abuse or neglect. Based on the concerns about commodification and harm highlighted in Chapter 3, I recommended that legislation expressly state that a risk of exploitation, abuse or neglect exists where: (a) the parents do not want a child in his/her own right; or (b) there is a serious risk of significant harm to the child. To ensure that due consideration is given to the welfare of the child to be born, I suggested that ethically complex cases, such as saviour sibling selection, be reviewed by a regional CEC.

My focus on saviour siblings in this book enabled me to draw comparisons between a relational framework and existing regulatory frameworks for selective reproduction in the UK and Australia. My proposed framework for regulating saviour sibling selection aims to be more responsive to individual cases than current UK and Australian regulation in several ways. First, my framework expressly articulates a broader range of interests relevant to saviour sibling selection, including those of the parents, any existing children and the collective interests of the family as a whole. Second, my framework devolves treatment decisions to prospective parents in consultation with their health-care team, subject to approval by a regional CEC. This is based on the idea that parents should be able to make their own decisions about selective reproduction, provided they fall within the parameters set by parliament. Third, my proposed framework removes some of the unjustifiable restrictions on saviour sibling selection that apply (or previously applied) under UK and Australian regulation. For example, no distinction is made between PGD for tissue typing in conjunction with screening for genetic disease and PGD for tissue typing alone. The use of tissue typing is also not restricted to siblings and could potentially be used for the benefit of a parent or other close relative. The welfare of the child remains a focus in my proposed regulatory framework, which expressly protects the child to be born from exploitation, abuse and neglect.

In addition to being responsive to individual cases, my proposed relational framework aims to canvass issues that will assist parents to make any future treatment decisions that may arise. For example, the decision to conceive a saviour sibling may be the first in a series of moral dilemmas faced by a family struggling to save the life of one of its members. The drama that unfolds in the fictional account of a saviour sibling in *My Sister's Keeper*[1] reveals the ongoing state of crisis that may be experienced by a family into which a saviour sibling is born. As Storrow points out, 'Whereas ethics pronouncements present the creation of a saviour sibling as a way to resolve a familial crisis, *My Sister's Keeper* demonstrates how the saviour's presence can actually intensify the crisis'.[2] If an initial cord blood donation does not cure the existing child, parents will need to consider other options such as peripheral blood or bone marrow donations by the saviour sibling. Decisions about subsequent donations may be less stressful if the parents have already explored both the individual and collective family interests in accordance with their own values and preferences through ethics counselling prior to conception.

There are three qualifications I wish to mention about my proposed relational framework for saviour sibling selection. First, my framework is potentially more burdensome than current regulatory frameworks as it introduces more variables into the equation about whether treatment should proceed than currently exist in UK and Australian regulation. For instance, it requires consideration of various individual and collective interests within a family and the nature of the relationships within the family. While this presents a difficult task, it is not impossible. Furthermore, these variables already exist whether or not they are openly acknowledged. In addition to being individuals in their own right, family members are 'relational and interdependent'.[3] Open acknowledgement of the complex interests and dynamics within families is an important first step in reconciling conflicting interests and achieving consensus. The decision to select a saviour sibling is complicated and regulation should at least attempt to accommodate the various interests at stake and support parents in the decision-making process. As Held argues, the 'messy concerns of morality' cannot be 'arranged along neat and clean lines' by being reduced to the categorical imperative or the principle of utility.[4]

Second, my relational framework is based on a largely theoretical analysis of the welfare of the child to be born. At various points throughout this book, I emphasise that ongoing empirical research into the short- and long-term impacts on children born as a result of PGD is needed to gain a better insight into how the welfare of the child is affected by selection. Third, my relational framework for saviour sibling selection is intended as a starting point for further discussion and analysis. If a relational framework is adopted, critical evaluation of the decision-making process should be carried out to identify ways in which the process itself might be improved. One key aspect of my proposed framework – clinical ethics consultation – is relatively new in the UK and Australia and is generally offered to physicians rather than parents. Australian clinics must currently seek advice from a CEC before providing saviour sibling selection although the advice of CECs is not binding. CECs are not as well established or regulated in the UK and Australia as human research ethics committees. I proposed a general framework for the operation of clinical ethicists and CECs in the context of saviour sibling selection. Ongoing empirical investigation into the operation and effectiveness of existing forms of clinical ethics consultation could further inform and improve my proposals. Clinical ethics consultation is more established in the US. Research into the operation of clinical ethics committees in the US could therefore be used to enlighten reform initiatives in the UK and Australia.[5]

Although the regulatory framework outlined in Chapter 6 is tailored to saviour sibling selection, the relational model on which it is based is relevant to other forms of selective reproduction. Belinda Bennett suggests that, '[t]he debate over saviour siblings can ... be seen not only as a debate over the ethics of creating tissue matched children, but also as a means of illustrating broader regulatory issues about contemporary biomedicine'.[6] A relational model is clearly relevant to saviour sibling selection where there are additional interests at stake that ought to be considered alongside the interests of the child to be born. A relational model also offers a new way to approach other ethically controversial cases, particularly those involving selection for non-therapeutic reasons, which are motivated by the interests of specific family members. The decision to select a child of a particular sex, for example, is driven by the interests of the prospective parents who desire a girl or a boy and may also impact on the interests of existing siblings who will grow up alongside the child selected. Similarly, deaf individuals may prefer to select a deaf child because, within their community, deafness is considered 'the norm' rather than a disability. The relationship between a deaf child and his/her parents and siblings may be different to that of a hearing child, depending on how important 'deafness' is to the cultural identity of family members.

As discussed in Chapter 2, PGD is currently prohibited in both the UK and Australia for social sex-selection and selecting a child with a disability. This is, at least in part, due to welfare of the child concerns. In Australia, the NHMRC has flagged these controversial treatments for further review following community discussion and debate. It would be interesting to consider how a relational model might apply in these contexts. Selecting a child for non-therapeutic reasons raises different challenges to those posed by saviour sibling selection and may be more difficult to justify. For example, the thought of enabling a deaf couple to use PGD to select a deaf child is confronting for many and raises important questions about how we view disability, whether impairment constitutes 'harm', and the nature of the parent/child relationship. In particular, the idea of allowing individuals to select a particular 'type' of child raises familiar concerns about 'designer babies', such as eugenics and slippery slopes. Further public debate is required to tease out the nature of concerns within the community associated with different types of selection using PGD. It is important, however, that this debate is ethically and empirically well-informed, and not based on mere speculation about how people will exercise reproductive choice and the impact such choices will have on society as a whole.

Many of the benefits of the relational model proposed in this book, which I identify for saviour sibling selection, are applicable to selective reproduction generally. It makes sense to consider not only the individual interests of the child to be born but also the interests of the child's parents, any existing siblings and the collective family interests that are likely to be affected by a decision about selective reproduction. The welfare of the child should be considered within the social context of the family into which he/she will be born because, for better or worse, that family will be the intimate community within which the child will grow and hopefully flourish. Provided the child to be born is not at risk of exploitation, abuse or neglect, the instrumental and inherent value of families provides a strong reason to limit state involvement in family decision-making, even if some reproductive decisions do not sit comfortably with particular sub-sections of society.

As discussed in Chapter 4, some bioethical writers have begun to argue for a greater role for the family in medical decision-making generally. This movement is an exciting one, as it recognises the moral import of the families that ultimately share the joys and bear the burdens involved in caring for loved ones. However, care must be taken to ensure that power imbalances that exist within families do not compromise the treatment of vulnerable parties. I have argued in this book that power imbalance is often a significant feature of intimate relationships, particularly families. In a sense, the protection of vulnerable individuals – the unborn, the young, the elderly and the ill – is the *raison d'être* of families. Returning to the words of Patricia Smith, 'family living is very probably a necessity for human existence'.[7] The relational model proposed in this book aims to support the families charged with protecting the child to be born and promoting the nucleus of well-being that is the touchstone of intimate families.

Selective reproduction challenges our assumptions about the role of parents and the nature of family relations. It also calls into question the extent to which biomedical advances should be used to engineer a desired family outcome. By exploring the ethics of selection, this book raises questions about why people choose to procreate and how much parents can ask of their children. The answers to these questions can be confronting as they reveal that the choices parents make are not necessarily made in the best interests of the child. Decisions are made within families for a multitude of reasons that are often inextricably connected and may affect the interests of more than one family member. Allowing parents to select the genetic traits of their child not only raises fears about a future in which babies are 'made to order', but also has the potential to undermine established notions about parental love. In the case of saviour sibling selection, selecting an embryo that will grow into a healthy child with the capacity to save the life of his/her sibling should not ordinarily detract from the nucleus of love or well-being within a family. Further debate and empirical analysis will shed more light on whether or not concerns about 'designer babies' are justified in relation to other forms of selective reproduction. Insofar as objections are based on the welfare of the child to be born, a relational approach provides a new perspective that contextualises the interests of the child within the family into which the child will be born.

Notes

1 Jodi Picoult, *My Sister's Keeper* (Allen & Unwin, 2005).
2 Richard F Storrow, 'Therapeutic Reproduction and Human Dignity' (2009) 21 *Law & Literature* 257, 270.
3 Virginia Held, *The Ethics of Care: Personal, Political, and Global* (Oxford University Press, 2006), 72.
4 Held, ibid, 73.
5 For an analysis of the operation of clinical ethics committees in the US, see Peter A Singer, Edmund D Pellegrino and Mark Siegler, 'Clinical Ethics Revisited' (2001) 2 *BMC Medical*

Ethics E1, <http://www.biomedcentral.com/content/pdf/1472-6939-2-1.pdf> (accessed 24 April 2013).

6 Belinda Bennett, 'Symbiotic Relationships: Saviour Siblings, Family Rights and Biomedicine' (2005) 19 *Australian Journal of Family Law* 195, 196.

7 Patricia Smith, 'Family Responsibility and the Nature of Obligation' in Diana Tietjens Meyers, Kenneth Kipnis and Cornelius F Murphy (eds), *Kindred Matters: Rethinking the Philosophy of the Family* (Cornell University Press, 1993), 54.

Bibliography

A Articles/books/reports

Aiken, William and Hugh LaFollette, *Whose Child? Children's Rights, Parental Authority, and State Power* (Rowman and Littlefield, 1980)

Alghrani, Amel and John Harris, 'Reproductive Liberty: Should the Foundation of Families Be Regulated?' (2006) 18 *Child and Family Law Quarterly* 191

American Academy of Pediatrics (AAP), 'Policy Statement – Children as Hematopoietic Stem Cell Donors' (2010) 125 *Pediatrics* 392

Archard, David William, *Children, Family and the State* (Ashgate, 2003)

Ashcroft, Richard E, Angus Dawson, Heather Draper and John R McMillan (eds), *Principles of Health Care Ethics* (Wiley, 2nd edn, 2007)

Baruch, Susannah, David Kaufman and Kathy Hudson, 'Genetic Testing of Embryos: Practices and Perspectives of US In Vitro Fertilization Clinics' (2008) 89 *Fertility and Sterility* 1053

Beauchamp, Tom L and James F Childress, *Principles of Biomedical Ethics* (Oxford University Press, 5th edn, 2001)

Benagioano, Giuseppe and Paola Bianchi, 'Sex Preselection: An Aid to Couples or a Threat to Humanity?' (1999) 14 *Human Reproduction* 868

Benatar, David, *Better Never to Have Been: The Harm of Coming into Existence* (Clarendon Press, 2006)

Bennett, Belinda, 'Symbiotic Relationships: Saviour Siblings, Family Rights and Biomedicine' (2005) 19 *Australian Journal of Family Law* 195

Biddulph, Steve, *Raising Babies: Should Under 3's go to Nursery?* (Harper Thorsons, 2006)

Birk, Dewinder, 'The Reform of the Human Fertilisation and Embryology Act 1990' (2005) 35 *Family Law* 563

Blackhall, Leslie J, *et al*, 'Ethnicity and Attitudes toward Patient Autonomy' (1995) 274 *Journal of American Medical Association* 820

Blustein, Jeffrey, 'The Family in Medical Decisionmaking' (1993) 23 *Hastings Center Report* 6

Boseley, Sarah, 'Green Light for "Designer Babies" to Save Siblings', *The Guardian* (online), 22 July 2004, <http://www.guardian.co.uk/science/2004/jul/22/sciencenews.health3?INTCMP=SRCH> (accessed 26 April 2013)

Boyle, Robert J and Julian Savulescu, 'Ethics of Using Preimplantation Genetic Diagnosis to Select a Stem Cell Donor for an Existing Person' (2001) 323 *British Medical Journal* 1240

Brazier, Margaret, 'Regulating the Reproduction Business?' (1999) 7 *Medical Law Review* 166

Brennan, Samantha, 'Recent Work in Feminist Ethics' (1999) 109 *Ethics* 858

Browett, Peter and Stephen Palmer, 'Legal Barriers Might Have Catastrophic Effects' (1996) 312 *British Medical Journal* 242

Brownsword, Roger, 'Bioethics Today, Bioethics Tomorrow: Stem Cell Research and the "Dignitarian Alliance"' (2003) 17 *Notre Dame Journal of Law, Ethics & Public Policy* 15

——, 'Regulating Human Genetics: New Dilemmas for a New Millennium' (2004) 12(1) *Medical Law Review* 14

——, 'Reproductive Opportunities and Regulatory Challenges' (2004) 67 *The Modern Law Review* 304

Buchanan, Allen E and Dan W Brock, *Deciding for Others: The Ethics of Surrogate Decision Making* (Cambridge University Press, 1989)

Cannold, Leslie and Lynn Gillam, 'Regulation, Consultation and Divergent Community Views: The Case of Access to ART by Lesbian and Single Women' (2002) 9 *Journal of Law and Medicine* 498

Casarett, David J, Frona Daskal and John Lantos, 'The Authority of the Clinical Ethicist' (1998) 28 *Hastings Center Report* 6

Chalmers, Don, 'Professional Self-regulation and Guidelines in Assisted Reproduction' (2002) 9 *Journal of Law and Medicine* 414

Cheyette, Cara, 'Organ Harvests from the Legally Incompetent: An Argument Against Compelled Altruism' (2000) 41 *Boston College Law Review* 465

Coady, Margaret, 'Families and Future Children: The Role of Rights and Interests in Determining Ethical Policy for Regulating Families' (2002) 9 *Journal of Law and Medicine* 449

Cohen, Cynthia B, '"Give Me Children or I Shall Die!" New Reproductive Technologies and Harm to Children' (1996) 26 *Hastings Center Report* 19

——, 'Wrestling with the Future: Should We Test Children for Adult Onset Genetic Conditions?' (1998) 8 *Kennedy Institute of Ethics Journal* 111

'Couple "Choose" to Have a Deaf Baby', *BBC News* (online), 8 April 2002, <http://news.bbc.co.uk/2/hi/health/1916462.stm> (accessed 26 April 2013)

Crouch, Robert A and Carl Elliott, 'Moral Agency and the Family: The Case of Living Related Organ Transplantation' (1999) 8 *Cambridge Quarterly of Healthcare Ethics* 275

Dahl, E *et al*, 'Preconception Sex Selection for Non-Medical Reasons: A Representative Survey from Germany' (2003) 18 *Human Reproduction* 2231

——, 'Preconception Sex Selection for Non-Medical Reasons: A Representative Survey from the UK' (2003) 18 *Human Reproduction* 2238

Daniels, J A, 'Adolescent Separation-Individuation and Family Transitions' (1990) 25 *Adolescence* 105

Davis, John, 'Selecting Potential Children and Unconditional Parental Love' (2008) 22 *Bioethics* 258

Devolder, K, 'Preimplantation HLA Typing: Having Children to Save Our Loved Ones' (2005) 31 *Journal of Medical Ethics* 582

'Doctor Plans UK "Designer Baby" Clinic', *BBC News* (online), 11 December 2001, <http://news.bbc.co.uk/1/hi/health/1702854.stm> (accessed 26 April 2013)

Donchin, Anne, 'Reworking Autonomy: Toward a Feminist Perspective' (1995) 4 *Cambridge Quarterly of Healthcare Ethics* 44

Doyal, Len, 'Clinical Ethics Committees and the Formulation of Health Care Policy' (2001) 27 *Journal of Medical Ethics* i44

Dutney, Andrew, 'Hope Takes Risks: Making Sense of the Interests of ART Offspring: the South Australian Experience' (Paper presented at the seminar Assisted Reproduction: Considering the Interests of the Child, Perth, WA, April 1999)

Dwyer, James and Elizabeth Vig, 'Rethinking Transplantation Between Siblings' (1995) 25 *Hastings Center Report* 7

Elliston, Sarah, *The Best Interests of the Child in Healthcare* (Routledge-Cavendish, 2007)

Elwyn, Glyn, Jonathon Gray and Angus Clarke, 'Shared Decision Making and Non-Directiveness in Genetic Counselling' (2000) 37 *Journal of Medical Genetics* 135

Erel, Osnat, Yael Oberman and Nurit Yirmiya, 'Maternal Versus Nonmaternal Care and Seven Domains of Children's Development' (2000) 126 *Psychological Bulletin* 727

Fain, Haskell, *Normative Politics and the Community of Nations* (Temple University Press, 1987)

Family Law Council of Australia, *Creating Children: A Uniform Approach to the Law and Practice of Reproductive Technology in Australia* (Australian Govt Pub Service, 1985)

Feinberg, Joel, *Harm to Others. Volume 1: The Moral Limits of the Criminal Law* (Oxford University Press, 1984)

——, 'Wrongful Life and the Counterfactual Element in Harming' (1986) 4 *Social Philosophy and Policy* 145

Fenton, Rachel Ann and Fiona Dabell, 'Time for Change (1)' (2007) 157 *New Law Journal* 848

Fiester, Autumn, 'Mediation and Advocacy' (2012) 12 *American Journal of Bioethics* 10

Fox, E, S Myers and R Pearlman, 'Ethics Consultation in United States Hospitals: A National Survey' (2007) 7 *American Journal of Bioethics* 13

Freckelton, Ian and Kerry Petersen (eds), *Controversies in Health Law* (Federation Press, 1999)

Freund, B L and K Siegel, 'Problems in Transition Following Bone Marrow Transplantation: Psychosocial Aspects' (1986) 56 *American Journal of Orthopsychiatry* 244

Friedman, Marilyn, 'Feminism and Modern Friendship: Dislocating the Community' (1989) 99 *Ethics* 275

——, *What are Friends For? Feminist Perspectives on Personal Relationships and Moral Theory* (Cornell University Press, 1993)

Fu-Chang Tsai, Daniel, 'How Should Doctors Approach Patients? A Confucian Reflection on Personhood' (2001) 27 *Journal of Medical Ethics* 44

Fukuyama, Francis, *Our Posthuman Future: Consequences of the Biotechnology Revolution* (Strauss & Giroux, 2002)

Gavaghan, Colin, *Defending the Genetic Supermarket: Law and Ethics of Selecting the Next Generation* (Routledge-Cavendish, 2007)

Gaylin, Willard and Ruth Macklin (eds), *Who Speaks for the Child: The Problems of Proxy Consent* (Plenum Press, 1982)

Gilbar, Roy and Ora Gilbar, 'The Medical Decision-Making Process and the Family: The Case of Breast Cancer Patients and their Husbands' (2009) 23 *Bioethics* 183

Gillam, Lynn, 'Prenatal Diagnosis and Discrimination Against the Disabled' (1999) 25 *Journal of Medical Ethics* 163

Gilligan, Carol, *In a Different Voice: Psychological Theory and Women's Development* (Harvard University Press, 1993)

Gillon, Raanan, 'Eugenics, Contraception, Abortion and Ethics' (1998) 24 *Journal of Medical Ethics* 219

Gillott, John, 'Screening for disability: a eugenic pursuit?' (2001) 27 *Journal of Medical Ethics*, Supp No 2, ii21

Glannon, Walter, *Genes and Future People: Philosophical Issues in Human Genetics* (Westview Press, 2001)

Glover, Jonathan, *Choosing Children: Genes, Disability and Design* (Clarendon Press, 2006)

Glover, Jonathan and European Commission of Human Rights, *Fertility and the Family: the Glover Report on reproductive technologies to the European Commission* (Fourth Estate, 1989)

Greer, Tyler, 'Medical Ethicist Examines How to Build a Better Human', *UAB Reporter* (Birmingham), 30 August 2012, <http://www.uab.edu/news/reporter/people/item/2697-medical-ethicist-examines-how-to-build-a-better-human> (accessed 26 April 2013)

Grundell, Erica, 'Tissue Typing for Bone Marrow Transplantation: An Ethical Examination of Some Arguments Concerning Harm to the Child' (2003) 22 *Monash Bioethics Review* 45

Gunning, Jennifer and Helen Szoke (eds), *The Regulation of Assisted Reproductive Technology* (Ashgate, 2003)

Habermas, Jürgen, *Moral Consciousness and Communicative Action* (Christian Lenhardt and Shierry Weber Nicholsen trans, MIT Press, 1990) [trans of: *Moralbewusstein und kommunikatives Handeln* (Suhrkamp Verlag, 1983)]

——, *The Future of Human Nature* (Polity, 2003)

Hansen, M *et al*, 'Assisted Reproductive Technology and Major Birth Defects in Western Australia' (2012) 120 *Obstetrics & Gynecology* 852

——, 'The risk of major birth defects after intracytoplasmic sperm injection and in vitro fertilisation' (2002) 346 *New England Journal of Medicine* 725

——, 'Twins Born Following Assisted Reproductive Technology: Perinatal Outcome and Admission to Hospital' (2009) 24 *Human Reproduction* 2321

Hardwig, John, 'What about the Family?' (1990) 20 *The Hastings Center Report* 5

Harris, J J, 'The Welfare of the Child' (2000) 8 *Health Care Analysis* 27

Harris, John, 'Sex Selection and Regulated Hatred' (2005) 31 *Journal of Medical Ethics* 291

Harris, John and Soren Holm (eds), *The Future of Human Reproduction: Ethics, Choice and Regulation* (Oxford University Press, 1998)

Hart, H L A, *Law, Liberty and Morality* (Oxford University Press, 1968)

Held, Virginia, *The Ethics of Care: Personal, Political, and Global* (Oxford University Press, 2006)

Horsey, Kirsty and Hazel Biggs (eds), *Human Fertilisation and Embryology: Reproducing Regulation* (Routledge-Cavendish, 2007)

House of Commons Science and Technology Committee, Fifth Report of Session 2004–5, *Human Reproductive Technologies and the Law*, HC7–1 and II (24 March 2005)

Hui, Edwin, 'Parental Refusal of Life-Saving Treatments for Adolescents: Chinese Familism in Medical Decision-Making Re-visited' (2008) 22 *Bioethics* 286

Human Fertilisation and Embryology Authority, *Sex Selection: Options for Regulation: A Report on the HFEA's 2002–03 Review of Sex Selection Including a Discussion of Legislative and Regulatory Options* (2003)

——, *Tomorrow's Children: Report of the Policy Review of Welfare of the Child Assessments in Licensed Assisted Conception Clinics* (November 2005)

Human Fertilisation and Embryology Authority and Human Genetics Commission Joint Working Party, *Outcome of the Public Consultation on Preimplantation Genetic Diagnosis* (November 2001)

Human Fertilisation and Embryology Authority Ethics & Law Committee, *Ethical Issues in the Creation and Selection of Preimplantation Embryos to Produce Tissue Donors* (22 November 2001)

Human Genetics Commission, *Making Babies: Reproductive Decisions and Genetic Technologies* (January 2006)

Huxley, Aldous, *Brave New World* (first published 1932; Flamingo, 1994 edn)

Infertility Treatment Authority, *Report on the Outcome of Consultation with Members of the Infertility Treatment Authority Ethics Panel* (February 2002) (document provided to the author by Tracey Petrillo (Policy Officer, VARTA) in July 2009)

Jackson, Emily, 'Conception and the Irrelevance of the Welfare Principle' (2002) 65 *Modern Law Review* 176

Jansen, Lynn A, 'Child Organ Donation, Family Autonomy, and Intimate Attachments' (2004) 13 *Cambridge Quarterly of Healthcare Ethics* 133

Jecker, Nancy S, 'Conceiving A Child to Save A Child: Reproductive and Filial Ethics' (1990) 1 *The Journal of Clinical Ethics* 99

Johnson, Martin H, 'The Art of Regulation and the Regulation of ART: The Impact of Regulation on Research and Clinical Practice' (2002) 9 *Journal of Law and Medicine* 399

Joint Committee on the Human Tissue and Embryos, (Draft) Bill Session 2006–7, *Human Tissues and Embryos (Draft) Bill*, HL 169/HC 630-I and II (August 2007)

Jost, Alison, 'Familiar? Yes. Flawed? Not Necessarily', (2009) *Bioethics Forum*, <http://www.thehastingscenter.org/Bioethicsforum/Post.aspx?id=3676&blogid=140/> (accessed 26 April 2013)

Källén, B *et al*, 'Cancer risk in children and young adults conceived by in vitro fertilisation' (2010) 126 *Pediatrics* e270

Kant, Immanuel, *Groundwork of the Metaphysics of Morals* (Cambridge University Press, first published 1785, 2005 edn)

Karpin, Isabel and Belinda Bennett, 'Genetic Technologies and the Regulation of Reproductive Decision-Making in Australia' (2006) 14 *Journal of Law and Medicine* 127

Karpin, Isabel and Kristin Savell, *Perfecting Pregnancy: Law, Disability, and the Future of Reproduction* (Cambridge University Press, 2012)

Kass, Leon R, *Life, Liberty and the Defense of Dignity: the Challenge for Bioethics* (Encounter Books, 2002)

——, 'Triumph or Tragedy? The Moral Meaning of Genetic Technology' (2000) 45 *American Journal of Jurisprudence* 1

Katari, S, 'DNA methylation and gene expression differences in children conceived in vitro or in vivo' (2009) 18 *Human Molecular Genetics* 3769

Katz, Jay, *The Silent World of Doctor and Patient* (Free Press, 1984)

Kavanagh, Matthew M, 'Rewriting the Legal Family: Beyond Exclusivity to a Care-Based Standard' (2004) 16 *Yale Journal of Law and Feminism* 83

Keenan, A and S Stock, '"Closed Future" for Saviour Siblings', *The Australian*, 17 April 2002, 3

Kent, Julie, 'Aussie Couple Fights to Have a Baby Girl through Selective IVF: Have Already Aborted Twin Boys', *Cleveland Leader* (online), 10 January 2011, <http://www.clevelandleader.com/node/15670> (accessed 26 April 2013)

King, David, 'The Case for Case-by-Case Regulation of PGD' (2010) 541 *BioNews*, <http://www.bionews.org.uk/page_53438.asp> (accessed 26 April 2013)

Kuczewski, Mark G, 'Reconceiving the Family: The Process of Consent in Medical Decisionmaking' (1996) 26 *The Hastings Center Report* 30

Kumar, Rahul, 'Who Can be Wronged?' (2003) 31 *Philosophy & Public Affairs* 99

Lauritzen, Paul *et al*, 'The Gift of Life and the Common Good: The Need for a Communal approach to Organ Procurement' (2001) 31 *The Hastings Center Report* 29

Lee, Ellie, Jan Macvarish and Sally Sheldon, 'Assessing Child Welfare under the Human Fertilisation and Embryology Act: The New Law: Summary of Findings' (University of Kent, September 2012), <http://blogs.kent.ac.uk/parentingculturestudies/files/2012/06/Summary_Assessing-Child-Welfare-final.pdf> (accessed 26 April 2013)

Liao, S Matthew, 'The Right of Children to be Loved' (2006) 14 *The Journal of Political Philosophy* 420

Mackenzie, Catriona and Natalie Stoljar (eds), *Relational Autonomy: Feminist Perspectives of Autonomy, Agency, and the Social Self* (Oxford University Press, 2000)

MacLeod, Kendra D *et al*, 'Pediatric Sibling Donors of Successful and Unsuccessful Hematopoietic Stem Cell Transplants (HSCT): A Qualitative Study of their Psychosocial Experience' (2003) 28 *Journal of Pediatric Psychology* 223

McDonald, Iain, Rachel Anne Fenton and Fiona Dabell, 'Treatment Provisions: Proposals for Reform of the Human Fertilisation and Embryology Act 1990' (2007) 29 *Journal of Social Welfare and Family Law* 293

McKibben, Bill, *Enough: Genetic Engineering and the End of Human Nature* (Bloomsbury, 2003)

McLean, Sheila, 'Clinical Ethics Committees, Due Process and the Right to a Fair Hearing' (2008) 15 *Journal of Law and Medicine* 520

McNair, Ruth, *Outcomes for Children Born of ART in a Diverse Range of Families* (Victorian Law Reform Commission Occasional Paper, August 2004)

Malek, Janet, 'Use or Refuse Reproductive Genetic Technologies: Which Would a "Good Parent" Do?' (2013) 27 *Bioethics* 59

Medew, Julia, 'Couples Use IVF to Pick Genes: "Designer Baby" Concerns', *The Age* (Melbourne), 3 July 2012, 1

Meslin, E M *et al*, 'Hospital Ethics Committees in the United Kingdom' (1996) 8 *HEC Forum* 301

Meyers, Diana Tietjens, Kenneth Kipnis and Cornelius F Murphy (eds), *Kindred Matters: Rethinking the Philosophy of the Family* (Cornell University Press, 1993)

Mill, John Stuart, 'On Liberty' in Mary Warnock (ed), *Utilitarianism and On Liberty* (Blackwell Publishing, 2nd edn, 2003), 88

——, *Utilitarianism* (Project Gutenberg EBook reprinted from Fraser's Magazine, 7th edn, Longmans, Green, and Co, 1879), <http://www.gutenberg.org/ebooks/11224> (accessed 26 April 2013)

Mnookin, Robert, 'Child-Custody Adjudication: Judicial Functions in the Face of Indeterminacy' (1975) 39 *Law and Contemporary Problems* 226

Month, S, 'Preventing Children from Donating May Not be in Their Best Interests' (1996) 312 *British Medical Journal* 240

Morrow, Lance, 'When One Body Can Save Another' (1991) 137 *Time Magazine* 54

Mumford, S E, E Corrigan and M G R Hull, 'Access to Assisted Conception: A Framework of Regulation' (1998) 13 *Human Reproduction* 2349

Murray, Thomas H, *The Worth of a Child* (University of California Press, 1996)

Nelson, Hilde Lindemann and James Lindemann Nelson, *The Patient in the Family: An Ethics of Medicine and Families* (Routledge, 1995)

Nelson, James Lindemann, 'Taking Families Seriously' (1992) 22 *The Hastings Center Report* 6

Nicholson, Alastair, 'Children's Rights in the Context of Infertility Treatment' (Speech delivered at the Infertility Treatment Authority One Day Symposium, Melbourne, 2 November 2006)

Ogus, Anthony, *Regulation: Legal Form and Economic Theory* (Clarendon Press, 1994)

Overall, Christine, *Why Have Children? The Ethical Debate* (The MIT Press, 2012)

Packman, W L, 'Psychosocial Impact of Pediatric BMT on Siblings' (1999) 24 *Bone Marrow Transplantation* 701

Parfit, Derek, *Reasons and Persons* (Clarendon Press, 1984)

Parker, Christine *et al* (eds), *Regulating Law* (Oxford University Press, 2004)

Parker, Stephen, 'The Best Interests of the Child – Principles and Problems' (1994) 8 *International Journal of Law and the Family* 26

Pearn, John H, 'Gatekeeping and Assisted Reproductive Technology: The Ethical Rights and Responsibilities of Doctors' (1997) 167 *Medical Journal of Australia* 318

Pence, Gregory E, *How to Build a Better Human: An Ethical Blueprint* (Rowman & Littlefield, 2012)

Pennings, Guido, 'Measuring the Welfare of the Child: In Search of the Appropriate Evaluation Principle' (1999) 14 *Human Reproduction* 1146

——, 'Saviour Siblings: Using Preimplantation Genetic Diagnosis for Tissue Typing' (2004) 1266 *International Congress Series* 311

Pennings, G, R Schots and I Liebaers, 'Ethical Considerations on Preimplantation Genetic Diagnosis for HLA Typing to Match a Future Child as a Donor of Haematopoietic Stem Cells to a Sibling' (2002) 17 *Human Reproduction* 534

People, Science & Policy Ltd, *Report on the Consultation on the Review of the Human Fertilisation & Embryology Act 1990* (March 2006)

Petersen, Kerry, 'Regulating Preimplantation Genetic Diagnosis: A Criminal Model Versus a Professional Model' (2009) 17 *Journal of Law and Medicine* 452

Picoult, Jodi, *My Sister's Keeper* (Allen & Unwin, 2005)

Progress Educational Trust (PET), 'Parents or Parliament: Embryo Testing, Who Decides?', Public Debate (London, July 2007)

Rachels, James 'When Philosophers Shoot From the Hip' (1991) 5 *Bioethics* 67

Ram, N R, 'Britain's New Preimplantation Tissue Typing Policy: An Ethical Defence' (2006) 32 *Journal of Medical Ethics* 278

Rawls, John, *A Theory of Justice* (Oxford University Press, 1971)

Robertson, J A, 'Extending Preimplantation Genetic Diagnosis: Medical and Non-medical Uses' (2003) 29 *Journal of Medical Ethics* 213

Robertson, John A, *Children of Choice: Freedom and the New Reproductive Technologies* (Princeton University Press, 1994)

——, 'Extending Preimplantation Genetic Diagnosis: The Ethical Debate: Ethical Issues in New Uses of Preimplantation Genetic Diagnosis' (2003) 18 *Human Reproduction* 465

Robertson, John, Helen Bequaert Holmes and Cynthia B Cohen, *Children of Choice: Freedom and the New Reproductive Technologies* (Princeton University Press, 1994)

Robertson, John A, Jeffrey P Khan and John E Wagner, 'Conception to Obtain Hematopoietic Stem Cells' (2002) 32 *Hastings Center Report* 34

Rosner, F, 'Hospital Medical Ethics Committees: A Review of their Development' (1985) 253 *Journal of American Medical Association* 2693

Ross, Lainie Friedman, *Children, Families, and Health Care Decision Making* (Clarendon Press, 1998)

——, 'Health Care Decisionmaking by Children: Is it in Their Best Interest?' (1997) 27 *The Hastings Center Report* 41

Ruddick, Sara, *Maternal Thinking: Toward a Politics of Peace* (Beacon Press, 1989)

Samuel, G N *et al*, 'Ethinicity, Equity and Public Benefit: A Critical Evaluation of Public Umbilical Cord Banking in Australia' (2007) 40 *Bone Marrow Transplantation* 729

Sandel, Michael J, *The Case Against Perfection: Ethics in the Age of Genetic Engineering* (Harvard University Press, 2007)

——, 'The Case Against Perfection: What's Wrong with Designer Children, Bionic Athletes, and Genetic Engineering' (2004) 292 *The Atlantic Monthly* 50

Savage, T *et al*, 'Childhood Outcomes of Assisted Reproductive Technology' (2011) 26 *Human Reproduction* 2392

Savulescu, Julian, 'Deaf Lesbians, "Designer Disability", and the Future of Medicine' (2002) 325 *British Medical Journal* 771

——, 'Sex Selection: The Case For' (1999) 171 *Medical Journal of Australia* 373

——, 'Substantial Harm But Substantial Benefit' (1996) 312 *British Medical Journal* 241

Savulescu, Julian and Guy Kahane, 'The Moral Obligation to Create Children with the Best Chance of the Best Life' (2009) 23 *Bioethics* 274

Schoeman, Ferdinand, 'Parental Discretion and Children's Rights: Background and Implications for Medical Decision-Making' (1985) 10 *The Journal of Medicine and Philosophy* 45

——, 'Rights of Children, Rights of Parents, and the Moral Basis of the Family' (1980) 91 *Ethics* 6

Scott, Rosamund, *Choosing between Possible Lives: Law and Ethics of Prenatal and Preimplantation Genetic Diagnosis* (Hart Publishing, 2007)

——, 'Choosing between Possible Lives: Legal and Ethical Issues in Preimplantation Genetic Diagnosis' (2006) 26 *Oxford Journal of Legal Studies* 153

Senate Community Affairs Legislation Committee, *Report on the Provisions of the Research Involving Embryos and Prohibition of Human Cloning Bill 2002*, October 2002, 2–8, <http://www.aph.gov.au/Parliamentary_Business/Committees/Senate_Committees?url=clac_ctte/completed_inquiries/2002–4/emb_cloning/report/index.htm> (accessed 26 April 2013)

Shakespeare, Tom, 'Choices and Rights: Eugenics, Genetics and Disability Equality' (1998) 13 *Disability and Society* 665

——, *Disability Rights and Wrongs* (Routledge, 2006)

Sharpe, Virginia A, 'To What Extent Should We Think of Our Intimates As "Persons"? Commentary on "Conceiving a Child"' (1990) 1 *The Journal of Clinical Ethics* 103

Sheldon, S and S Wilkinson, 'Should Selecting Saviour Siblings be Banned?' (2004) 30 *Journal of Medical Ethics* 533

Sheldon, Sally and Stephen Wilkinson, 'Hashmi and Whitaker: An Unjustifiable and Misguided Distinction?' (2004) 12 *Medical Law Review* 137

Sherman, Nancy, 'The Virtues of Common Pursuit' (1993) 53 *Philosophical and Phenomenological Research* 277

Singer, Peter, Edmund D Pellegrino and Mark Siegler, 'Clinical Ethics Revisited' (2001) 2 *BMC Medical Ethics* E1, <http://www.biomedcentral.com/content/pdf/1472-6939-2-1.pdf> (accessed 26 April 2013)

Slowther, Anne *et al*, 'Clinical Ethics Support Services in the UK: An Investigation of the Current Provision of Ethics Support to Health Professionals in the UK' (2001) 27 (Suppl 1) *Journal of Medical Ethics* i2

Slowther, Anne, Leah McClimans and Charlotte Price, 'Development of Clinical Ethics Services in the UK: A National Survey' (2012) 38 *Journal of Medical Ethics* 210

Smajdor, Anna, 'The Review of the HFE Act: Ethical Expertise or Moral Cowardice?' (2007) 432 *Bionews*, <http://www.bionews.org.uk/page_37959.asp> (accessed 26 April 2013)

Smith, Malcolm, 'Reviewing Regulation of Assisted Reproductive Technology in New South Wales: The Assisted Reproductive Technology Act 2007 (NSW)' (2008) 16 *Journal of Law and Medicine* 120

Smith, Rebecca, 'Britain's Only Saviour Sibling Twins', *The Daily Telegraph* (online), 9 August 2009, <http://www.telegraph.co.uk/health/children_shealth/5998991/Britains-only-saviour-sibling-twins.html> (accessed 26 April 2013)

Sokol, Daniel, 'The Unpalatable Truth about Ethics Committees' (2009) 339 *British Medical Journal* 891

Sparrow, Robert and David Cram, 'Saviour Embryos? Preimplantation Genetic Diagnosis as a Therapeutic Technology' (2010) 20 *Reproductive Biomedicine Online* 667

Spriggs, M and J Savulescu, 'Saviour Siblings' (2002) 28 *Journal of Medical Ethics* 289

Storrow, Richard F, 'Therapeutic Reproduction and Human Dignity' (2009) 21 *Law & Literature* 257

Sureau, Claude, 'Gender Selection: A Crime Against Humanity or the Exercise of a Fundamental Right?' (1999) 14 *Human Reproduction* 867

Szoke, Helen, 'The Nanny State or Responsible Government?' (2002) 9 *Journal of Law and Medicine* 470

Taylor, Charles, 'Hegel's Ambiguous Legacy for Modern Liberalism' (1988–89) 10 *Cardozo Law Review* 857

Ten, C L, 'A Child's Right to a Father' (2000) 19 *Monash Bioethics Review* 33

Thomas, Cordelia, 'Pre-Implantation Testing and the Protection of the "Saviour Sibling"' (2004) 9 *Deakin Law Review* 119

Tobin, John, *The Convention on the Rights of the Child: The Rights and Best Interests of Children Conceived Through Assisted Reproduction* (Victorian Law Reform Commission Occasional Paper, August 2004)

Tolosa, Jose N *et al*, 'Mankind's First Natural Stem Cell Transplant' (2010) 14 *Journal of Cellular and Molecular Medicine* 488

Turillazzi, E and V Fineschi, 'Preimplantation Genetic Diagnosis: A Step By Step Guide to Recent Italian Ethical and Legislative Troubles' (2008) 34 *Journal of Medical Ethics* e21

United Kingdom, Committee of Inquiry into Human Fertilisation and Embryology, *Report of the Committee of Inquiry into Human Fertilisation and Embryology*, Cmnd 9314 (1984) (The Warnock Report)

United Kingdom, Department of Health, *Government Response to the Consultation on Proposals to Transfer Functions from the Human Fertilisation and Embryology Authority and the Human Tissue Authority* (January 2013)

United Kingdom, Department of Health and Social Security, *Human Fertilisation and Embryology: A Framework for Legislation*, Cm 259 (1987)

Verlinksy, Y *et al*, 'Preimplantation Diagnosis for Fancomi Anemia combined with HLA Matching' (2001) 285 *Journal of the American Medical Association* 3130

Victorian Law Reform Commission, *Assisted Reproductive Technology & Adoption: Position Paper One – Access* (2005)

——, *Assisted Reproductive Technology & Adoption*, Final Report (2007)

Viot, G, S Epelboin and F Olivennes, 'Is there an Increased Risk of Congenital Malformations after Assisted Reproductive Technologies (ART)? Results of a French Cohort Composed of 15 162 Children' (2010) 25 *Human Reproduction* I54

Walker, Margaret Urban, 'Keeping Moral Space Open: New Images of Ethics Consulting' (1993) 23 *Hastings Center Report* 33

Warnock, Mary (ed), *Utilitarianism and On Liberty* (Blackwell Publishing, 2nd edn, 2003)

Weil, Jon *et al*, 'The Relationship of Nondirectiveness to Genetic Counselling: Report of a Workshop at the 2003 NSGC Annual Education Conference' (2006) 15 *Journal of Genetic Counseling* 85

Wertz, D C and J C Fletcher, 'Feminist Criticism of Prenatal Diagnosis: A Response' (1993) 36 *Clinical Obstetrics and Gynaecology* 541

Wikler, Daniel 'Can We Learn from Eugenics' (1999) 25 *Journal of Medical Ethics* 183

Wilkinson, Stephen, *Choosing Tomorrow's Children: The Ethics of Selective Reproduction* (Clarendon Press, 2010)

Williams, Bernard, *Moral Luck: Philosophical Papers, 1973–1980* (Cambridge University Press, 1981)

Williams, Clare, Priscilla Alderson and Bobbie Farsides, 'Is Nondirectiveness Possible within the Context of Antenatal Screening and Testing?' (2002) 54 *Social Sciences & Medicine* 339

Wisborg, K, H J Ingerslev and T B Henriksen, 'IVF and Stillbirth: a Prospective Follow-Up Study' (2010) 25 *Human Reproduction* 1312

Wolf, S M, 'Ethics Committees and Due Process: Nesting Rights in a Community of Caring' (1991) 50 *Maryland Law Review* 798

Wolf, Susan M (ed), *Feminism & Bioethics: Beyond Reproduction* (Oxford University Press, 1996)

Yang, Y *et al*, 'Evaluation of blastomere biopsy using a mouse model indicates the potential high risk of neurodegenerative disorders in the offspring' (2009) 8 *Molecular & Cellular Proteomics* 1490

B Book chapters

Asch, Adrienne and Gail Geller, 'Feminism, Bioethics and Genetics' in Susan M Wolf (ed), *Feminism & Bioethics: Beyond Reproduction* (Oxford University Press, 1996), 318

Blyth, Eric, 'Conceptions of Welfare' in Kirsty Horsey and Hazel Biggs (eds), *Human Fertilisation and Embryology: Reproducing Regulation* (Routledge-Cavendish, 2007), 17

Buxton, Jess, 'Unforseen Uses of Preimplantation Genetic Diagnosis – Ethical and Legal Issues' in Kirsty Horsey and Hazel Biggs (eds), *Human Fertilisation and Embryology: Reproducing Regulation* (Routledge-Cavendish, 2007), 109

Donchin, Anne, 'Autonomy and Interdependence: Quandaries in Genetic Decision Making' in Catriona Mackenzie and Natalie Stoljar (eds), *Relational Autonomy: Feminist Perspectives of Autonomy, Agency, and the Social Self* (Oxford University Press, 2000), 236

Feinberg, Joel, 'The Child's Right to an Open Future' in William Aiken and Hugh LaFollette (eds), *Whose Child? Children's Rights, Parental Authority, and State Power* (Rowman and Littlefield, 1980), 124

Harris, John, 'Rights and Reproductive Choice' in John Harris and Soren Holm, *The Future of Human Reproduction: ethics, choice, and regulation* (Oxford University Press, 1998), 5

Jackson, Emily, 'Rethinking the Pre-Conception Welfare Principle' in Kirsty Horsey and Hazel Biggs (eds), *Human Fertilisation and Embryology: Reproducing Regulation* (Routledge-Cavendish, 2007), 47

Jecker, Nancy S, 'Impartiality and Special Relations' in Diana Tietjens Meyers, Kenneth Kipnis and Cornelius F Murphy (eds), *Kindred Matters: Rethinking the Philosophy of the Family* (Cornell University Press, 1993), 74

Levine, Carol, 'Family Caregiving' in Mary Crowley (ed), *From Birth to Death and Bench to Clinic: The Hastings Bioethics Center Briefing Book for Journalists, Policymakers, and Campaigns* (The Hastings Center, 2008), 63, 65

Meyers, Diana Tietjens, 'Introduction' in Diana Tietjens Meyers, Kenneth Kipnis and Cornelius F Murphy (eds), *Kindred Matters: Rethinking the Philosophy of the Family* (Cornell University Press, 1993), 13

O'Neill, Onora, 'Kantian Ethics' in R E Ashcroft *et al* (eds), *Principles of Health Care Ethics* (Wiley, 2nd edn, 2007), 73

Skene, Loane, 'Why Legislate on Assisted Reproduction?' in Ian Freckelton and Kerry Petersen (eds), *Controversies in Health Law* (Federation Press, 1999), 267

Smith, Janet Farrell, 'Communicative Ethics in Medicine: The Physician-Patient Relationship' in Susan M Wolf (ed), *Feminism & Bioethics: Beyond Reproduction* (Oxford University Press, 1996), 184

Smith, Patricia, 'Family Responsibility and the Nature of Obligation' in Diana Tietjens Meyers, Kenneth Kipnis and Cornelius F Murphy Jr (eds), *Kindred Matters: Rethinking the Philosophy of the Family* (Cornell University Press, 1993), 41

Steinfels, Margaret O'Brien, 'Children's Rights, Parental Rights, Family Privacy and Family Autonomy' in Willard Gaylin and Ruth Macklin (eds), *Who Speaks for the Child: The Problems of Proxy Consent* (Plenum Press, 1982), 253

Szoke, Helen, 'Australia – A Federated Structure of Statutory Regulation of ART' in Jennifer Gunning and Helen Szoke (eds), *The Regulation of Assisted Reproductive Technology* (Ashgate, 2003), 75

Walker, Kristen, 'Should There Be Limits on Who May Access Assisted Reproductive Services? A Legal Perspective' in Jennifer Gunning and Helen Szoke (eds), *The Regulation of Assisted Reproductive Technology* (Ashgate, 2003), 123

Williams, Bernard, 'Persons, Character and Morality', in *Moral Luck: Philosophical Papers, 1973–1980* (Cambridge University Press, 1981), 18

C Cases

Australia

Harriton v Stephens (2006) 226 CLR 52
In the Marriage of GWW and CMW (1997) 136 FLR 421
JS and LS v Patient Review Panel (Health and Privacy) [2011] VCAT 856 (8 April 2011)
R v Hughes (2000) 202 CLR 535
Re Inaya (special medical procedure) (2007) 213 FLR 278

Europe

Costa v Italy (European Court of Human Rights, Chamber, Application No 54270/10, 28
   August 2012

UK

McKay v Essex Area Health Authority [1982] QB 1166
*Quintavalle (on behalf of Comment on Reproductive Ethics) v Human Fertilisation and Embryology
   Authority* [2005] UKHL 28, [2005] 2 AC 561 (House of Lords)
R (on the application of Quintavalle) v Human Fertilisation and Embryology Authority [2002] EWHC
   3000 (Admin), [2003] 2 All ER 105 (High Court)
R (on the application of Quintavalle) v Human Fertilisation and Embryology Authority [2003] EWCA
   Civ 667, [2004] QB 168 (Court of Appeal)
Re B (A Minor) (Wardship: Medical Treatment) [1990] 3 All ER 927
Re J (A Minor) (Wardship: Medical Treatment) [1990] 3 All ER 930
Re Y (Mental Incapacity: Bone Marrow Transplant) [1996] 2 FLR 787

US

Re *AC* (1990) 573 A 2d 1235
Re Quinlan (1976) 355 A 2d 647
Strunk v Strunk 445 S W 2d 145 (Ky 1969)
Turpin v Sortini, 31 Cal 3d 220 (1982)
Wisconsin v Yoder, 406 US 205 (1972)

D Legislation

Australia

Assisted Reproductive Technology Act 2007 (NSW)
Assisted Reproductive Treatment Act 2008 (Vic)
Assisted Reproductive Treatment Regulations 2009 (Vic)
Assisted Reproductive Treatment Act 1988 (SA)
Australian Constitution 1900
Children, Youth and Families Act 2005 (Vic)
Crimes Act 1958 (Vic)
Family Law Act 1975 (Cth)
Health Practitioner Regulation National Law [Various jurisdictions] Act
Human Reproductive Technology Act 1991 (WA)
Human Tissue Act 1982 (Vic)

Infertility (Medical Procedures) Act 1984 (Vic)
Infertility Treatment Act 1995 (Vic)
National Health and Medical Research Council Act 1992 (Cth)
Prohibition of Human Cloning for Reproduction Act 2002 (Cth)
Research Involving Human Embryos Act 2002 (Cth)
Transplantation and Anatomy Act 1978 (ACT)

UK

Children Act 1989 (UK)
Female Genital Mutilation Act 2003 (UK)
Human Fertilisation and Embryology Act 1990 (UK)
Human Fertilisation and Embryology Act 2008 (UK)
Human Fertilisation and Embryology (Research Purposes) Regulations 2001 (SI 2001/188) (UK)
Medical Act 1983 (UK)
Prohibition of Female Circumcision Act 1985 (UK)

US

18 USC § 116

E Treaties

Convention on the Rights of the Child, opened for signature 20 November 1989, [1991] ATS 4 (entered into force 2 September 1990)

F Other sources

Reference

The American Heritage Dictionary of the English Language (Houghton Mifflin Company, 4th edn, 2003) cited in *The Free Dictionary* by Farlex, <http://www.thefreedictionary.com/family> (accessed 26 April 2013), definitions 1a and b
Butler, S (ed), *Macquarie Dictionary* (Macquarie Dictionary Publishers, 5th edn, 2009)
Simpson, JA and E C Weiner, *The Oxford English Dictionary* (Oxford University Press, 1989)

Australia

Code of practice/guidelines/schemes

Australian Medical Association, *Code of Ethics of the Australian Medical Association* (2004, revised 2006), <http://ama.com.au/node/2521> (accessed 26 April 2013)
Australian and New Zealand Infertility Counsellors Association, *Guidelines for Professional Standards of Practice Infertility Counselling* (October 2003)
Fertility Society of Australia, Reproductive Technology Accreditation Committee, *Code of Practice for Assisted Reproductive Technology Units* (revised October 2010)
Infertility Treatment Authority, *Tissue Typing in Conjunction with Preimplantation Genetic Diagnosis* (adopted February 2003, updated January 2004)

National Health and Medical Research Council, *Ethical Guidelines on the Use of Assisted Reproductive Technology in Clinical Practice and Research 2004 (as revised in 2007 to take into account the changes in legislation)* (June 2007)

WA Select Committee on the Human Reproductive Technology Act 1991, *Report* (1999)

Written correspondence

Email from Margaret Coady (Committee Member, Royal Womens' Hospital Clinical Ethics Advisory Group) to Michelle Taylor-Sands, 25 March 2010

Email from Tracey Petrillo (Policy Officer, Victorian Assisted Reproductive Treatment Authority) to Michelle Taylor-Sands, 13 May 2010

Legislative materials and government documents

Family Law Council, *Creating Children: a Uniform Approach to the Law and Practice of Reproductive Technology in Australia*, 1985

Scully, Sharon, 'Does the Commonwealth have constitutional power to take over the administration of public hospitals?' (Research Paper No 36, Parliamentary Library, Parliament of Australia, 2009)

Victoria, *Parliamentary Debates*, Legislative Assembly, 4 May 1995, 1243–48 (Mrs Tehan (Minister for Health))

——, *Parliamentary Debates*, Legislative Assembly, 30 May 1995, 1917–32 (Mrs Tehan (Minister for Health))

——, *Parliamentary Debates*, Legislative Assembly, 1 June 1995, 2103–17 (Mr Doyle)

——, *Parliamentary Debates*, Legislative Council, 6 June 1995, 1213–18 (R I Knowles)

Consultation documents

Victorian Law Reform Commission, *Assisted Reproductive Technology & Adoption* Consultation Paper (20 January 2004)

Presentations

Gillam, Lynne, 'Human Research Ethics Committees' (Paper presented at the Centre for Human Bioethics Intensive Bioethics Course, Alexandra, Victoria, 3 December 2009)

Websites

Fertility Society of Australia, *About FSA* (c 2013), < http://www.fertilitysociety.com.au/home/about/> (accessed 26 April 2013)

Leukaemia Foundation, *Fact Sheet: Stem Cell Transplants* (February 2011), <http://www.leukaemia.org.au/fileadmin/dl-docs/factsheets4/FACTSHEET-StemCellTransplants.pdf> (accessed 26 April 2013)

National Health and Medical Research Council, *Assisted Reproductive Technology (ART)* (2012), <http://www.nhmrc.gov.au/health-ethics/australian-health-ethics-committee-ahec/assisted-reproductive-technology-art/assisted-> (accessed 26 April 2013)

——, *Assisted Reproductive Technology (ART): Sex Selection though Pre-implantation Genetic Diagnosis* (13 February 2013), <http://www.nhmrc.gov.au/health_ethics/health/art.htm> (accessed 26 April 2013)

——, *Australian Health Ethics Committee (AHEC)* (2012), <http://www.nhmrc.gov.au/about/committees/ahec/index.htm> (accessed 26 April 2013)

National Tay-Sachs & Allied Diseases Association of Delaware Valley, *Tay-Sachs Disease* (n.d.), <http://www.tay-sachs.org/taysachs_disease.php> (accessed 23 April 2013)

Royal Children's Hospital Melbourne, Children's Bioethics Centre, *Clinical Ethics Service* (15 March 2013), <http://www.rch.org.au/bioethics/clinical_ethics_service/> (accessed 26 April 2013)

International

United Nations Resolution on Intensifying Global Efforts for the Elimination of Female Genital Mutilations, UN GA/11331, 67th Session, UN Doc A/RES/67/146 (20 December, 2012)

New Zealand

Human Genome Research Project, *Choosing Genes for Future Children: The Regulatory Implications of Preimplantation Genetic Diagnosis* (2006) Dunedin, New Zealand

UK

Code of practice/guidelines/schemes

Human Fertilisation and Embryology Authority, *Code of Practice* (1st edn) (1991), <http://www.hfea.gov.uk/docs/1st_Edition_Code_of_Practice.pdf> (accessed 26 April 2013)

——, *Code of Practice* (8th edn, first published 2009, revised October 2011), <http://www.hfea.gov.uk/docs/8th_Code_of_Practice.pdf> (accessed 26 April 2013)

Minutes of meetings/papers submitted

Human Fertilisation and Embryology Authority, *Minutes of Authority Meeting* (20 January 2010)

——, *Minutes of the 139th Open Authority Committee Meeting (Part 2 – Open Meeting)* (21 July 2004), <http://www.hfea.gov.uk/docs/AM_Minutes_Jul04.pdf> (accessed 26 April 2013)

Legislative materials and government documents

Department of Health (UK), *Review of the Human Fertilisation and Embryology Act: Proposals for Revised Legislation (Including Establishment of the Regulatory Authority for Tissue and Embryos)*, Cm 6989 (2006)

Human Fertilisation and Embryology Act 1990, As amended: an illustrative text (1990)

Human Fertilisation and Embryology HL Bill (2007–8) (UK)

United Kingdom, *Human Reproductive Technologies and the Law: Government Response to the Report from the House of Commons Science and Technology Committee*, Cm 6641 (2005)

——, *Parliamentary Debates*, House of Lords, 7 December 1989, vol 513, col 1002 (James Mackay)

——, *Parliamentary Debates*, House of Lords, 6 February 1990, vol 515, col 787 (James Mackay)

White, Edward, 'Human Fertilisation and Embryology Bill [HL]: Committee Stage Report' (Research Paper 08/62, House of Commons Library, UK Parliament, 9 July 2008)

Consultation documents

Department of Health (UK), *Consultation on Proposals to Transfer Functions from the Human Fertilisation and Embryology Authority and the Human Tissue Authority*, Consultation Paper (June 2012)

——, *Review of the Human Fertilisation and Embryology Act: A Public Consultation* (16 August 2005)

Human Fertilisation and Embryology Authority, *Tomorrow's Children: A Consultation on Guidance to Licensed Fertility Clinics on Taking in Account the Welfare of Children to be Born of Assisted Conception Treatment* (January 2005)

Websites

General Medical Council, *Good Medical Practice* (13 November 2006), <http://www.gmc-uk.org/static/documents/content/GMP_0910.pdf> (accessed 1 February 2013)

US

Leukemia and Lymphoma Society, The, 'Cord Blood Stem Cell Transplantation' (Fact Sheet No 2, August 2007), <http://www.lls.org/resourcecenter/freeeducationmaterials/treatment/cordblood> (accessed 26 April 2013)

President's Council on Bioethics, The, *Human Cloning and Human Dignity: An Ethical Inquiry*, (Washington), July 2002, <http://bioethics.georgetown.edu/pcbe/reports/cloningreport/pcbe_cloning_report.pdf> (accessed 26 April 2013)

Index

Lightning Source UK Ltd.
Milton Keynes UK
UKOW06f0335031116
286741UK00014B/336/P